# FRIEND OF
# GOD

# RAY C. STEDMAN

# FRIEND OF GOD

## THE LEGACY OF ABRAHAM, MAN OF FAITH

DISCOVERY HOUSE
PUBLISHERS®

Discovery House Publishers is affiliated with RBC Ministries, Grand Rapids, Michigan.

Requests for permission to quote from this book should be directed to: Permissions Department, Discovery House Publishers, P.O. Box 3566, Grand Rapids, MI 49501, or contact us by e-mail at permissionsdept@dhp.org

All Scripture quotations, unless otherwise indicated, are taken from the Holy Bible, New International Version®, NIV®. Copyright ©1973, 1978, 1984 by Biblica, Inc.™ Used by permission of Zondervan. All rights reserved worldwide. www.zondervan.com

*Interior design by* Michelle Espinoza

**Library of Congress Cataloging-in-Publication Data**

Stedman, Ray C.
Friend of God : the legacy of Abraham, man of faith / Ray C. Stedman.
    p. cm.
Previously published: Man of faith. Portland, Or. : Multnomah Press, c1986.
    ISBN 978-1-57293-371-2
    1. Abraham (Biblical patriarch)—Sermons. 2. Bible. O.T. Genesis
    XI, 31-XXV, 8—Sermons. I. Stedman, Ray C. Man of faith.
    II. Title.
    BS580.A3S75 2010
    222'.11092--dc22                                    2010022351

Printed in the United States of America
Second printing 2011

# CONTENTS

# PUBLISHER'S PREFACE

Ray Stedman (1917–1992) served as pastor of the Peninsula Bible Church from 1950 to 1990, where he was known and loved as a man of outstanding Bible knowledge, Christian integrity, warmth, and humility. Born in Temvik, North Dakota, Ray grew up on the rugged landscape of Montana. When he was a small child, his mother became ill, and his father, a railroad man, abandoned the family. Ray grew up on his aunt's Montana farm from the time he was six. He came to know the Lord at age ten.

As a young man, Ray lived in Chicago, Denver, Hawaii, and elsewhere. He enlisted in the Navy during World War II and often led Bible studies for civilians and Navy personnel. He sometimes preached on the radio in Hawaii. At the close of the war, Ray was married in Honolulu (he and his wife, Elaine, had first met in Great Falls, Montana). They returned to the mainland in 1946, and Ray graduated from Dallas Theological Seminary in 1950. After two summers interning with Dr. J. Vernon McGee, Ray traveled for several months with Dr. H. A. Ironside, pastor of the Moody Church in Chicago.

In 1950, Ray was called by the two-year-old Peninsula Bible Fellowship in Palo Alto, California, to serve as its first pastor. Peninsula Bible Fellowship became Peninsula Bible Church, and Ray served a forty-year tenure, retiring on April 30, 1990. During those years, Ray Stedman authored a number of life-changing Christian books, including the classic work on the meaning and mission of the church, *Body Life*. He went into the presence of his Lord on October 7, 1992.

This book, *Friend of God*, is based on a series of messages Pastor Stedman delivered at Peninsula Bible Church in 1968. The text has been completely rewritten and updated for the new millennium. In these pages, Ray Stedman takes us on a rewarding and fascinating journey through the life of Abraham. His unique blend of insightful Bible teaching, delightful storytelling, and conversational style will draw you into the mind, soul, and faith of the greatest of all Old Testament heroes, Abraham.

You'll experience each episode of Abraham's life in a new and life-changing way—and you'll discover that every event in this ancient man's life has profound meaning for your life as a twenty-first-century follower of Christ. As Pastor Stedman has said, "Each of the incidences in Abraham's life [is] a luminous illustration of some New Testament event or truth."

So turn the page, and take a four-thousand-year journey back in time—a journey that brings you right back to your own life today. Rediscover the adventure of faith alongside this remarkable man known as Abraham, *Friend of God*.

# 1

# THE BEGINNING
# OF FAITH

*Genesis 11:31–12:9*

You are lost in the desert. Your throat is parched, and your dry tongue sticks to the roof of your mouth. *Just one sip of water,* you tell yourself. *I'd sell myself into slavery for just one sip!*

Then you see something up ahead—a water pump shaded by a canopy. As you stagger closer, you see something hanging on a strap from the pump handle—a canteen. And beside the pump is a sign that reads: "Beneath your feet is all the fresh, cool water you will ever need. But the pump will not work unless it is primed with water. The canteen contains exactly enough water to prime the pump."

You take the canteen in your hand, shake it, and feel the water sloshing inside. Now what do you do? Should you believe the promise written on the sign? What if the sign is a hoax? What if there is nothing but dry sand beneath that pump? What if the only water for miles is in that canteen? If you trust that sign, you could be pouring your life away.

You must make a decision: Will you drink from the canteen? Or will you take the only water you have seen for days and pour it down the throat of that pump? Will you place your trust in what you can touch and see and hear, or will you have faith in a promise?

Abraham was a man who believed the promise of God. Many times in his life, he came to a point where all he had to go on was the equivalent of a canteen and a promise. Yet he repeatedly proved himself willing to believe that promise, pour out his canteen, and prime the pump of God's blessing in his own life and the life of his physical and spiritual descendants. Abraham was an ordinary man with an extraordinary willingness to place his trust in the promises of God.

## FAITH IS THE SECRET

There's a simple secret linking the Old and the New Testaments together into a unified whole, a single consistent story. That secret is faith. The unifying principle of faith makes the study of the Old Testament a never-ending delight.

The Old Testament is designed as a picture book. The books of the Old Testament illustrate spiritual truths with fascinating stories, which could be called word pictures. Then those same spiritual truths are presented as principles and teachings in the New Testament. This is especially true of the Old Testament books of Moses (Genesis through Deuteronomy), plus the book of Joshua. In the biographies of people like Abraham, Jacob, Joseph, Moses, and Joshua, God gives us powerful images and riveting stories that symbolize for us what the godly life— the life of spiritual obedience, growth, and progress—should look like.

As the apostle Paul wrote, "All Scripture is God-breathed" (2 Timothy 3:16). In other words, the Bible is directly inspired by God (that is literally what "God-breathed" means). God has revealed His mind through His Word. One of the most convincing proofs that the Bible is inspired by God is the profound way in which the Spirit of God has transformed the historical facts of the Old Testament into a symbolic pattern for spiritual living. The events of the Old Testament form a picture for us of what takes place as we grow spiritually mature in God's grace.

Abraham's life is a beautiful portrait of justification by faith. The story of Isaac teaches us what it means to be a child of God. Jacob's life vividly demonstrates how God works to purify us, sanctify us, and deliver us from the power of sin. And the story of Joseph is a moving story of what it means to suffer for God, to die to self, and to experience glorious resurrection and a completely new life of service to God.

Skeptics might say that we are superimposing our own interpretation on the Old Testament. But the New Testament itself shows us that God planned and structured the Old Testament to be read, studied, and interpreted in exactly this manner. In 1 Corinthians 10, Paul refers to a number of incidents in the history of Israel, then concludes with these words: "These things happened to them as examples and were written down as warnings for us, on whom the fulfillment of the ages has come" (1 Corinthians 10:11). And in the book of Romans, he wrote: "For everything that was written in the past was written to teach us, so that through endurance and the encouragement of the Scriptures we might have hope" (Romans 15:4).

There are numerous New Testament passages, notably in Paul's letter to the Galatians and in the Lord's teaching, that clearly show that the Old Testament events are to be regarded as spiritual analogy as well as literal history.

At the same time, we should remember to guard against wild and fanciful interpretations. We must remember to observe the rules of sound biblical interpretation so that we will always rightly divide the Word of truth. It would be a tragic loss to miss the rich spiritual truths that are embedded in these Old Testament illustrations. But if we extract interpretations that God never placed there, we risk straying into spiritual error.

## THE GOD OF GLORY APPEARED

One of the clearest Old Testament portraits of spiritual truth is the story of Abraham, from his origins in distant Ur of the Chaldeans to his final resting place in the cave of Machpelah near Hebron, in Canaan. Abraham is the quintessential role model of faith. Again and again, the writers of the New Testament hold him up as an example of how God works in the life of obedient, believing people to fulfill His promises of grace. Abraham is clearly chief among all the heroes of faith recorded in Hebrews 11.

The life of Abraham is a mirror in which we behold a reflection of our own lives. In tracing the story of Abraham, we discover the secrets by which the Spirit of God intends to transform us from faltering, stumbling pilgrims into men and women of stalwart faith. By applying the secrets of Abraham's life to our own lives, we will be made worthy to take our place beside the great heroes of faith in the Bible.

Abraham was originally called Abram, and it was not until years later that God changed his name (his name change will prove to be deeply significant). We meet Abram for the first time in the closing verses of Genesis 11 and the opening verses of Genesis 12:

> This is the account of Terah.
>
> Terah became the father of Abram, Nahor and Haran. And Haran became the father of Lot. While his father Terah was still alive, Haran died in Ur of the Chaldeans, in the land of his birth. Abram and Nahor both married. The name of Abram's wife was Sarai, and the name of Nahor's wife was Milcah; she was the daughter of Haran, the father of both Milcah and Iscah. Now Sarai was barren; she had no children.
>
> Terah took his son Abram, his grandson Lot son of Haran, and his daughter-in-law Sarai, the wife of his son Abram, and together they set out from Ur of the Chaldeans to go to Canaan. But when they came to Haran, they settled there.
>
> Terah lived 205 years, and he died in Haran. (Genesis 11:27–32)

Abram was born in the Chaldean city of Ur in Mesopotamia. At that time, Ur was one of the largest cities in the world, with a population in excess of fifty thousand people. It was located at Tell el-Mukayyar, Iraq, on the south (right) bank of the Euphrates, a short distance from the modern Iraqi city of Nasiriyah.

The Scriptures pass over Abram's early life in Ur with only a brief mention. It is as if the Spirit of God wants us to know that the life of Abram did not truly begin until his momentous encounter with God.

In Acts 7, Stephen, the first Christian martyr, gives a speech in which he tells us that the call of God came to Abraham while he was still living in Ur of the Chaldeans. The city of Ur was once thought to be the dwelling place of a primitive people living in mud-walled houses. Accordingly, some scholars once regarded Abram as a primitive and unlearned man. But the spade of the archaeologist has since turned up the ruins of Ur and dispelled this false impression. We now know that Ur was a city of great wealth and culture, home to a library and a university. The people of Ur were devoted to commerce, learning, and the pagan worship of the moon goddess.

Abram may have been a worshiper of the moon. Or it may be that God chose Abram and spoke to him because Abram had already rejected the moon worship of his surrounding culture. The Scriptures do not speak clearly of his beliefs prior to his encounter with God. However, we do know that once God called Abram, this man of ancient Ur responded in obedient faith. The writer of Hebrews tells us that he left the idolatrous city of Ur and ventured out in faith, "looking forward to the city with foundations, whose architect and builder is God" (see Hebrews 11:8–10).

Stephen, in Acts 7, declared, "The God of glory appeared to our father Abraham while he was still in Mesopotamia, before he lived in Haran. 'Leave your country and your people,' God said, 'and go to the land I will show you' " (Acts 7:2b–3).

So the God of glory appeared to Abram while he still lived in Ur in Mesopotamia. We don't know in what form or appearance God manifested himself. But we do know that God took the initiative in reaching out to Abram. That is always the pattern of God's interactions with human beings. People often think that they are searching after God, but those searching feelings are nothing but a response to God as He draws them to himself.

Whether Abram had rejected the religion of Ur or was actively worshiping idols of the moon goddess, we cannot say. But we do know that it was God who sought Abram, not Abram who sought God. And this is also true of your life and mine. God sought us out while we were still strangers and enemies to Him. In the relationship between God and human beings, God is always the initiator.

## GOD'S THREEFOLD COMMAND

In his encounter with God, Abram came face to face with a command and a promise. In the opening verses of Genesis 12, we read:

> The LORD had said to Abram, "Leave your country, your people and your father's household and go to the land I will show you.
> "I will make you into a great nation
>     and I will bless you;
>     I will make your name great,
>     and you will be a blessing.
> "I will bless those who bless you,
>     and whoever curses you I will curse;
>     and all peoples on earth
>     will be blessed through you." (Genesis 12:1–3)

First, Abram was commanded to go. Second, Abram was promised a land. The promise of the land was not symbolic or metaphorical. Abram was promised a literal place in which to dwell—a place for himself and his descendants.

God also promised to make Abram's name great and to make him the father of a great nation and a blessing to all nations. This promise has been literally fulfilled and amply confirmed through the reestablishment of the nation of Israel. All the nations and peoples of the earth are blessed by the nation and people of Israel. God will keep His promise to Abram: anyone who blesses Israel and the Jewish people will be blessed, and anyone who curses the same shall be cursed.

But beyond the literal promises God made to Abram, we wish to discover another dimension of this historical account. Throughout our study, we will follow the warrant given to us by the New Testament, and we will apply the spiritual principles embedded in the story of Abram to our lives.

At the outset, let us make sure that we do not make the mistake (which is so common) of taking these promises of the Old Testament and applying them literally to believers and the church today. For example, Israel was told not to intermarry with other races, and God meant what He said to Israel. But anyone who applies that instruction in the church today will run into all sorts of absurdities and even tragic injustices.

False doctrines of racial segregation have arisen from the misapplication of God's literal instructions to Israel. Those Old Testament instructions were intended to keep God's people spiritually pure and separate from the idolatrous practices of the pagan nations. It was never intended to separate Christians of different races from each other. Such a misapplication of Old Testament instructions to New Testament times makes no rational or theological sense. Indeed, the New Testament makes it clear that racism is unacceptable in the church: "There is neither Jew nor Greek, slave nor free, male nor female, for you are all one in Christ Jesus" (Galatians 3:28).

To avoid drawing false conclusions from the Old Testament, we need to continually compare Scripture with Scripture.

## THE DECISION WE MUST MAKE

God commanded Abram to do three things: leave his country, leave his kindred, and leave his father's house. This is exactly the command God issues to every person who hears the call of the gospel today.

First, God told Abram to leave his country. Similarly, God also calls you and me out of our country, our place of residence since birth. Abram had to leave his physical residence, a place of idolatry, commerce, political power, and pleasure. But you and I are called to leave the old life with all of its ambition, rebellion, and worship of wealth, power, and pleasure. The old life is characterized by a selfish demand for supposed independence, which is really slavery. We are to turn our backs on the dying and condemned social system of this world, with its humanistic values and satanic philosophies.

Second, God told Abram to leave his people—that is, his culture, the social environment that sought to conform him to its mold. God also commands you and me to separate ourselves from our people and our culture. This doesn't mean we are to shun non-Christians and live as hermits. It means that we are not to allow the surrounding culture to shape our thinking and behavior. When God confronts us with His call, we must turn our backs on the lures and moral traps of our society. We are to renounce all concern about what others think and be preeminently concerned with what God thinks.

Third, God told Abram to leave his father's house—that is, he was to break his ties with the old man or the old self. Our father, in this sense, is Adam, the father of us all. What theologians call our Adamic nature is the father's house in which we all live. God calls us to leave this, no longer putting any dependence upon our natural talents and resources. Instead, we must begin to walk in dependence upon God, our heavenly Father. He can do through us what we cannot do ourselves.

Many of us, when we first hear the gospel, have grown tired of the land of Ur, for it is a land of darkness, a place of great weariness of soul, a realm of spiritual hunger and death. Yet, even though we feel empty and unsatisfied in this land, part of us resists God's call to leave that land. There is much that seems desirable in the old life. Abram probably felt this sense of hesitancy. God was calling him out of his familiar old life to a land that was unknown. But regardless of any trepidation and insecurity Abram felt, he knew he could not deny the reality of God. He chose to obey God's command: "Leave your country, your people and your father's household and go to the land I will show you."

Have you heard this command of God in your life? Have you heard the living God call your name and say, "You must no longer depend on the old crutches that once supported you—the worldly attitudes and philosophy in which you were reared. They are based on the lies of Satan, and you must not live on that basis any longer. Accept the truth reflected in my Word, the truth which saws across the grain of this world. Leave your old country, your people, your old ways. Seek a new country, a new people, a new home, a new Father."

The decision we must make is simple to understand but often hard to implement. It means letting go. You cannot have one foot in the world and one foot in heaven. You cannot stay in Ur and moved to the land of promise at the same time. To choose one, you must forsake the other. There is no middle course.

## GOD'S THREEFOLD PROMISE

Following this command to Abram, God gives him a mighty promise. Like the command, the promise is threefold:

> "I will make you into a great nation
> and I will bless you;
> I will make your name great,
> and you will be a blessing.
> "I will bless those who bless you,
> and whoever curses you I will curse;
> and all peoples on earth
> will be blessed through you." (Genesis 12:2–3)

The first of these three promises is that God would make of Abram a great nation. God literally fulfilled this promise through the nation of Israel—not merely the biblical kingdom of Israel or the current state of Israel, but the people of Israel, including all the Jewish people who are scattered around the world.

But what does the nation of Israel symbolize to us in a spiritual sense? What is a nation? It is the life of a man, enlarged to vast proportions. In our day, a nation may be made up of a millions of families, all living together in a heterogeneous society. But that is not what a nation is according to the Bible. In God's Word, every nation begins with a man. The man starts a family. The family grows and expands. Generation by generation, the family enlarges to a point where it is finally a nation. In a biblical sense, a nation is the continuation and expansion of the life of a single man—in this case, a man named Abram.

God's promise to Abram—the promise that He will make Abram a great nation—is a picture of eternal life. This is the first promise of the gospel. As Paul writes, "For the wages of sin is death" (symbolized in Abram's life by his former homeland, Ur), "but the gift of God is eternal life in Christ Jesus our Lord" (Romans 6:23). If you receive the gift of eternal life and leave your country, your people, and your father's household, what will God do for you? He will give you eternal life. He will make of you a great nation. He will expand and enlarge your life to an infinite degree.

## "YOU WILL BE A BLESSING"

God's second promise to Abram is, "I will bless you; I will make your name great, and you will be a blessing." This promise had a profound and specific meaning to Abram. As we trace the story of his life, we find that it meant that God would bless him with riches and honor. It meant that God would use Abram to bless the lives of others. He would become influential and effective for God.

God makes this same promise to us today, but in the spiritual realm. If you are thinking about riches and honor and being a blessing in terms of dollars and cents and material goods, you are on the wrong track. Despite what many proponents of the prosperity gospel would have you believe, God does not promise a life of prosperity to any believer today. God does not commit himself to make us wealthy when we become Christians, but He does promise us all the riches of Christ Jesus. As the apostle Paul tells us:

> Oh, the depth of the riches of the wisdom and knowledge of God!
> How unsearchable his judgments,
> and his paths beyond tracing out! (Romans 11:33)

This is the rewarding life of adventure and joy the world is looking for. Money cannot buy these riches. Only in Jesus can you become what God intended you to be. Only in Him can women fulfill the beauty of their womanhood. Only in Him can men experience the glory of their manhood. These are the riches of Christ.

And there is still more that God offers us. He offers honor, but not the honor of people. If you are looking for crowds and fame and your photo on magazine covers, then you should become a politician or a movie star. But if you want genuine honor, which comes from God alone, then listen to the words of Christ: "Whoever serves me must follow me; and where I am, my servant also will be. My Father will honor the one who serves me" (John 12:26).

Finally, God offers this promise, the choicest of all: "You will be a blessing." This is the glory of being used by God to bless others—the joy of a fruitful life. There is nothing more wonderful than the experience of being God's instrument to bring blessing to other lives.

Niccolò Paganini (1782–1840) has been called the greatest violinist who ever lived. He astounded audiences by performing an entire sonata on a single string. In one piece, "Variations for the Fourth String," he used a harmonic technique to reach a note three octaves beyond what that string could normally produce—a note no other violinist could reach. He amazed and delighted thousands of music lovers during his lifetime.

Paganini willed his favorite violin, which he called *il mio cannone violino* ("my cannon violin"), to the city of Genoa. He placed only one condition on his bequest: No one would ever be allowed to play it. So the cherished violin was displayed in a glass case. Unfortunately, violins do not age well in a display case. A finely crafted instrument needs to be exercised regularly to maintain its beauty and tone. Paganini's violin was drying out and cracking from lack of use until the city decided to violate the terms of the will and allow the instrument to be played from time to time.

So it is with you and me. God did not create us to be museum pieces, placed behind glass as silent exhibits of His grace. He created us to be used daily for His glory and for the blessing of others. We can never become what He intends us to be until we allow Him to use us as He intends.

I have been privileged on a number of occasions to have God use my life in a way that has blessed the hearts of others, and there is no joy like it on earth. It's a moving and thrilling experience to know that God has used your words, deeds, or prayers to bring hope and healing into someone's life. God offers this kind of meaningful, joyful life to everyone who believes in Jesus Christ. These are the riches, honors, and blessings that are part of the second promise of God to Abram.

## BLESSING AND CURSING

And there is yet a third part to this promise:

> "I will bless those who bless you,
>     and whoever curses you I will curse;
>     and all peoples on earth
>     will be blessed through you." (Genesis 12:3)

This promise speaks of identification and sonship. God expresses here what every parent feels toward his or her children: If anyone blesses my children, then I will bless them—and if anyone harms my kids, they'll have to deal with me! We are wrapped up in our children. Whatever touches them touches us. That's why John writes, "How great is the love the Father has lavished on us, that we should be called children of God! And that is what we are!" (1 John 3:1a).

In this blessing, God says, "I will identify myself with you. What concerns you, concerns me. I will bless those who bless you, and curse those who curse you." We are identified with God, and wherever we go, we will be either a blessing or a curse. The world will not ignore us. When we live truly godly lives, the people around us must choose to either bless us and receive us or reject us and curse us. There is no middle ground.

This was the case with God's own Son, Jesus of Nazareth. No one who met Him remained neutral. If we are living truly Christlike lives, we will have the same effect on the people we encounter. This is why Paul writes: "For we are to God the aroma of Christ among those who are being saved and those who are perishing. To the one we are the smell of death; to the other, the fragrance of life. And who is equal to such a task?" (2 Corinthians 2:15–16).

Our lives are to be vibrant with the vitality that God possesses. When our character reflects His character, then all the families of earth will be blessed through us. He will touch the world through our lives.

## THE HARAN INTERLUDE

This promise is entirely a work of God, not Abram. All Abram has to do is obey. God will do everything else. If Abram will step out in faith toward the land of promise, God will do the rest.

What, then, is the land of promise? This is an important question, because the land of promise is spoken of throughout the Word of God. In the most literal sense, of course, it is the land of Canaan.

You may have heard it said that the promised land is heaven, but that's not true (except in the symbolic sense that heaven truly begins here on earth). The promised land is not a state or dimension we enter when we die. God wants us to know that we, like Abraham, enter the land of promise at the beginning of the Christian life. We live in this land of promise throughout our days.

So, in a symbolic sense, the promised land is a life that is lived in Christ. The New Testament calls this life "the fullness of the Spirit." It is a life controlled by the Spirit of God, reflecting the glory of Christ. We enter into this life by conversion, but we do not experience the fullness of its blessing until we, like Abram, learn to adjust ourselves to its demands. Our life in Christ is truly the land of promise, the land of God's blessing and power. The entire Bible is written for no other purpose than to bring the people of God into the land of God.

At this point in Genesis, we come to an important interlude. We learn that Abram obediently started out for the land, but he stopped along the way. As a result, Abram went through a lengthy period of wasted years at a place called Haran:

> Terah took his son Abram, his grandson Lot son of Haran, and his daughter-in-law Sarai, the wife of his son Abram, and together they set out from Ur of the Chaldeans to go to Canaan. But when they came to Haran, they settled there.
>
> Terah lived 205 years, and he died in Haran. (Genesis 11:31–32)

God told Abram to leave Ur, but Abram didn't just get up and leave.

In fact, it was Terah, Abram's father, who apparently took the initiative. Terah packed up his family—Abram and Sarai, along with Abram's nephew Lot—and together they set off from Ur to go to Canaan. The account does not say that Terah heard God's call as Abram did. In fact, it appears that Terah set out for Canaan to get away from Ur.

It may well be that Abram told his father Terah about God's call to him, and at that point, Terah may have recognized that Ur did not offer anything that truly satisfies the heart. When Terah saw that his son Abram was determined to leave, he may well have said, "All right, I'll go along." As the head of the family, he went out of Ur and headed for Canaan, but he only got as far as the land of Haran. He stopped halfway to Canaan.

Here we see a powerful illustration of the spiritual state of those who try to gain the promise of the gospel by leaving Ur but who never enter Canaan. Ur represents the world and its ways, and there are many people who seek to gain God's promise by leaving their old worldly life behind—but they never enter into the promised land of living by God's grace.

Many Christians have left Ur but have never reached the land of promise. They have only gone as far as Haran, and there they will die. They may have joined a church. They may have gotten religion. They live moral lives and go through the outward motions of the Christian faith. But they will never go farther than Haran. They are religious but not born again.

It's important to note that the word *haran* means "parched." The literal, historical Haran was indeed a parched and dismal place to live, and a Haran spiritual experience is a parched and dismal way to live.

But Terah didn't settle in Haran alone. Abram was there, too. He left Ur by faith and was on his way to Canaan. but he wasted many years in Haran. While he was in that place, halfway between his old life and the promised land, there was no discernible difference between Abram and his father. He was not ready to fully obey God—not yet. Remember, God had commanded Abram to leave his father's house, but Abraham had not done so. As a result, Abram wasted 75 of his 175 years in Haran. When Terah died, Abram decided he was free to go on to Canaan.

Do you see the symbolic significance of Abram's Haran experience? This story speaks to us across the ages, reminding us that if we depend upon our own resources to be acceptable to God, then we force Him to take those resources away. God will let us go on for a long time, until we learn the weakness and folly of our way of life. But ultimately, He will take them all away.

I'm sure that Abram felt a deep loss at the death of his father. Yet that was truly one of the most important days of Abram's life. It was the day he became free to follow God's command, free to leave Haran, free to press on to the promised land.

In the same way, the day that God takes from us all of our resources will seem like a dreary and miserable day. Suddenly, the things we have counted on to make us acceptable to God have vanished from our lives. We are miserable. We feel lost. Yet that is truly one of the greatest days of our lives, because we are now free to enter the promised land, free to depend on God alone.

What are the resources you cling to? What is your Haran? Perhaps it is your career, your beautiful home, your material possessions. Perhaps it is your reputation, your standing in the community, your position as a teacher or leader in the church. Perhaps it is your health, your marriage, or some cherished dream. Suddenly, those resources have been removed from your life, and you feel empty and alone. You have nothing left to depend on but God.

It's time to leave Haran, my friend. It's time to believe the promise of God and to set forth on your journey to the land He has promised you.

## THE LAND OF PROMISE

As Abram enters the land God has promised him, the Genesis account gives us a revealing description of conditions in that land:

So Abram left, as the LORD had told him; and Lot went with him. Abram was seventy-five years old when he set out from Haran. He took his wife Sarai, his nephew Lot, all the possessions they had accumulated and the people they had acquired in Haran, and they set out for the land of Canaan, and they arrived there.

Abram traveled through the land as far as the site of the great tree of Moreh at Shechem. At that time the Canaanites were in the land. The LORD appeared to Abram and said, "To your offspring I will give this land." So he built an altar there to the LORD, who had appeared to him.

From there he went on toward the hills east of Bethel and pitched his tent, with Bethel on the west and Ai on the east. There he built an altar to the LORD and called on the name of the LORD. Then Abram set out and continued toward the Negev. (Genesis 12:4–9)

This is more than just a record of what Abram did when he first entered the land. It is truly a picture of the conditions of a Spirit-filled life.

First, Abram passed through the land to the place at Shechem, to the great tree of Moreh. These names are quite revealing. Shechem means "shoulder," and to the Hebrews the shoulder is a symbol of strength. The name Moreh means "instruction." When we combine these two words, we get a glimpse of an important spiritual principle: Only as we receive the instruction of God's Word, as revealed to us by the teaching of the Spirit of God, do we find strength to live. As the apostle Peter writes: "Like newborn babies, crave pure spiritual milk, so that by it you may grow up in your salvation" (1 Peter 2:2).

Second, Abram encountered opponents when he entered the land of promise. "At that time," Genesis tells us, "the Canaanites were in the land." This speaks to the fact that life in the land of promise is full of conflict and opposition.

The Canaanites were a number of pagan tribes that afflicted Israel throughout its history. One such tribe, for example, was the Philistine nation, a people who lived along the southern coast of Canaan. The word *Palestine* is a corruption of "Philistine," and the Palestinian people, who have been locked in conflict with the Jews ever since the reestablishment of Israel in 1948, claim to be direct descendants of the Philistines. So the conflict between Abram and the Canaanites continues to this day.

The Canaanites symbolize the opposition we continually face in the spiritual land of promise. The spiritual forces that oppose us have such names as lust, envy, jealousy, impatience, intemperance, greed, rage, slander, bitterness, and so forth. These are our daily enemies—the temptations without, the weakness within.

## CLEANSING AND CHOOSING

Third, life in the land of promise is a life of continual cleansing. Genesis tells us that Abram "built an altar to the Lord and called on the name of the Lord." We tend to think of an altar as a symbol of worship, and it is. But the most essential purpose of an altar is cleansing, because cleansing is the foundation of true worship.

Abram built an altar to the Lord, and so should we. Every day, we should have an altar experience with God. As pilgrims in the Christian life, we urgently need God's daily cleansing in our lives. Every pilgrim needs the cleansing of the blood of Christ, which was shed upon the cross. When we come before the cross and rightly judge the reality of our lives, acknowledging and confessing our sins to God, He cleanses us. We need to experience this cleansing every day.

Many Christians seem to feel they need the cleansing of the cross only at the beginning of the Christian life. This is not true. Just as we daily need to cleanse our bodies and brush our teeth and dry behind our ears, so we also need to cleanse ourselves spiritually on a regular and continual basis. The power of the cross is the power of God to cleanse us every day.

Fourth, life in the land of promise is a life of choices and decisions. This passage tells us that Abram pitched his tent between Bethel and Ai. Bethel means "the house of God"; Ai means "ruin." That is where the Christian life is lived. We must continually make choices between the path that leads to God and His blessings and the path that leads to the ruin of the flesh. We must choose: Bethel or Ai, Christ or self. We cannot have both. To choose one is to reject the other.

In this story, we find a fitting symbol of the Christian life: the tent of Abram. When Abram came to the promised land, he did not build a mansion. He pitched a tent, a temporary dwelling place. Why? Because he never stopped in one place for long. He was a pilgrim, a sojourner.

And so are we. All through the New Testament, we, as Christian pilgrims, are exhorted to walk in the Spirit. Walk, walk, walk! No matter how many lessons you've learned in the Christian life, God always has another lesson to teach you. You took a step today, and you learned a lesson. But tomorrow, there is another step to be taken, another lesson to be learned. And after that, another and another and another.

How the flesh resents this! We want to experience victory and be done with it. We want to close escrow on our nice big house in the promised land, but God tells us, "No, it's not time to settle down. Pick up your tent and keep moving."

Everyone is living in one of three places—Ur, Haran, or Canaan. Where do you live? Ur is the land of death and darkness, the land into which we were born. Haran is the halfway house where we gain the outward appearance of being religious but where there is no inward reality. Canaan is the land of power and blessing, the place of the Spirit's fullness. Have you entered the land?

# 2

# A FAILURE OF FAITH

*Genesis 12:10–13:4*

Benjamin Harrison served as president of the United States from 1889 to 1893. He and his wife, Caroline, were the first couple to occupy the White House after it was wired for electricity. President Harrison was a brave man who had faced death many times as a brigadier general in the Civil War. But there was one thing that both President and Mrs. Harrison feared: the light switches on the White House walls.

Electricity was such a new and mysterious force that the Harrisons feared they might be electrocuted just by touching the switches. How did they turn the White House lights on and off? Simple: They had the servants do it. If there were no servants handy when the Harrisons retired for the night, they slept with the bedroom lights on all night.

Fear is a powerful force. Our fears sometimes drive us to do foolish things. God calls us to turn on the light switch of faith. All too often, however, instead of turning on the light switch, we press the panic button. As we continue our journey, we will discover that even Abraham, our role model of faith, knew what it felt like to push the panic button and retreat from the light of faith.

## FEAR VERSUS FAITH

We pick up the story of Abram in Genesis 12, where we discover the reasons for Abram's failure of faith. Those reasons are traced for us in three movements: the famine in Canaan, the folly of Egypt, and the fullness of God in the land. We read: "Now there was a famine in the land, and Abram went down to Egypt to live there for a while because the famine was severe" (Genesis 12:10).

In those days, the land of Canaan had a moderate climate much like parts of California. In good years, when there was rain, the land produced an abundant harvest. But in drought years, the land could become parched and dry, and the grass would wither. For those whose livelihood depended on pasturing flocks, the dry years were difficult, dangerous times. Abram was a man with flocks and herds, and when the rains failed, his livelihood suffered. When food became scarce in Canaan, Abram felt driven to leave, even though God had called him to be there.

The Scriptures do not tell us that Abram asked God's permission to go to Egypt. It appears that Abram took counsel not from God but from his fears. He pushed the panic button and fled to Egypt to escape the uncertainty of the drought in Canaan. Fear drove him.

As we have already seen, the land of Canaan symbolizes a life of fellowship with Jesus Christ. A famine in the land, therefore, symbolizes any circumstance that would threaten our dependence on Him and our fellowship with Him. Have you ever experienced a famine in your relationship with Christ? Often, we will seem to live a life of joy and fellowship with Him—then, unexpectedly, circumstances arise that make us feel cut off from the Lord.

Those circumstances may be as serious as a major catastrophe in our lives, something that causes us to question our faith or doubt God's love for us. Or it may be something as minor as a car that won't start or a problem at the office or an argument with a friend—some experience that robs us of our joy, leaving us with little strength to pray and seek God's fellowship. Or it may be a lengthy trial of depressing circumstances that never seem to end and that make us question our relationship with God.

All of these can be times of spiritual famine. We become fearful, and we are tempted to flee our Canaan instead of remaining in the promised land and trusting God to provide for us. We would rather go to Egypt, a place where life seems more pleasant.

Our escape to Egypt can take many forms. Some people escape through drugs, alcohol, overeating, overspending, gambling, or other addictions. Some choose to immerse themselves in a whirling social life. Some choose a sexual affair or pornography. Some seek money or status or fame to escape their spiritual famine. Whenever we try to satisfy our spiritual needs with worldly resources, we have fled from Canaan and escaped to Egypt.

It is not wrong to seek a momentary escape—that is, a time of rest and recreation. God understands that we need to pace ourselves and take time to recharge our physical and spiritual batteries. As Jesus said, "Come with me by yourselves to a quiet place and get some rest" (Mark 6:31). When we take time to rest and reflect with the Lord, we are retreating even more deeply into Jesus, not running away from Him and escaping into Egypt.

The issue at stake in the story of Abram's flight to Egypt as the issue of fear versus faith. When we experience fear, God calls us to turn that fear over to Him and trust Him. That is faith. When we rely on Him in total trust and faith, there is no room for fear. Faith cancels fear.

## FALSEHOOD VERSUS FAITH

Next, Abram's experience demonstrates for us the unutterable folly of Egypt:

> As he was about to enter Egypt, he said to his wife Sarai, "I know what a beautiful woman you are. When the Egyptians see you, they will say, 'This is his wife.' Then they will kill me but will let you live. Say you are my sister, so that I will be treated well for your sake and my life will be spared because of you."
>
> When Abram came to Egypt, the Egyptians saw that she was a very beautiful woman. And when Pharaoh's officials saw her, they praised her to Pharaoh, and she was taken into his palace. He treated Abram well for her sake, and Abram acquired sheep and cattle, male and female donkeys, menservants and maidservants, and camels.

But the LORD inflicted serious diseases on Pharaoh and his household because of Abram's wife Sarai. So Pharaoh summoned Abram. "What have you done to me?" he said. "Why didn't you tell me she was your wife? Why did you say, 'She is my sister,' so that I took her to be my wife? Now then, here is your wife. Take her and go!" Then Pharaoh gave orders about Abram to his men, and they sent him on his way, with his wife and everything he had. (Genesis 12:11–20)

Here Abram turns away from faith and toward falsehood. He has gone to Egypt and escaped the pressure of famine in Canaan. He has found in Egypt the relief he was seeking. In Egypt, there was plenty of food, comfort, and security. Abram was able to acquire wealth and servants and a beautiful home, but it all came at the price of his integrity.

True, it's more comfortable to live in a mansion in Egypt than a tent in Canaan. But the pleasures of Egypt always come with a heavy price tag.

When Abram lost his courage and compromised his faith. He sacrificed his integrity. In his fear, he took refuge in cowardice and falsehood. He told what some today would call a little white lie. He said to his beautiful wife, "Look, dear, I know these Egyptians. I read about them in the library in Ur. They're all wolves, and you are a beautiful woman. I know what will happen when we get there. The Egyptians will want to take you—and if they know you are my wife, they'll kill me to get you. So I have a plan: Tell them you're my sister."

You may say, "That's not a little white lie! That's a whopper!" What Abram told the Egyptians was not altogether false. Sarai was Abram's half-sister. She was the daughter of a woman who married Abram's father after Abram was born. So even though Abram and Sarai were not genetically related, Abram's claim was a half-truth.

But a half-truth is always a total lie. We often lie to ourselves, pretending that if there is some little grain of truth mixed in with our lie, then the lie isn't so bad. The fact is, whenever we set out to deceive, we take refuge in falsehood. If we have lied even a little, then we have deceived to the nth degree. If you compromise even a tiny particle of your integrity, you have compromised it all.

So Abram clearly intended to deceive. He undoubtedly rationalized his lie as necessary to save his own life and protect his beautiful wife. And here we come to one of the most startling aspects of the story.

It's important to remember that Sarai was sixty-five years old at the time, yet her beauty was so exquisite that Abram feared he might be killed because of her. We cannot assume that Abram was viewing his sixty-five-year-old bride through rosy-tinted glasses of love. After all, the Egyptians were also astonished at her beauty. When they saw her, they immediately rushed to Pharaoh and told him of this beautiful woman who had come into their country from Canaan.

So Abram feels he must protect himself, and in his fear he thinks his only recourse is to lie. This is the first result of moving out of Canaan and out of fellowship with Christ. When we leave the promised land and move away from the tent and the altar, the old self comes to the fore and assumes control of our lives. The immediate result is hypocrisy and deceit. I'm sure that in your experience, you have found this principle to be true. The moment you move away from the control of God, your old self asserts its control—and you soon find yourself mired in deception.

The result of Abram's lie was that he put Sarai in real danger. Unaware that Sarai was Abram's wife, the Egyptian pharaoh claimed Sarai for his harem. Abram's lie opened this door. Abram's lie, which he intended to protect himself, put his wife and his marriage at risk. He exposed his wife to immorality, humiliation, and danger. This, too, is the folly of Egypt: Our loved ones suffer because of our cowardice and deceit.

And the harm of Abram's lie did not end with Sarai. Abram's nephew, Lot, was harmed as well. Lot went to Egypt with Abram, and there he became captivated by the worldly riches and comforts of that land. Later, when the allurements and enticements of the cities of Sodom and Gomorrah cast their spell over Lot, the Scriptures tell us that those cities seem to him like the land of Egypt. The lust for comfort and worldly glory was born in Lot during his stay in Egypt, and it nearly destroyed him.

When you flee to Egypt, you harm not only yourself but your loved ones as well.

## A CURSE TO THE WORLDLINGS

Abram became vulnerable to the folly of Egypt by becoming rich in that land. Is there anything wrong with being rich? Not necessarily. Riches can be a blessing, especially if we use our riches to bless the lives of others.

But we need to remember that riches can deceive us. Jesus warned that "the deceitfulness of wealth" can choke out the truth of God's Word in us (see Mark 4:19). In Egypt, Abram acquired flocks, herds, and servants—all symbols of great wealth in the ancient Middle East. When Abram returned to the land of Canaan, what was the first thing that took place? Strife! There was an intense conflict between Abram's herdsmen and Lot's herdsmen over the riches they had acquired in Egypt.

It's significant that among the many servants Abram acquired in Egypt was a maidservant named Hagar. As we shall see, Abram will later have a child named Ishmael with Hagar. This is extremely significant, because Ishmael will become the father of all the Arab nations— and the Arab people have been a thorn in the side of Israel ever since. The price of living in Egypt is always a higher price than we realize, and a higher price than we would knowingly want to pay.

And that is not all. By choosing to leave the promised land and live in Egypt, Abram became a curse and a source of trouble to the worldlings around him, the unbelieving people of Egypt—people we would think of today as unsaved. Because Pharaoh had taken Sarai, Abram's wife, into his house, the Lord afflicted Pharaoh and his entire household with plagues.

Just as God calls you and me to be a blessing to the unsaved people around us, God called Abram to be a blessing wherever he was. But when Abram went to Egypt, he made himself a curse to those around him. A Christian out of fellowship with Christ cannot help the lost people around him. Such Christians become a curse, not a blessing. If you are not walking in the fullness of the Spirit, please do not attempt to share Christ with anyone. Your witness would not be authentic, and you would do more harm than good.

But please understand, I'm not suggesting you should be silent and go on sinning. My urgent counsel to you is to stop sinning, to revive your love relationship with the Lord, and then to become a bold and vibrant witness for Him!

## REBUKE AND HUMILIATION

The Scriptures tell us that after Pharaoh and his household suffered plagues from the Lord, Pharaoh summoned Abram before him and said, "What have you done to me? Why didn't you tell me she was your wife? Why did you say, 'She is my sister,' so that I took her to be my wife? Now then, here is your wife. Take her and go!"

The great irony of this story is that God used a pagan king to rebuke Abram. Pharaoh demonstrates more character and better morals than God's chosen servant, Abram! It should be Abram, the man of faith, who teaches Pharaoh about God's ways. Instead, Abram discovers that Egypt is, for him, a place of rebuke and humiliation.

When I was a young Christian living in Denver, I accepted a job soliciting advertisements for a small church paper. The pastor of the church felt that some businesses that dealt with the church would be willing to advertise in our little paper. So I called on those businesses to sell ad space.

I phoned the manager of a popular restaurant near the church, saying, "I'm calling on behalf of Mr. Hewitt, the pastor of the church." And that was true; Mr. Hewitt had given me permission to speak on his behalf. But the woman who managed the restaurant misunderstood and thought I was Mr. Hewitt. Throughout the conversation, she addressed me as Mr. Hewitt. It took me by surprise, and not knowing how best to respond, I didn't correct her. She placed the ad.

The following month, I called her again to renew the ad. Her mistaken impression had worked so well the first time that I continued the ruse and identified myself as Mr. Hewitt. I lied—and I placed another ad.

The third month, I tried the same ploy again. When she spoke to me, her voice was chilly and harsh. "I don't know who you are," she said, "but you are not Mr. Hewitt. From where I am sitting, I can see Mr. Hewitt and his wife eating lunch. I don't know what kind of church you run, but if this is how you do business, you don't need to call me anymore." With that, she hung up the phone.

As I write these words, I can still feel the shame and humiliation I felt at that moment. I had called this woman as a representative of the church and of the Lord, but she had rebuked me for my folly. And it was a rebuke I richly deserved.

For you and me, just as it was for Abram, Egypt is a place not only of folly but also of rebuke and humiliation. That is why we must live our spiritual lives in the land of promise, not in the land of Egypt.

## WHAT ABRAM FOUND IN CANAAN

Finally, God brings Abram's painful lesson to an end. He leads Abram out of Egypt and back into the land of Canaan. Abram is crushed and humiliated, but he is also wiser, having learned the painful lessons of his folly in Egypt. The Scriptures tell us:

> Then Pharaoh gave orders about Abram to his men, and they sent him on his way, with his wife and everything he had.
>
> So Abram went up from Egypt to the Negev, with his wife and everything he had, and Lot went with him. Abram had become very wealthy in livestock and in silver and gold.
>
> From the Negev he went from place to place until he came to Bethel, to the place between Bethel and Ai where his tent had been earlier and where he had first built an altar. There Abram called on the name of the LORD. (Genesis 12:20–13:4)

Abram didn't leave of his own accord. Pharaoh sent him packing! The Egyptian king gave orders to his men to make sure that Abram and his wife and all their belongings were gone for good. We get a clear sense from God's Word that Pharaoh was enraged with Abram and told him, in effect, "Get out! And good riddance!"

So Abram was kicked out of Egypt and made his way back into Canaan. He went to the place between Bethel and Ai, the place where he had once pitched his tent. And what did he find there? He found the altar he first built to God.

Abram had no altar in Egypt. While in the land of Egypt, he didn't live as God intended. He had no place of worship or cleansing. But when Abram returned to Canaan, he was back where God wanted him. He was back in fellowship with God, living in a pilgrim's tent, worshiping at a pilgrim's altar. And there, Abram called upon the name of the Lord.

What do we learn from Abram's experience? We learn that time spent in Egypt is wasted time. We do not grow in grace when we are outside of God's will for our lives. We do not achieve the things He wants us to achieve. We cannot be a blessing to others when we have departed from His will. Abram may have grown materially rich in Egypt, but in a spiritual sense, he had nothing to show for his time in Egypt except barrenness and weakness.

And so it is with you and me. When we forsake the path of faith and neglect to walk in fellowship with God, we waste the life God has given us. Years spent away from Him are wasted years. I know Christians who have lived almost all of their Christian lives in Egypt. They have nothing to show for it but barren, empty lives, full of regret.

We have to ask ourselves: What were the conditions in Canaan when Abram returned there? The Scriptures do not mention the famine again, but I think it is reasonable to conclude that the famine was still going on. Remember, Abram did not leave Egypt by his own free will. He was driven out of that country by Pharaoh. I believe that if Abram had received word that the famine had ended in Canaan, he would have left Egypt of his own accord and gone back to that land. The fact that he had to be forced out of the country strongly suggests that life in Canaan was still very hard.

Notice also that a quarrel developed between the herdsmen of Lot and the herdsmen of Abram. The reason for the quarrel: There was a severe shortage of feed for the herds. This is another indication that the land was still in the grip of a famine.

But even though the famine continued, Abram was no longer afraid of being without food. Why not? Because his perspective had changed. When Abram returned to the promised land, the first thing he did was call upon the name of the Lord. This, of course, is what he should have done when the famine first overshadowed the land. If he had focused on God instead of focusing on his difficult circumstances, he would have saved himself from the humiliation and regret of those wasted years in Egypt.

What does it mean to call upon the name of the Lord? God's name has a powerful meaning for your life and mine. It symbolizes the wealth and resources of God. Think of it this way: When you write a check, you sign your name in the bottom right corner. By signing your name, you authorize the bank to draw the amount of the check out of your account—your resources—that have been deposited in the bank. Your name is your guarantee that those resources are available.

When Abram called on the name of the Lord, he was laying claim to the resources of the Lord—resources that the Lord had promised to him. In calling upon God's name, Abram discovered that God's resources are more than sufficient for his needs, even in times of famine and harsh circumstances. The apostle Paul put it this way in the New Testament: "And my God will meet all your needs according to his glorious riches in Christ Jesus" (Philippians 4:19).

## FACING YOUR FAMINE

Hudson Taylor was a pioneering missionary in China during the late nineteenth century. Near the close of his life, the Boxer Uprising broke out in China—a violent attack upon all foreigners and foreign influences in China. The uprising began in northern China in 1898 and continued through the summer of 1901. The attacks were aimed especially at Christian missionaries and Chinese Christian converts. While the government of China looked the other way, so-called boxers (gangs of Chinese street thugs) attacked foreign embassies, missionary compounds, and churches, terrorizing, pillaging, raping, and killing.

Every day, new reports came to Hudson Taylor's missionary headquarters of the death and persecution of missionaries, pastors, and Chinese Christians. Taylor had given his life to evangelizing China and building up the Chinese church. Suddenly, it all seemed to be crumbling before his eyes. One day, when the news was particularly bleak, Taylor's associates wondered if the discouragement would be too much for the old man. He spent the morning alone in his house. When his associates came to see him in the afternoon, they feared they would find him steeped in depression.

But as they approached the house, they were astonished to hear him singing aloud this hymn of trusting faith:

*Jesus, I am resting, resting,*
*In the joy of what Thou art;*
*I am finding out the greatness,*
*Of Thy loving heart.*
*Thou hast bade me gaze upon Thee,*
*And Thy beauty fills my soul,*
*For by Thy transforming power,*
*Thou hast made me whole.*

Are you going through a time of testing and trial that makes it difficult to cling to faith in God? Are you facing a famine in some area of your life? Are you tempted to escape your famine experience by fleeing to Egypt? You may find some temporary relief there, but I assure you, the price is more than you would ever want to pay.

If we remain in the promised land, even in times of famine, we can say, "I trust you, Lord. I know you will see me through this experience. I will live in this tent, and I will worship you at this altar. I will not be moved from my trust in you."

# 3

# LETTING GOD CHOOSE

*Genesis 13:5–18*

Life must be lived forward, though it often seems arranged backwards.

We must make the most crucial and important choices of our lives at a time when we have the least experience to guide us. We must make decisions about our college education and even our careers when we are teenagers, knowing next to nothing about the world. And most of us choose the person we will marry while we are in our twenties—still too young to have gained much wisdom about relationships.

Because we must make these important decisions while we lack experience and the wisdom that experience brings, we often hear people say, "If only I had known!" or, "If I had it to do it over again!" And it is not just the young who often regret their decisions, but on into our forties, fifties, and sixties, we discover that we have made mistakes raising our children or investing our money or purchasing real estate or starting a business. It seems we constantly make decisions we later regret.

What does this aspect of human life reveal to us? It tells us that we are all incapable of handling life by ourselves. We all lack the wisdom necessary to truly master the adventure of living. It's a wise person indeed who learns this lesson early and heeds the admonition of God's Word, "Trust in the LORD with all your heart, and lean not on your own understanding; in all your ways acknowledge him, and he will make your paths straight" (Proverbs 3:5–6).

That is the lesson Abram learns next.

## THE TRAP OF PROSPERITY

After the temporary lapse of faith that took Abram from Canaan into Egypt, we find him back in the land of promise. He's living in his tent and worshiping at his altar. He's enjoying the fullness of God's provision for his life.

But as we have already seen, life in the promised land is an experience of continual conflict. If we stop moving forward with God, we immediately slip backwards. So we must press on from one victory to the next.

Moreover, life in the promised land is an experience of unending choice. We are continually faced with decisions. As we shall soon see, the conflicts that are a part of life in the promised land confront us with decisions that must be made in reliance upon God's wisdom. Abram must make just such a decision when he comes into conflict with his nephew Lot:

> Now Lot, who was moving about with Abram, also had flocks and herds and tents. But the land could not support them while they stayed together, for their possessions were so great that they were not able to stay together. And quarreling arose between Abram's herdsmen and the herdsmen of Lot. The Canaanites and Perizzites were also living in the land at that time. (Genesis 13:5–7)

The story of Lot, Abram's nephew, can be summed up in one phrase in Genesis 13:5: "Lot, who was moving about with Abram." Wherever Abram was, Lot was. When Abram stopped, Lot stopped. "With Abram"—that's about all that can be said of Lot.

Some Bible commentators are critical of Abram for taking Lot with him out of the land of Ur. As we examine the story of Abram, it's clear that Lot was a continual weight around his neck. Even so, the Bible never implies that Abram was wrong to bring Lot along. Lot evidently responded when God spoke to Abram and called him to go to the promised land. Lot wanted to go along, and Abram, wishing to help him, agreed.

Though Abram was not wrong to bring Lot along, he did find himself repeatedly hindered by his nephew. Why? Because Lot repeatedly made poor choices. Lot is a symbol of a common sort of Christian—the kind of Christian who depends on others for faith and inspiration to act. You are probably acquainted with Christians like Lot. They don't seem to have their own walk with God. They lean on the church or on other Christians or on Christian radio and television shows. Their faith derives from other people, not from a deep and intimate connection with God.

Lot's dependence on Abram limited his own spiritual life. When Abram's faith failed, Lot's also failed. Abram became Lot's crutch, and when the crutch that props you up is weak, you are destined to fall.

You might say that Lot was a secondhand Christian. This doesn't mean that Lot's faith was counterfeit. The New Testament tells us clearly that Lot was a righteous man (see 2 Peter 2:7). But Lot was spiritually ineffective because he was dependent on Abram for his faith.

Lot's dependence on Abram also made him unstable. When he experienced pressure and uncertainty, he stuck close to Abram, because he sensed his need of Abram's strength, courage, and faith. Lot knew that he himself was spiritually weak—too weak to trust in his own character and faith. In this respect, Lot was like many Christians today. They will cling to their Christian friends in times of pressure and trial, drawing upon the spiritual resources of others, knowing they lack spiritual resources of their own.

But there is one test that this kind of believer cannot withstand— the test of prosperity. Material prosperity always exposes a spiritually dependent person for what he or she truly is. That is what happened to Lot.

The Bible tells us that Lot "had flocks and herds and tents," but the land could not support both Abram and Lot because "their possessions were so great that they were not able to stay together." As a result, conflict arose between Abram and Lot—what we would today call a conflict of interests.

We often see similar situations arise among Christians. For

example, two believers go into business together. The one who is spiritually stronger and more committed sees the business as a means to benefit the work of God. He has dedicated his business to the Lord. While he knows God expects him to take his normal living from the business, this man is not trying to build the business in order to gain worldly wealth. He sees the business as a way of investing in eternity, investing in lives, and making money that can help advance the work of God.

At first, both partners share this approach to their business. Both want to use their business to serve God and others. Then prosperity comes. The business begins making money. The second man is able to raise his standard of living, and he is lured by the material things of life. He becomes increasingly more concerned about enlarging his profits and growing the business—and he loses his original perspective.

So it was with Abram and Lot. Prosperity came between the uncle and nephew. The time had come for a dividing of the ways.

## ABRAM'S WISE SOLUTION

It was the man of faith, Abram, who took the initiative in solving the conflict between Lot and himself. Lot would have allowed the conflict between himself and his uncle to deteriorate until war broke out, but Abram acted wisely to bring the simmering conflict to an end. He said, in effect, "There's only one thing to do. We must separate now before the conflict between us grows any worse."

The previous passage ended with these words: "The Canaanites and Perizzites were also living in the land at that time." Why does the passage mention these two ethnic groups? The Canaanites and Perizzites were enemies who constantly made war against God's people. This is a warning to us that whenever strife looms between believers, the enemies of the Lord are ready to take full advantage of it.

The Canaanites and Perizzites represent the evils of the flesh that are continually at war with the believer's spirit. These enemies lurk in every Christian heart: jealousy, envy, resentment, malice, and other forms of bitterness. Whenever there is discord and disunity among

Christians, these enemies are ready to take advantage of the situation. They seek to defeat us through a strategy of divide and conquer.

The reference to the Canaanites and Perizzites in the context of the conflict between Abram and Lot suggests that these enemies threatened to take advantage of the quarrel between the two men. Abram understood the danger, so the Scriptures tell us that he proposed a solution to the problem:

> So Abram said to Lot, "Let's not have any quarreling between you and me, or between your herdsmen and mine, for we are brothers. Is not the whole land before you? Let's part company. If you go to the left, I'll go to the right; if you go to the right, I'll go to the left." (Genesis 13:8–9)

Abram clearly states the reasons for this separation, and every word he speaks is important. Abram knew that the Canaanites and the Perizzites would take advantage of any strife between Lot and himself. So he acted preemptively, making sure that he resolved the conflict before his enemies could strike. As believers, we must act preemptively, resolving conflicts before feelings of bitterness attack and destroy us from within.

Notice, too, that Abram acted to end the strife as a matter of personal integrity and family honor. He said, "Let's not have any quarreling between you and me . . . for we are brothers." They were kinsman, tied together in the same stream of life, members of the same family. If Abram hurt Lot, he injured a part of himself, and vice versa. Brothers cannot injure brothers without harming themselves and the entire family.

The same is true in the body of Christ, the church. Fellow Christians are brothers and sisters, members of one family of faith. Brothers and sisters cannot injure one another without wounding themselves and the entire body of Christ. Whenever strife erupts among Christians, the entire church is harmed, and the gospel of peace, love, and forgiveness is brought down in shame and disgrace. Abram, in his God-given wisdom, said, "Let's not have any more strife. We're kinsman, so let's calmly settle the matter now before it divides the family."

Then Abram did a magnificent, Christlike thing: He willingly surrendered his own rights without complaint. Though he was the elder of the two, the leader, and certainly entitled to the greater portion, Abram gave Lot the first choice. Abram's godly, selfless decision shows that the altar of worship was at work in this man's heart.

When I was training for the ministry, I traveled for several months as an assistant to Dr. Harry A. Ironside, pastor of the Moody Church in Chicago. I once heard Dr. Ironside relate an experience from his early life. His mother took him to a church meeting. During the meeting, conflict erupted between two Christian men. The situation became so heated that the two men nearly came to blows.

One man stood and shouted, "I don't care what you do—I insist on my rights!"

Hearing that, an older man who was partially deaf leaned forward in his chair, cupped his ear in his hand, and said, "What did you say, brother? You demand your rights, do you? Ah, brother, if you had your rights, you'd be in hell! The Lord Jesus didn't come to get His rights— He came to get His wrongs, and He got them."

The angry fellow blushed and tugged at his collar. "Sir, you are absolutely correct. I've behaved foolishly and selfishly. I humbly apologize. Settle the matter as you think best."

Soon, there was perfect agreement. Why? Because a man who had been behaving like Lot was reminded of what Christlikeness is all about, and he experienced a change of heart. He became like Abram instead. He gave the first choice to the others in that meeting. May you and I always remember, in times of conflict, to respond as Abram did— and may we always follow the selfless example of our Lord Jesus Christ.

## LOT'S CHOICE

Next, we learn what happens when Lot chooses:

> Lot looked up and saw that the whole plain of the Jordan was well watered, like the garden of the LORD, like the land of Egypt, toward Zoar. (This was before the LORD destroyed Sodom and Gomorrah.) So Lot chose for himself the whole

plain of the Jordan and set out toward the east. The two men parted company: Abram lived in the land of Canaan, while Lot lived among the cities of the plain and pitched his tents near Sodom. Now the men of Sodom were wicked and were sinning greatly against the LORD. (Genesis 13:10–13)

The text suggests that Abram and Lot stood upon a promontory overlooking the valley. Lot lifted up his eyes—and what did he see? A lush, green, well-watered plain. In the midst of the drought-parched desert, those garden-like plains looked like Eden itself. He saw the Jordan River winding through a great gorge at the deepest point on the face of the earth. On either side of the Jordan, the grass grew lush and green, and the variety of palm trees along the banks made his mouth water.

Lot also saw the cities of the plain, like the great cities of Egypt. Lot remembered Egypt as a place where one could get rich quick—a place of endless commercial possibilities.

But there were some things about that land that Lot did not see. Although the Jordan River flowed through the land, Lot did not grasp the significance of the river's name. The word *Jordan* means "death." It comes from the Hebrew *yarden*, meaning "descender" (from *yarad*, meaning "to descend" or "to sink down"). When John the Baptist baptized people in the Jordan River, it signified the death of the old life as the person was plunged beneath the waters of death and rising again to a new life when that person was raised up out of the waters of death.

The River Jordan descended out of the living waters of Galilee and dropped far below sea level into the Dead Sea, from which there is no outlet. The river, flowing in its steep-walled, canyon-like channel, was grand to look upon. But it flowed to a dead end. Its waters were doomed to end up in a salty sea in which nothing could live. In choosing the land through which the Jordan flowed, Lot chose death instead of life.

Lot also chose to move his herds into the land near Sodom. The passage tells us, "Now the men of Sodom were wicked and were sinning greatly against the Lord." Lot saw the wealth of Sodom and other nearby cities, but he did not take into account their moral corruption.

Today, the name of Sodom is linked to a particular form of unnatural sexual activity, and the reason will become apparent as we continue our study. But it is important to remember that the wickedness and sin of Sodom extended far beyond the sexual depravity of its people. Elsewhere, the Word of God tells us that Sodom was "arrogant, overfed and unconcerned" and "did not help the poor and needy." The people of Sodom "were haughty and did detestable things before [God]" (see Ezekiel 16:49–50).

We live in a Sodom-like culture today. Moral corruption permeates our society, not only in the sexual depravity that surrounds us but also in the arrogance, extravagance, and unconcern for the poor and needy. Those whom society exalts as the trendsetters of our day—from government leaders to corporate leaders to the entertainers and celebrities on our magazine covers and television screens—tend to be arrogant and haughty, and they do detestable things before the Lord.

God warns us not to fall into the snare of Lot. He was lured by the riches and the life of power and pleasure that Sodom offered. We should not be too quick to judge Lot, as if we are immune from the enticements that captured his heart. We, too, are prone to chase after the false values of Sodom.

The passage tells one other thing about the land Lot chose: He didn't understand that cities of that land were doomed to destruction. Genesis tells us that Lot made his fateful choice "before the LORD destroyed Sodom and Gomorrah." Lot saw only the great prosperity and natural beauty of that land. He didn't realize that judgment was coming upon Sodom and Gomorrah. The land and its inhabitants were about to be swept away.

Human beings cannot foresee what God will do. Neither Lot nor Abraham could foresee the death and judgment that awaited Sodom— and that is the point of this passage of Scripture. Lot, presuming to run his own life, chose for himself. Deceived by the enticing riches of Sodom, he stumbled blindly into heartache and judgment. By contrast, Abram was content to let God choose for him. Though the land Abram received looked second-best, it was God's best plan for his life.

Long before the true nature of Sodom became apparent to Lot, Abram chose to entrust his future to God. He had learned that the only true Reality, the only Source of the knowledge of things as they really are, is revealed to the man with the tent and the altar. Riches, power, and pleasure are deceptive; they entice us and lead us to corruption and death. But the tent and the altar lead us to life and God's truth.

"Lot chose for himself." What a telling phrase that is! As he looked out over the land, the fallen self within him said, "This is what I want! This will give me power and position and praise among people." So he chose for himself and pitched his tents near Sodom. And every time he moved his tent, he moved it a little bit closer to Sodom—to the city that was under the shadow of God's judgment.

We shall see more of what Lot's choice will cost him in a later chapter.

## GOD'S CHOICE FOR ABRAM

Now, what of Abram? How did it go with the man who was willing to let God make the choices for him? We read:

> The LORD said to Abram after Lot had parted from him, "Lift up your eyes from where you are and look north and south, east and west. All the land that you see I will give to you and your offspring forever. I will make your offspring like the dust of the earth, so that if anyone could count the dust, then your offspring could be counted. Go, walk through the length and breadth of the land, for I am giving it to you."
>
> So Abram moved his tents and went to live near the great trees of Mamre at Hebron, where he built an altar to the LORD. (Genesis 13:14–18)

Lot lifted up his eyes and chose for himself. But now God says to Abram, the man of faith, "Lift up your eyes." Where does God tell him to look? Everywhere! To the north, the south, the east, and the west. All the land is his—even the portion Lot chose!

This land is a symbol of the fullness of life in the Spirit of God—the life of joy, power, love, and glory. This is the life Paul longs for us when he prays that we "may have power, together with all the saints, to grasp how wide and long and high and deep is the love of Christ, and to know this love that surpasses knowledge—that you may be filled to the measure of all the fullness of God" (Ephesians 3:18–19). All of this is ours, if we are willing to let God make the choices of life for us.

Lot, in his selfishness, will never know the joy that is Abram's. Nor will we, if we make our choices on the basis of what we see, on the basis of the materialistic values of this dying culture. But if, like Abram, we are content to have what God gives us in life, all the fullness of Christ will be ours. As Paul writes, "All things are yours . . . and you are of Christ, and Christ is of God" (see 1 Corinthians 3:21–23).

Then God said to Abram, "All the land that you see I will give to you and your offspring forever. I will make your offspring like the dust of the earth." In other words, "Not only do I give this land to you, but also I will fill the land with your descendants. I will make you fruitful beyond your imagination. I will make your life one of such blessing that after you are gone there will be those who will stand up and say, 'I received my spiritual life through Abram, the man of faith.'"

Next, God told Abram to rise up and walk the length and breadth of the land. This symbolizes all that Christ will be to us through the eternal ages to come. God says to us, as He told Abram, "Don't wait for some future promise—possess it now! It is yours! Walk through the promised land. Set your feet upon it. Possess it and enjoy it now!"

Understand, when God told Abram to walk the length and breadth of the land, this didn't change the fact that there were Canaanites and Perizzites in the land. Abram's enemies were still there, ready to do him harm. But wherever Abram went in that land, God opened the door. The whole land was his. He could go where he wanted. He could live where he chose. When Abram moved in, the Canaanites and the Perizzites had to move out.

The same is true for you and me in the spiritual realm. As God tells us in Romans 6:14: "For sin shall not be your master, because you are not under law, but under grace." Whenever you want to be free from the power of sin, you can. The land of promise lies open before you, and your enemies must give way before you. So go forth and possess the land God has given you.

We read that Abram moved his tent and came down to great trees of Mamre. The word *mamre* means "fatness," the place where the soul is made fat with the fullness of God's rich supply. Mamre was at Hebron, a word that means "fellowship." There, in the place of fatness and fellowship, Abram built an altar to the Lord. He confessed again by the building of an altar that he was nothing but a fallible human being, with no power in himself. He acknowledged that he needed the continual cleansing of God.

You and I live in a world like that of Abram and Lot, a world in which sin and materialistic values constantly clamor at us. We are tempted to act selfishly, to grab the best for ourselves while we can. We are tempted to seize what the world offers, the riches and enticements of the cities of the plain. We must make a choice.

God implores us to learn from Abram, to be content with our tent and altar, to enjoy the blessings of the land by faith, trusting that His promises to us will be fulfilled. Like Abram, the man of faith, let us trust God and let Him make the choices for our lives.

# 4

# WHEN YOU NEED
# A FRIEND

*Genesis 14:1–16*

"Sometimes I wonder what it really means to be a Christian," the young man said. He was raised in a Christian home and grew up in the church, but now, in his teens, he was beginning to question the reality of his faith. "If being a Christian means growing up in a dull environment, living a boring life, and talking about long spiritual words all day, I don't know if I am into it. Somehow I know there must be more."

This young man, whose story Ron Luce tells in *Inspire the Fire: Giving Today's Youth Something Real to Believe In* (Lake Mary, FL: Creation House, 1994, 14–15), is not alone. Many people, including many in the church, think of the Christian life as a dull, dreary, uneventful existence. If that is your perception of Christianity, then I have good news for you: Genuine, authentic Christianity is anything but dull. It is truly the adventure of a lifetime.

If you see the Christian life as boring and unchallenging, then your vision of reality is out of focus. You do not understand true spirituality. This view of Christianity as a dull and humdrum existence is common among non-Christians and among church-going people who have bought into a worldly, carnal view of life. Such people view life as Lot did. But those who view life as Abram did are destined for a life of genuine excitement, lasting meaning, and high adventure.

As we have seen, whenever Abram is living in a tent and worshiping at an altar in the land of Canaan, he is a symbolic picture of a Christian living in the power of God and the joy of the pilgrim life. A truly godly man or woman lives in this world but is not of this world. As Christians, we are meant to live by the daily cleansing of the cross.

Lot, by contrast, is a symbolic picture of the carnal (fleshly, worldly) Christian, who lives for the flesh and is governed by the flesh and its appetites. He has forsaken the place of fellowship with Christ. After leaving Abram on the hillside, Lot eagerly moved toward Sodom and Gomorrah, the cities of the plain. He was drawn by the enticements of the world and began to live for himself and for the pleasures of the senses. Lot symbolizes the Christian who is born again but who remains enmeshed in the enticements of the materialistic world system.

## ENEMIES WITHOUT, ENEMIES WITHIN

Abram's quiet and pleasant life is about to be shattered. Life in the Spirit is like that. We are never permitted to rest beside the still waters very long, nor would we want to. The life in the Spirit is a life of adventure.

In Genesis 14, we are introduced to the first war ever recorded in Scripture. It is a stirring account, vividly contrasting the noisy, vaunted armies of earth against the quiet but invincible power of faith:

> At this time Amraphel king of Shinar, Arioch king of Ellasar, Kedorlaomer king of Elam and Tidal king of Goiim went to war against Bera king of Sodom, Birsha king of Gomorrah, Shinab king of Admah, Shemeber king of Zeboiim, and the king of Bela (that is, Zoar). All these latter kings joined forces in the Valley of Siddim (the Salt Sea). (Genesis 14:1–3)

Archaeologists have amply verified the existence of the kings named here. Long before the rise of the Babylonian Empire, these kings made a military foray into the land of Canaan, perhaps to defend their trade routes with Egypt or to subdue the warlike tribes of the area. When these invaders threatened the rich cities of the plains, the kings of those cities became greatly alarmed.

The chief of these invading armies was Kedorlaomer, the king of Elam, a land between Babylonia and Persia, along the northern coast of the Persian Gulf. Kedorlaomer headed a confederacy of five monarchs from the east. He represents the world's power to harass and enslave Christians. But more than one worldly king is required to adequately illustrate the world's hostility to God's people. Bera, king of Sodom, along with the other kings of the cities of the plains, pictures the world in its lust for sensual pleasure.

So here we see Abram and Lot caught between two wicked forces— the kings of the plains and the invading kings from the east. Both forces illustrate the naked power of the world to tyrannize us and take away our liberty. These forces are often found in opposition throughout history.

In fact, we in the United States live in similar circumstances today: Most Americans today live under the tyranny of the enemies within— materialism, greed, and the sexual appetites. These forces dominate the life of our culture. Meanwhile, America is also threatened by outside forces, from tyrannical militaristic states like Russia, China, and Iran, as well as the ruthless bands of terrorists who seek to destroy our way of life.

The enemies of our political freedom are symbolic of the enemies of our spiritual freedom. Just as the United States is threatened from without and within, so we as Christians face both external and internal forces which seek to destroy us. All of the enemies have their genesis in the fallen nature of humanity.

This is the situation in which Lot found himself as he dwelt in Sodom. He had become enmeshed in the commercialism and material-ism of Sodom, even though he had kept himself free from the sexual degradation of the place. Though he viewed himself as a follower of God, he had made compromises with the world. He had placed himself in a position of spiritual danger. Sodom was the enemy within.

Then came news of invading armies from the east—a direct threat from the enemy without. This enemy threatened to deprive Lot of his freedom and perhaps of life itself.

What is the enemy without that you face? Perhaps you are being unfairly attacked by opposition and hostility from other people. Or perhaps you are facing a financial catastrophe. Maybe some important relationship in your life is strained or broken. Or you may be facing attacks of doubt as your university professor or a book you've been reading seeks to undermine your faith.

You feel attacked and threatened from without at the same time you face temptations and difficult moral choices within. You are caught in the jaws of a vise. Like Lot, you are being squeezed between the enticements of Sodom and the outright hostility and tyranny of Kedorlaomer.

## THE HELPLESSNESS OF LOT

Next, we learn more of these invaders from the east, and we discover that they seem more than merely fierce. They truly appear to be invincible:

> In the fourteenth year, Kedorlaomer and the kings allied with him went out and defeated the Rephaites in Ashteroth Karnaim, the Zuzites in Ham, the Emites in Shaveh Kiriathaim and the Horites in the hill country of Seir, as far as El Paran near the desert. Then they turned back and went to En Mishpat (that is, Kadesh), and they conquered the whole territory of the Amalekites, as well as the Amorites who were living in Hazazon Tamar. (Genesis 14:5–7)

The Rephaites and Zuzites were families of giants—men who were eight to ten feet tall and feared by everyone around. Yet the powerful kings from the east swept away even these giants. The territory in which this war was fought is a vast region, from the north and west of the Sea of Galilee, down the Jordan Valley, all the way south to the Red Sea. This seemingly invincible and unstoppable enemy struck fear into every heart and relentlessly crushed all opposition.

In the next few verses, Lot takes center stage. If not for him, we would know nothing of these events, because the Bible never reports on any human history except that which relates to God's people. Here is Lot's role in the story:

> Then the king of Sodom, the king of Gomorrah, the king of Admah, the king of Zeboiim and the king of Bela (that is, Zoar) marched out and drew up their battle lines in the Valley of Siddim against Kedorlaomer king of Elam, Tidal king of Goiim, Amraphel king of Shinar and Arioch king of Ellasar— four kings against five. Now the Valley of Siddim was full of tar pits, and when the kings of Sodom and Gomorrah fled, some of the men fell into them and the rest fled to the hills. The four kings seized all the goods of Sodom and Gomorrah and all their food; then they went away. They also carried off Abram's nephew Lot and his possessions, since he was living in Sodom. (Genesis 14:8–12)

Notice that the text underscores the existence of many tar or bitumen pits in the Valley of Siddim, the valley of the Dead Sea. These pits were filled with natural asphalt, much like the La Brea Tar Pits in Los Angeles. The desert winds would blow sand over these open pits of sticky asphalt, giving the appearance of firm desert ground. But anyone venturing into that place would be trapped and drawn into the tar as if it were quicksand. When the tide of battle turned against the five kings of the plains of Canaan, forcing them to retreat, the four invading kings from the east used those tar pits as a trap, herding the fleeing armies into a kill zone of tar. The soldiers of the kings of Sodom and Gomorrah either sank in the pits or fled to the hills.

So Kedorlaomer and the other kings from the east fell upon Sodom and Gomorrah, plundered the cities, and took captives, including Lot and all of his possessions. Lot was powerless to fight back. You may know how Lot felt if you've ever found yourself in the grip of forces and circumstances over which you have absolutely no control. If you've ever been burdened by a frightening medical diagnosis, or the loss of a career, or the loss of your reputation, or a destructive habit that enslaves you, then you have a sense of the helplessness Lot felt.

## PRAYER SETS CAPTIVES FREE

The story of Lot has become a cliffhanger. Lot is in the hands of the invading kings from the east—and now the scene shifts to Abram, who is up on the mountainside. The Holy Spirit, the author of this story, wants us to see the overcoming power of faith. From a human perspective, all hope for Lot seems lost. But there is still once chance to save him. Lot's only hope is his uncle, Abram: "One who had escaped came and reported this to Abram the Hebrew. Now Abram was living near the great trees of Mamre the Amorite, a brother of Eshcol and Aner, all of whom were allied with Abram" (Genesis 14:13).

During the siege of Sodom, a messenger escaped from the city. He went to Hebron, the place of fellowship, and there he found Abram and three of Abram's friends and allies. Mamre, as we have seen, means "fatness" or "richness." Eshcol means "group" or "bunch," and Aner means "exile," one who withdraws himself. Taking these three names together, they seem to suggest a prayer meeting.

Abram the Hebrew leads the meeting. Since this is the only place in Scripture where Abram is called a Hebrew, the term must have special significance. The word *Hebrew* comes from the word *ivriy*, from the root word `*avar*, which means "to cross over." So the word *Hebrew* means "one who crosses over, one who travels or traverses, a pilgrim." In this passage, the Spirit of God highlights for us the character of the man to whom Lot looks for rescue. If Lot is to be saved from the enemy, he must be rescued by the Hebrew, the pilgrim, the man who dwells in a tent and holds lightly the things of this life.

Here is a group of people who live in the richness of fellowship with God, and they have withdrawn themselves from the ordinary demands of life for a specific purpose. Abram the Hebrew lives in rich, godly fellowship with these three brothers, Mamre, Eshcol, and Aner. They have withdrawn themselves to devote themselves to prayer and worship. This is exactly what the Lord Jesus bids us do in the New Testament: "But when you pray, go into your room, close the door and pray to your Father, who is unseen" (Matthew 6:6).

So, as the text tells us, one person escaped from Sodom and came to Abram and his friends on the hillside and told Abram that Lot had been captured. When one of God's children becomes captured and enslaved by some outside force—whether it happens because of the persecution of the righteous or because of that Christian's own folly and sin—the only solution to that crisis is for the people of God to pray the prayer of faith.

We see a New Testament parallel to this Old Testament incident in the account of the imprisonment of the apostle Peter by King Herod. In that account we are told, "So Peter was kept in prison, but the church was earnestly praying to God for him" (Acts 12:5). As a result of the prayers of God's people, Peter's shackles fell off and the doors of the prison were flung open. Peter was led out of the prison by an angel—a free man. The prayer of God's people is the key to victory whenever one of God's children is held captive by any physical, emotional, or spiritual force.

Next, let's see how Lot was delivered from captivity:

> When Abram heard that his relative had been taken captive, he called out the 318 trained men born in his household and went in pursuit as far as Dan. During the night Abram divided his men to attack them and he routed them, pursuing them as far as Hobah, north of Damascus. (Genesis 14:14–15)

Here is the key to victory—318 trained and committed men, Abram's elite fighting force. There were many other soldiers in the armies of Abram and his allies that he could have called upon. But Abram chose to go to war with a fighting force that made up in skill, training, and discipline what it may have lacked in numbers. To put it in today's terms, Abram called in "the few, the proud, the Marines." And these 318 elite troops were all he needed.

This is the first recorded instance of war in the Bible, yet Abram appears to be a master of the art of warfare. No doubt, his modest forces must have seemed pitiful and small, stacked up against the vast armies of Kedorlaomer and the other invading kings from the east. But God has a lesson for us in this story—a lesson He repeats in various ways in a number of passages of Scripture: Never be intimidated by the superior numbers of the enemy. One believer plus God is always an overwhelming force.

Throughout Scripture we see that God's victories are never won by force of numbers. His secret weapon is nothing less than the Spirit of Almighty God himself. As God said to Zerubbabel, king of Judah, "'Not by might nor by power, but by my Spirit,' says the LORD Almighty" (Zechariah 4:6).

Think of all the threats to life and freedom in the world today, from terrorism to murderous totalitarian regimes to the nightmare scenario of nuclear war. In country after country around the world, our Christian brothers and sisters are threatened with imprisonment, torture, and death if they take a stand for their faith. The fastest-growing religion in the world is not Christianity but Islam—and the most extreme factions of Islam are intensely committed to the destruction of all infidels, including Christians.

If we look at all of the forces that threaten our way of life, our faith, and our lives, it is easy to become frightened and discouraged. Christians are clearly outnumbered. The world is hostile to us and our message. But God wants us to know that we have a secret weapon with which to defeat our enemies. That weapon is the Spirit of God.

He wants us to know that the secret to defeating our enemy lies not in numbers nor in military might and weapons but in men and women of faith. He calls us to live as pilgrims and strangers in this world and to continually separate ourselves from the enticements and demands of this life so that we can seek the face of God. Through prayer and faith in Him, a small number of believers can break the chains that have enslaved the souls of men and women around the world. A handful of believers, agreeing together in prayer, is more powerful than all the armies and all the nuclear arsenals of the world's great nations.

Now let's examine Abram's strategy.

As was the custom with armies of that day, when the pagan invaders had withdrawn to a place they considered safe, they made camp for several days and indulged in a time of carousing and reveling in celebration of their victory over Sodom. It was at such a moment that Abram and his allies found them. Abram divided his forces by night and launched a two-pronged attack, surrounding the unsuspecting enemy camp on both sides. At a signal, both forces sprang upon the surprised enemy camp with spears and swords. The element of surprise gave them a great victory over the invaders from the east. Abram's small army sent Kedorlaomer's forces fleeing in disarray.

The division of Abram's forces into a two-pronged attack suggests the Christian's weapons in spiritual warfare. In Ephesians 6, we are reminded that we possess two effective weapons: the Word of God and the power of the Spirit through prayer. As the apostle Paul tells us, "Take . . . the sword of the Spirit, which is the word of God. And pray in the Spirit on all occasions with all kinds of prayers and requests. With this in mind, be alert and always keep on praying for all the saints" (Ephesians 6:17–18).

## A GREAT AND MIGHTY DELIVERANCE

Abram pursued the invading forces as far as Hobah, north of Damascus. Through prayer and persistence, he won a great victory over the kings from the east. The next verse reveals the extent of the victory Abram has won: "He recovered all the goods and brought back his relative Lot and his possessions, together with the women and the other people" (Genesis 14:16).

As Christians, we live in a network of relationships. Our sins and folly can bring harm to the people closest to us. Lot, in choosing the enticements and city life of Sodom instead of the pilgrim's life of the tent and the altar, placed his family in great peril. When the kings from the east took Lot captive, they took his entire household captive.

At the same time, because we live in this network of relationships, one Christian can sometimes become the means of deliverance for others, especially for a weaker brother or sister. There was nothing Abram could do to deliver Lot from Sodom. The city of Sodom represented an inward choice in the heart of Lot. He chose to live in the materialistic, sensualized atmosphere of Sodom. If a child of God chooses to be materialistic, fleshly, and greedy for things of the world, there is not much anyone can do for him. Abram could not force Lot to leave Sodom.

But when the kings from the east attacked Sodom and threatened Lot's life and liberty, Abram was able to act—and his resources were sufficient. As the New Testament tells us, "The prayer of a righteous man is powerful and effective" (James 5:16b). The history of the church is replete with examples of deliverances through faithful prayer.

Is there someone you know who is held captive by some force beyond his or her control? Are you held captive by circumstances or habits or sins beyond your control? The key that unlocks that prison is prayer. It is the intercession of one righteous Christian on behalf of another child of God.

A wise and experienced missionary leader once came to our church to speak about prayer. He talked about the problem of habits, compulsions, addictions, and circumstances that overwhelm us and frustrate us in our walk with God. He said, "Perhaps you are held captive by some sand in your life. You cannot break free of its grip, yet you feel it is so shameful that you cannot bring yourself to confess it publicly. Let me suggest to you a way of deliverance. If you are a woman, seek out some older woman of God, someone you can trust to pray for you, counsel you, and keep everything in strictest confidence. If you are a man, seek out an older man of God with those same qualifications. Lay the whole matter out before that person, and say, 'Please pray for me.'"

That's good advice.

When Lot was held captive, he was powerless to help himself. He needed a rescuer, someone to deliver him from the clutches of the enemy. Abram was that rescuer. By faith and by prayer, Abram gained access to the power of God, and he brought about a mighty deliverance.

5

# THE PERIL OF VICTORY

*Genesis 14:17–24*

Following Abram's stunning victory over Kedorlaomer and the other kings from the east, we come to a curious incident involving a strange and enigmatic king. This king, Melchizedek, is mentioned only twice in the Old Testament—once here in Genesis 14 and again in Psalm 110:4. Because Melchizedek receives such brief mention in the Old Testament, you might think of him as a minor biblical character.

Yet the New Testament book of Hebrews dwells at such length on the encounter between Abram and Melchizedek that our curiosity is awakened regarding this ancient man of mystery (see Hebrews 5–7). Without question, Abram's meeting with Melchizedek was arranged by the Spirit of God as a message to believers down through the centuries.

## MELCHIZEDEK, PRIEST AND KING

Having defeated Kedorlaomer, Abram turns toward Sodom. He brings with him all the stolen goods and freed captives, including Lot and his family. It is a time of victory for Abram, and therefore a time of peril. The enemy of our souls loves to attack us when we least expect it, when we are off-guard and elated over a great spiritual victory. Satan's attack is rarely obvious; rather, he prefers to take advantage of us when our defenses are down.

And so it is with Abram. Here, we see him confronted with a subtle temptation on his way back to Sodom. But deliverance will come to

Abram from an unexpected source: "After Abram returned from defeating Kedorlaomer and the kings allied with him, the king of Sodom came out to meet him in the Valley of Shaveh (that is, the King's Valley)" (Genesis 14:17).

The scene is a valley somewhere between the city of Sodom and the battlefield where Abram defeated Kedorlaomer. In Genesis, this valley was called the Valley of Shaveh. This same valley later became known as the Kidron Valley—the same valley Jesus and the disciples crossed on their way to the Garden of Gethsemane on the night He was betrayed.

In Abram's day, what we now know as the city of Jerusalem was a tiny village called Salem. The village was ruled by a priestly king whose name was Melchizedek. We meet this mysterious king in the next few verses:

> Then Melchizedek king of Salem brought out bread and wine. He was priest of God Most High, and he blessed Abram, saying,
>> "Blessed be Abram by God Most High,
>> Creator of heaven and earth.
> And blessed be God Most High,
>> who delivered your enemies into your hand."
> Then Abram gave him a tenth of everything. (Genesis 14:18–20)

Melchizedek, king of Salem, steps forth from the shadows, ministers to Abraham with bread and wine, and speaks words of blessing for Abram and praise for God. Then, he disappears from the pages of Genesis just as suddenly and mysteriously as he appeared. The next appearance of Melchizedek is a brief mention in one of the psalms of David:

> The LORD has sworn
>> and will not change his mind:
>> "You are a priest forever,
>> in the order of Melchizedek." (Psalm 110:4)

What does David the psalmist mean by those words? This psalm is addressed to the coming Messiah, Jesus of Nazareth. In this psalm, David declares that the Messiah shall be made a priest forever after the order of Melchizedek. He will fulfill the same priestly function as this king of Salem.

Then another thousand years roll by, and in the book of Hebrews we have another, more extended reference to this strange individual. Who was Melchizedek? Some Bible scholars suggest that he was Shem, the son of Noah. The biblical chronology suggests that Shem could still have been living at that time. Other scholars believe that Melchizedek was a theophany, an appearance of the pre-incarnate Christ in human form.

We do not know for sure. All we are positively told about Melchizedek is that he filled a duel role as both the king of Salem (or Jerusalem) and the priest of the Most High God (in Hebrew, *El Elyon*). The name Melchizedek means "king of righteousness." He appears suddenly in the biblical record without any mention of father or mother and without any account of his birth or death.

Because of these omissions from the Genesis record, the writer of Hebrews tells us that, since we have no record of his genealogy, Melchizedek is a symbol or type of the eternal priesthood of our Lord Jesus Christ. After all, Jesus had no beginning or ending of days; rather, He lives eternally to make intercession for all those who come to God through Him. So the Melchizedek priesthood is a ministry of help to those who face trials and troubles.

Melchizedek was evidently a Gentile king. The original knowledge of God as the maker and possessor of the heavens and the earth had evidently come to him unchanged, handed down from Adam and Noah. Melchizedek worshiped the one true God and served as a priest before God. The Lord Jesus is our heavenly Melchizedek, ready to minister to us in our times of need. His ministry is to reveal El Elyon, the Most High God, to us. He reveals God as the one who is more than adequate to meet our needs. As the apostle Paul tells us, "And my God will meet all your needs according to his glorious riches in Christ Jesus" (Philippians 4:19).

## TEMPTED BY THE KING OF SODOM

Following this meeting between Abram and Melchizedek, another encounter takes place, this time between Abram and the king of Sodom:

> The king of Sodom said to Abram, "Give me the people and keep the goods for yourself."
>
> But Abram said to the king of Sodom, "I have raised my hand to the LORD, God Most High, Creator of heaven and earth, and have taken an oath that I will accept nothing belonging to you, not even a thread or the thong of a sandal, so that you will never be able to say, 'I made Abram rich.'" (Genesis 14:21–23)

Here we see the temptation that threatens Abram. After meeting Melchizedek, Abram encounters the king of Sodom, who somehow escaped capture. This king was in the city when news of Abram's triumph reached the city gates. Abram was returning to the city of Sodom, along with the freed captives and the spoils of war.

So the king of Sodom went to Abram and made him an offer: "Give me the people and keep the goods for yourself." The king's offer seemed like a fitting and justifiable reward. Of course, Abram had not fought his battle against the kings from the east on behalf of wicked Sodom. He had fought solely for the sake of Lot and his family.

Nevertheless, Abram's victory benefited Sodom. As a result, the king of the city led a welcoming committee to reward Abram with the usual payment reserved for conquering heroes. The king asked only for the return of the citizens who were taken captive by the invaders. All of the riches Abram had taken from the enemy were his to keep. This was an amazing offer because Sodom was a fabulously wealthy city.

Though the text does not explicitly say so, I think it's safe to say that we can see the hand of Satan behind this offer. Abram might well have said, "I earned these riches. I deserve them. The king offers them to me, no strings attached. I can take this wealth and return to my tent and altar. It's not as if I am going to live in Sodom, as Lot has done. I can still be God's servant, living as a pilgrim in the land of promise, yet enjoying all of these glittering riches."

If you were in Abram's place, what would you have done? You have to admit, such an offer would be almost too tempting to pass up.

The king of Sodom has freely offered this gift to Abram, and that is why it is such an inviting trap. For a man of Abram's character, accepting such a gift would have meant he was obligated to the giver. From that day forward, the king of Sodom could say, "Abram is in my debt. If I ever need military help, I know where to turn. My military ally is on that hillside."

This seemingly free gift posed an insidious threat to Abram's independence. Up to that point, Abram took orders only from God. But if he accepted the gift from the king of Sodom, he would never be wholly God's man again.

Note the timing of the temptation: It came when Abram might well be off-guard, enjoying the exhilaration of his triumph. After the stress and danger of battle, Abram had certainly earned a rest, and even a reward. And it was at this moment, when he was most vulnerable, that this temptation came to Abram.

Have you ever had an experience like this? I have seen Christian college students surrounded throughout the school year by subtle and perilous dangers to their faith and their walk with Jesus Christ. Again and again they resist temptation, keeping their guard up throughout the school year. Then they go home on vacation, they relax, they let their guard down—and they succumb to moral failure. Satan knows the best moment to attack, and it's always the moment when we least expect it, when we have let down our defenses.

The pressure on Abram to accept the king's gift was great. The king was expressing his gratitude. For Abram to reject this gift was to risk angering the king. You can probably identify with Abram. There have probably been times when you have felt trapped into accepting a gift you didn't want. You didn't want to offend that person by saying no. Often, we seem to care more about what others think than what God thinks.

If you say yes to an offer today, will you be indebted? The easiest time to say no is now, as the apostle Paul observed: " 'Everything is permissible for me'—but not everything is beneficial. 'Everything is permissible for me'—but I will not be mastered by anything" (1 Corinthians 6:12).

Paul is saying, "My only wish is to serve Christ. I reject any lesser thing that would threaten to control me or limit me. It may be lawful and permissible, but if it makes any demand on me that is not His demand, I want no part of it." That is the attitude Abram demonstrates here.

Abram replies to the king of Sodom that he has sworn a solemn oath to God "that I will accept nothing belonging to you, not even a thread or the thong of a sandal, so that you will never be able to say, 'I made Abram rich.' " In other words, "I will take nothing; not a thread, not even a shoestring! I don't care what you offer me, I want no part of it, end of discussion." It is not possible for Abram to make it any more emphatic.

And take note of Abram's boldness and frankness when addressing the king of Sodom. He tells the king exactly why he rejects the offer: "so that you will never be able to say, 'I made Abram rich.' " In effect, he tells the king, "I know what your motive is. I can see the trap you are laying for me. But I can serve only one king at a time, and I choose to serve Almighty God with a single, undivided heart. Thanks—but no thanks."

This is a bold and positive declaration, and it represents a victory, an even greater victory than Abram has recently won on the battlefield. His battlefield victory involved the defeat of a human enemy, but this victory represents a triumph over Satan and his schemes.

How did Abram see through the satanic strategy with such clarity? If you or I were in Abram's sandals that day, would we have stepped into the satanic trap, or would we have rejected the king's offer as Abram did? I'm sure my own devious heart would have found a hundred ways to rationalize the king's gift as an added bonus from God, as a just reward for my courage and faithfulness in battle.

But Abram wasn't fooled by the king's offer. He didn't step into Satan's trap. Certainly, as we have seen, Abram was quite capable of making foolish choices. Yet here, in Genesis 14, he passes the test with flying colors. How was that possible?

## THE MINISTRY OF MELCHIZEDEK

Now we understand why God led Abram back to his home by way of the Valley of Shaveh, the King's Valley. The king of Sodom was coming to meet Abram, and Abram was not prepared for the temptation the king had planned for him. Abram was no different from you and me. This unsuspecting man would undoubtedly have fallen into Satan's trap.

But God intervened. He sent Melchizedek to meet Abram.

Melchizedek's first act of ministry toward Abram was to remind him of the character and limitless resources of the God he served. Melchizedek said, in effect, "Abram, your God is the creator and possessor of heaven and earth. He made it all. He owns the whole universe. All the riches of the world belong to Him. If anyone were to offer you the riches of a kingdom, remember the limitless riches of the God you serve."

Next, Melchizedek served Abram bread and wine. We need no interpreter for these symbols. Not only do they prefigure the bread and cup of the Lord's Supper, but also they speak eloquently of the strength and joy that flow from acts of self-giving love. We experience the meaning and power of the bread and the cup whenever we as Christians partake of these symbols of the suffering of our Lord. He gave himself in the fullness of His life and poured out all that He was and all that He possessed.

When we remember His sacrifice for us and feast upon these symbols of His life and death, we draw strength and power that enables us to reject the insidious traps and snares that this world offers us. When we partake of the bread and the cup, and we do this in remembrance of Him, we strengthen ourselves in order to maintain our independence and single-mindedness as servants of Christ.

So, Abram worships God through the ministry of Melchizedek. The Scriptures tell us that Abram gave Melchizedek "a tenth of everything." In other words, Abram gave a tithe of everything he had to Melchizedek, the king of Salem. Whether you view Melchizedek as merely a human king who symbolized the priestly and kingly role of Jesus the Messiah, or whether you view Melchizedek as a theophany, an Old Testament appearance of the pre-incarnate Christ, one thing is clear: Abram viewed Melchizedek as God's personal representative.

So Abram paid a tithe of everything he had to God's representative, Melchizedek. This tithe symbolized Abram's recognition that everything Abram had belonged to God. This is the same spirit in which we should give to God. New Testament giving is not a debt that we pay to God but a symbolic action we perform in recognition of the fact that all we are and all we have belongs to Him. This is one of the ways we worship Him.

Centuries later, a much greater Melchizedek, Jesus the Lord, would pray in bloody agony in the garden at the edge of the King's Valley. But here in Genesis 14, Abram experienced by faith the high-priestly ministry of Jesus Christ, expressed to him through Melchizedek, the king of Salem. And as Melchizedek ministered to him, Abram's heart overflowed with the love of Christ. Strengthened in spirit, he understood that nothing but God could satisfy his heart. Riches would not satisfy. The favor of an earthly king would not satisfy. Nothing satisfies but God alone.

There in that valley, Abram swore an oath to the Lord that he would not touch a single thing that Sodom could offer him. Strengthened by this encounter with Melchizedek, Abram rose up and went out to meet the king of Sodom. He was ready for any trap that Satan and the king might set for him.

## WHY DO WE FALL FOR IT?

If you are as old as I am, you are probably aware of the television quiz show scandals of the late 1950s. The scandals erupted when a number of television game show contestants revealed that they had been coached by producers, that the results of the shows had been rigged, and that the public had been deceived.

One young man, who earned more than $129,000 on the game show *Twenty-One*, testified before a congressional subcommittee that he had originally wanted to go on the show without any help or coaching, relying on his knowledge alone. A brilliant young man who had earned a master's degree in astrophysics and a doctorate in English at Columbia University, he knew he could win without cheating. But the show's producer told him that the quiz contests were mere entertainment and giving help to certain contestants to rig the outcome was a common practice—it was just show business.

"This, of course, was not true," the young man told the subcommittee members, "but I wanted to believe him. He said I would do a great service for teachers and education. In the end, I realized I had actually done a great disservice."

During his more than two-month run on the game show, this young man amazed the public with his apparently endless knowledge of many difficult subjects. He even appeared on the cover of *Time* magazine. But in the end, he was disgraced. He accepted the offer, and it proved to be a trap that led to his downfall.

Life is full of subtle temptations and seemingly innocent offers. We are eager to rationalize and justify choices that, deep down, we know are wrong. Why do we so easily surrender our integrity to the king of Sodom? It's because we do not go to our Melchizedek, the Lord Jesus Christ, and ask him to minister to us and open our eyes. We do not come to the throne of grace to find help in time of need.

So we fail and we fall.

Abram would never have passed this test in his own strength. He passed the test because God intervened and sent Melchizedek to meet him in his time of need. The king of Salem opened Abram's eyes to the trap of the king of Sodom. Melchizedek reminded Abram that the greatest treasures of this world are like cereal box prizes compared with the true riches that belong to God, the maker of heaven and earth.

After Melchizedek ministered to Abram, he could say to the king of Sodom, "Thanks but no thanks. I want nothing from you. I want no man to claim that he made Abram rich. If I am rich, the glory goes to God alone. He is the maker and possessor of the world."

At the close of this story, Abram displays a caring and sensible attitude toward the others who were his allies in the battle against the kings from the east. He tells the king of Sodom: "I will accept nothing but what my men have eaten and the share that belongs to the men who went with me—to Aner, Eshcol and Mamre. Let them have their share" (Genesis 14:24).

Abram seems to say that what would be wrong for him to take would be all right for his three allies—Aner, Eshcol and Mamre—to accept. Is Abram practicing a double standard? Is he saying that what is right for one person could be wrong for another? What lesson would God have us learn from this?

These men had not reached Abram's level of spiritual maturity. The Scriptures do not tell us if they also encountered Melchizedek, or if Abram and Melchizedek met in private, away from the other three. In any case, it is clear that these three men did not have the same depth of spiritual perception that Abram did. So Abram was content to allow God to deal with them directly in these spiritual gray areas. Abram was not going to require his three friends to walk according to his own conscience.

Apparently God had revealed to this Old Testament saint the truth of Romans 14—the principle that we are not to judge our brothers and sisters in matters where the Scriptures do not give us clear and unambiguous guidance. Paul writes:

> Accept him whose faith is weak, without passing judgment on disputable matters. . . . Each one should be fully convinced in his own mind. . . . You, then, why do you judge your brother? Or why do you look down on your brother? For we will all stand before God's judgment seat. (Romans 14:1, 5b, 10)

On a number of occasions, well-meaning Christians have come to me and said, "The Lord has spoken to my heart and told me it's wrong to drink coffee. And I believe you should stop drinking coffee, too." While I respect their convictions, I have not received the same word from the Lord that they have.

I recall one dear old Nazarene evangelist known as Uncle Bud. A number of people who had strong views on various borderline issues had encouraged him to give up drinking coffee. Whenever one of these Christians would ask, "How can you drink coffee and still be a Christian?" he would grin and reply, "Just bring me a cup, and I'll show you."

God wants us to act in accordance with our convictions. But He does not want us to force our views on others. So Abram says, in effect, "Let these three allies of mine have their share. It would be wrong for me to take anything. But they are not standing in the same place I am. They have earned a share. Let them have the reward they have earned."

This incident in the life of Abram reminds us of our deep need to remain in continual fellowship with God. We cannot hope to triumph over the dangers and temptations of this world unless we regularly go to the King's Valley, partake of the bread and cup, and remember what our heavenly Melchizedek has done for us.

Apart from Him, we are no match for the snares of Satan. But we can always pass the test as long as we are delivered daily from Satan's traps by the love and strength of the Lord Jesus Christ.

# 6

# FAITH CONQUERS FEAR

*Genesis 15:1–6*

If you are a city dweller in the twenty-first century, what do you see when you look up at the night sky? Probably a starless gray dome. You know that somewhere above that blanket of dirty air, there's an immense starry realm. Why can't you see the stars? Because they are obscured by a combination of air pollution and light pollution.

In Abram's day, however, every night brought forth a glittering spectacle of thousands of stars scattered across the heavens. Of course, the greatest concentration of stars was that gauzy band of light called the Milky Way—our local galaxy, a collection of approximately 250 billion stars. As we come to Genesis 15, we encounter a startling promise that God makes to Abram, a promise that draws upon the imagery of the vast numbers of stars in the night sky.

## FOUR KEY PHRASES

The opening paragraph of Genesis 15 illustrates what Bible scholars call the law of first occurrence. This principle states that the first time a word or phrase is used in the Bible, that usage establishes its basic meaning throughout Scripture. As we shall see, four such phrases appear for the first time in these verses. Those four phrases will be repeated many times again throughout the Word of God. As we study this passage together, see if you can recognize all four.

The chapter begins with these words:

> After this, the word of the LORD came to Abram in a vision:
>
> "Do not be afraid, Abram.
> I am your shield,
> your very great reward."
>
> But Abram said, "O Sovereign LORD, what can you give me since I remain childless and the one who will inherit my estate is Eliezer of Damascus?" And Abram said, "You have given me no children; so a servant in my household will be my heir."
>
> Then the word of the LORD came to him: "This man will not be your heir, but a son coming from your own body will be your heir." He took him outside and said, "Look up at the heavens and count the stars—if indeed you can count them." Then he said to him, "So shall your offspring be."
>
> Abram believed the LORD, and he credited it to him as righteousness. (Genesis 15:1–6)

Did you notice the first of those four phrases? In verse 1, we read, "After this, the word of the LORD came to Abram in a vision." That phrase, "the word of the Lord came," will appear many times afterward in Scripture. This phrase underscores the God-breathed character of the Bible. The word of the Lord came to many people in Scripture, just as it came to Abram. These individuals were borne along and inspired by the Holy Spirit, and they wrote down the words that were given to them by the Spirit. Then they sat down and studied the pages they had written to learn what God had said through them. The apostle Peter explained it this way:

> Concerning this salvation, the prophets, who spoke of the grace that was to come to you, searched intently and with the greatest care, trying to find out the time and circumstances to which the Spirit of Christ in them was pointing when he predicted the sufferings of Christ and the glories that would follow. It was revealed to them that they were not serving

themselves but you, when they spoke of the things that have now been told you by those who have preached the gospel to you by the Holy Spirit sent from heaven. Even angels long to look into these things. (1 Peter 1:10–12)

Did you notice the second of those four phrases in Genesis 15? The Lord says to this man of faith, "Do not be afraid." In some versions, this is translated simply, "Fear not!" Again and again throughout the Scriptures, this is God's message to humanity.

The third of those four phrases is, "I am your shield." This statement is the first description of God's character anywhere in the Bible. In many ways, we find this thought repeated throughout Scripture. God is our fortress, our strength, our shield, our tower of refuge. As the psalmist tells us: "He who dwells in the shelter of the Most High will rest in the shadow of the Almighty" (Psalm 91:1).

The last of these four phrases is found in the last verse of this section: "Abram believed the Lord, and he credited it to him as righteousness." This is the earliest statement found in Scripture of the essence of the gospel: Salvation is by grace through faith. We cannot earn favor with God. We receive His favor as a free gift when we place our trust in him. The moment we place our faith in the Lord, He credits our faith to us as righteousness.

## ABRAM'S FEAR

When God appears to Abram in a vision, his first words are, "Do not be afraid, Abram." What does this tell us? Clearly, it reveals the state of this man's heart: Abram was afraid. In all likelihood, he was having a fitful, sleepless night because of his fear. What was he afraid of? The Scriptures do not tell us, but there are several obvious possibilities.

We know that this incident took place immediately after Abram's encounter with the king of Sodom. Abram might have been fearful of the king's wrath. In the light of day, immediately after being ministered to by Melchizedek, Abram spoke boldly and bluntly to the king of Sodom, and the king may well have felt insulted by Abram's words. Perhaps Abram was second-guessing himself in the middle of the night.

He may have thought, "Oh, why wasn't I more diplomatic? Did I have to speak so sharply to the king? What if he sends an army out after me?"

Or Abram might have tossed and turned because of anxious thoughts over Kedorlaomer, the king from the east whom Abram had defeated on the field of battle. Abram had overthrown a vast invading army with a mere handful of men. Though Kedorlaomer had been defeated and routed, there is no indication that he was killed. It may well be that this dictator had sworn vengeance upon Abram, and that may be why Abram was so afraid.

Abram probably said to himself, "What have I gotten myself into? I'm almost sorry I won this battle. When Kedorlaomer comes back to get his revenge, what will I do? I caught him off guard the first time. Next time, he'll be ready for me." So Abram was tormented in the middle of the night with fearful, anxious thoughts.

At the same time, I'm sure that there was a much deeper fear lurking in the depths of Abram's heart—a gnawing sense that he had somehow misunderstood the promises of God. Ten years earlier, God had told Abram: "All the land that you see I will give to you and your offspring forever. I will make your offspring like the dust of the earth, so that if anyone could count the dust, then your offspring could be counted" (Genesis 13:15–16). Ten years of waiting had passed after Abram received that promise. "Hope deferred makes the heart sick," says Proverbs 13:12. The sickness was beginning to creep into Abram's soul.

"O Sovereign LORD," Abram said to God, "what can you give me since I remain childless and the one who will inherit my estate is Eliezer of Damascus? . . . You have given me no children; so a servant in my household will be my heir." From these words, we can tell what Abram is thinking. He has begun to wonder if the children God had promised him would be his genetic descendants or the descendents of his servant, Eliezer.

As he lay on his bed, unable to sleep, the old man pondered the possibility that he had misinterpreted God's promise. He felt lonely, disappointed, and disillusioned—and he was deeply afraid that his hopes for future descendants had been dashed.

At that point, Abram became aware that he was not alone. A Presence was with him. In his heart, he heard the word of the Lord come to him. Sometimes, God spoke audibly to the saints of the Old Testament, and sometimes He spoke quietly within their hearts. The Scriptures do not tell us how God spoke to Abram in this vision. But we do know that in the midst of Abram's fear and doubt, he experienced a sense of God's presence. The word of the Lord came to him, saying, "Do not be afraid, Abram. I am your shield, your very great reward." God wanted Abram to know that He was present with him, and Abram had nothing to fear.

If God is for us, who can be against us? If God is our shield, whom should we fear? As the writer to the Hebrews tells us:

> God has said,
>> "Never will I leave you;
>>> never will I forsake you." So we say with
>>> confidence,
>> "The Lord is my helper; I will not be afraid.
>> What can man do to me?" (Hebrews 13:5b–6)

That is the thought that comforted Abram's heart during his time of fear and darkness. Those words of encouragement from the Lord were all Abram needed to settle his worries, whether he fretted about Kedorlaomer or the king of Sodom or his future descendants.

## TRUSTING IN OUR SHIELD

Have you learned to count on the invisible protection of God? Can you stand before your enemies as our Lord stood before Pilate, saying, "You would have no power over me if it were not given to you from above" (John 19:11)? Jesus trusted in the shield of the Lord, and so should we. Someone once said, "Christians are immortal until their work is done." Nothing can touch us or hurt us, except by permission of God, who is our living shield. If we would place our complete trust in our all-powerful shield, we would lose all fears.

Have you ever noticed that you seem to have lived a charmed life? Most people, looking back over their lives, can point to a number of instances where they easily could have lost their lives in an accident or an illness. Most of us can recall times when we seemingly escaped death by the skin of our teeth. Where you merely lucky? Or were you being protected by the hand of God?

One time, my wife, Elaine, and I drove across New Mexico. We were in desolate and lonely country, moving along at about sixty miles an hour. As we drove, I noticed a continuous grinding noise. The noise grew louder and louder. It was not unusual for that old car to groan and grumble as it rolled along. But this noise was becoming so loud and annoying that it demanded my full attention.

I stopped by the side of the road to investigate. Stepping out of the car, I immediately noticed that the hub of the right front wheel was hot and smoking. I jacked up the car, and the moment the right front wheel came up off the ground, the wheel fell off and rolled into a ditch.

At that point, I realized that Elaine and I had narrowly avoided a serious, if not deadly, accident. We had driven for miles on a wheel that was not even secured to the car. I'm certain that the wheel was held in place by the protective hand of God. He was our shield that day.

And that was God's message to Abram: "I am your shield, Abram. I am your defense against any force that would seek to destroy you. Do not be afraid. Nothing can touch you without my permission."

When I read through the gospel accounts, I'm struck by the number of times our Lord Jesus calmed His disciples with the words, "Do not be afraid." These are not empty words. He constantly reassured His disciples with the promise of His presence. When the storm threatened to sink the disciples' boat, or when the disciples shuddered in fear as He spoke of the impending cross, His message to them again and again was, "Do not be afraid; I am with you." As the Lord told His disciples in the final hours before his arrest, "Do not let your hearts be troubled. Trust in God; trust also in me" (John 14:1).

## OUR GREAT REWARD

And God is not only our shield. He says to Abram that He is "your very great reward." God is our great reward, our dearest treasure, the only genuinely satisfying joy we will ever know.

One evening, Elaine and I were invited to a neighborhood party. We welcomed the opportunity to become better acquainted with our neighbors. When we arrived, we discovered that it was a cocktail party, and it had been in progress for an hour or so. We were greeted warmly (even hilariously), and our host introduced us to many of our new neighbors. To all appearances, everyone appeared to be having a great time, but it soon became obvious that much of the apparent happiness was artificial.

As I talked to people, it became clear that many of the people of that party were covering up a haunting sense of emptiness, meaninglessness, and futility. The alcohol in their glasses was an anesthetic to numb their fear and pain. Elaine and I left that party feeling deeply sorry for those people. We prayed together for opportunities to be salt and light in that neighborhood and a witness for Christ among our neighbors. We said afterwards that we would not trade one moment of the riches of Christ for an entire lifetime of the superficial happiness those people so desperately sought.

The joy of knowing God is the "very great reward" He gave to Abram. After God spoke to Abram that night, we never again read that Abram experienced fear about Kedorlaomer or worries over the king of Sodom. Those pressures and anxieties were fully met by the reality of God's presence with him.

But there was one concern that still weighed heavy on Abram's heart—that vacuum of loneliness within, that deep longing for descendants to fulfill the promise that God had made to him a decade before. Could God meet that longing as well? So Abram blurted out his deepest fear to God—his fear of dying childless, of leaving this life without any physical descendants of his own.

In reply, God, Abram's almighty friend, led Abram out of his tent and into the warm night. And God drew Abram's attention to the stars overhead. The man gazed up at the stars, which wheeled in their silent courses above. He undoubtedly felt that deep sense of awe that comes over anyone at the sight of the Milky Way galaxy.

And God said, "A son coming from your own body will be your

heir. . . . Look up at the heavens and count the stars—if indeed you can count them. So shall your offspring be."

Abram must have been deeply comforted and reassured to hear God reaffirm His promise. And if his doubts ever returned to trouble his sleep, Abram could step out of his tent and gaze up at the night sky. The starlit heavens would remind him of the promise God had made.

The previous time God made this promise to Abram, He said that Abram's descendants would be like the dust of the earth. Here in Genesis 15, God chose a different metaphor. He promised that Abram's descendants would be like the stars of heaven in their multitude.

These two metaphors imply two distinct lines of descendants. First, Abram would have an earthly line of descent—the nation Israel (descended through his son Isaac) and the Arab people (descended through his son Ishmael). Second, Abram would have a heavenly or spiritual line of descent—Jesus the Messiah and all who, by faith in Him, would be called the sons of God. As Paul wrote, "If you belong to Christ, then you are Abraham's seed, and heirs according to the promise" (Galatians 3:29).

Looking back from our vantage point in the twenty-first century, we can see that God has fulfilled these promises to the letter. Abram truly has an earthly line of descendants, yet he also has a heavenly line of spiritual descendants. These descendants number in multitudes like the dust of the earth or the stars of the heavens.

Finally, Genesis 15 tells us, "Abram believed the Lord, and he credited it to him as righteousness." Paul cited this passage in his letter to the Galatians: "Consider Abraham: 'He believed God, and it was credited to him as righteousness.' Understand, then, that those who believe are children of Abraham" (Galatians 3:6–7). In other words, Paul is telling us that when we believe God as Abram did, our faith is credited to us as righteousness as well.

As we read these words, we need to avoid the mistake of assuming that Abram was a super saint who possessed a mighty faith far beyond our ability to attain. Abram was a flesh-and-blood man, prone to the same failings and weaknesses as you and I. If we compare our faith with Abram's and try to work up a superfaith within us, we will become spiritual hypochondriacs, always going about taking our spiritual temperature and feeling our spiritual pulse—and always thinking we are sickly and weak when we are just human. Abram was a weak and faltering human being just like us, and his faith was credited to him as righteousness. And we are his spiritual descendants.

We are spiritually inadequate, it's true, but God is more than adequate, and He will keep His promises toward us. Yes, we are weak and our faith is often weak, but He is strong. When our faith falters, He will pick us up and carry us in His arms. The reality of our faith is not based on our feelings. There will be times when we don't feel very strong in our faith. But feelings rise and fall. God's love for us is constant and unchanging, and He will carry us through those nights of doubt and fear. As Charles Wesley wrote:

> *Faith, mighty faith, the promise sees*
> *And looks to God alone,*
> *Laughs at impossibilities,*
> *And cries: It shall be done!*

From the first book of the Bible to the last, God presents only one way of salvation—the way of faith. We cannot work our way to favor with God. We cannot earn our salvation; we can only receive it as a free and undeserved gift. We are accepted by God on the basis of faith alone. As the apostle Paul wrote to the Ephesians: "For it is by grace you have been saved, through faith—and this not from yourselves, it is the gift of God—not by works, so that no one can boast" (Ephesians 2:8–9).

And we find that same faith principle at work here in the pages of Genesis: "Abram believed the Lord, and he credited it to him as righteousness" (Genesis 15:1–6). Abram could never earn God's favor. He could only receive it by faith as a free gift of grace.

It's important to note that this statement in Genesis 15:6 does not mean that this was the first moment Abram ever believed God and was counted as righteous before Him. This was not the moment of

Abram's spiritual regeneration. The New Testament book of Hebrews makes it clear that Abram's faith relationship with God went back to a much earlier point in life. When Abram left Ur of the Chaldeans in response to God's command, his obedient faith was credited to him as righteousness:

> By faith Abraham, when called to go to a place he would later receive as his inheritance, obeyed and went, even though he did not know where he was going. By faith he made his home in the promised land like a stranger in a foreign country. (Hebrews 11:8–9a)

So this incident under the stars in Genesis 15 does not represent the moment of Abram's regeneration. It is one instance out of many in which God reaffirmed Abram's faith and his imputed (credited) righteousness. It's important to note that this affirmation does not come after some work or achievement of Abram's. It comes after a time of doubting and fear, when Abram was clinging to faith by his fingernails. It was at that moment, when Abram was weak and fearful, that God reaffirmed His promise, and Abram's faith was strengthened. And that faith in God, which Abram had lived by since leaving Ur, was credited to him as righteousness.

Abram believed God regarding His promise of a coming Son, and the righteousness of Christ was credited to him. Two thousand years ago, that long-promised Son appeared in human history. Today, God calls us to believe in the Son who has already come. If we will cease trying to please God with our works and start living in dependence on the living Son, then our faith, like Abram's, will be credited to us as righteousness.

Do not think you have come to the end of the road when you place your faith in Jesus Christ. The moment you receive Him as Lord of your life, you stand at the beginning of an exciting adventure—just as Abram began a life of adventure the moment he set forth from Ur. In every moment of fear and doubt, let us cast ourselves upon Almighty God, trusting that His promise shall be our shield and our great reward.

# 7

# THE FURNACE AND THE LAMP

*Genesis 15:7–21*

In the country schoolhouses of an earlier era, students learned to write by using a copybook. The copybook produced a sample line of handwriting, and every student would laboriously try to reproduce the sample on the line below it. It's not hard to tell who has learned to write by the copybook method because they all have a similar style of penmanship.

The relationship between the Old and New Testaments demonstrates a similar principle. The Old Testament's record of how God dealt with Israel is a metaphorical copybook that the New Testament uses as a pattern.

In our study of Abraham, we see God's initial dealings with Israel. Now, with the benefit of hindsight, we can see that these stories serve as patterns of faith for today's believer. What literally and physically occurred in the life of Abraham now occurs spiritually in our lives as Christians. That is why these stories remain so fascinating and beneficial after all these years. That is also why the Christians in the early church, with nothing more than the Old Testament in their hands, could test and prove the doctrines of the apostles. The teachings of the New Testament reaffirm the pattern set down in the Old Testament.

## GENESIS AND ROMANS

Genesis 15 condenses for us the doctrinal themes of Romans 4 through 8. That section of Romans is one of the most doctrinally important sections of the entire New Testament. Accordingly, Genesis 15 represents an extremely important period in Abram's life.

This passage begins with the great principle that governed Abram's life: his daily trust in God. Abram had faith that God was able to do through him what He had promised. Because of this faith, Abram was credited with righteousness, even though he had no righteousness of his own.

These are the same principles Paul declares for us in Romans 4 through 8. In Romans 4 and 5, Paul makes a clear strong argument for the doctrine that we are justified and made righteous by grace through faith alone. No one can attain righteousness by good works. Abraham couldn't, and neither can we. Paul writes:

> If, in fact, Abraham was justified by works, he had something to boast about—but not before God. What does the Scripture say? "Abraham believed God, and it was credited to him as righteousness." . . . The words "it was credited to him" were written not for him alone, but also for us, to whom God will credit righteousness—for us who believe in him who raised Jesus our Lord from the dead. (Romans 4:2–3, 23–24)

This, of course, is a small sampling of Paul's argument. He makes the case for justification by grace through faith with great clarity throughout Romans 4 and 5.

Then, in Romans 6 through 8, Paul explains how to be delivered from the reigning power of sin. If our Christian experience ended with Romans 4 and 5, we would be miserable failures as Christians, because we would not have entered fully into the power for victorious living that Christ purchased for us.

Salvation is just the beginning. We need to move from salvation to sanctification to become all that God created us to be. Sanctification means to be set apart and made fit for God's intended purpose. As Paul makes clear in Romans 6 through 8, sanctification is a process by which we grow into the image of Christ and display the fruit of the Spirit. When we receive Christ, His righteousness is instantly credited to us; but as we grow in Christ day by day, we become more and more righteous in our thoughts and behavior. That is sanctification.

Just as sanctification is the theme of Romans 6 through 8, it is also the theme of Genesis 15:7–21. The process of sanctification begins with nothing less than a hunger of the heart for God and His righteousness. That is what we see in the first two verses of this section of Abram's story:

> He also said to him, "I am the LORD, who brought you out of Ur of the Chaldeans to give you this land to take possession of it."
> But Abram said, "O Sovereign LORD, how can I know that I will gain possession of it?" (Genesis 15:7–8)

Here, God reminds Abram that He called Abram out of Ur and brought him into the land of Canaan. Abram responded by asking, in effect, "Lord, how will I know that this land is truly mine? I have been walking the length and breadth of this land now for ten years, as you told me to. I have been living here as a pilgrim. How can I truly possess the land you said you would give to me?" In these words, we glimpse Abram's intense desire to possess what God has promised him. Though the land is his by promise, Abram longs to make it his by ownership.

## HOW TO POSSESS THE LAND

The land has both literal and spiritual significance. God intends for Abram to possess the land in a literal sense through his descendants, his natural seed. But God also intends for Abram to possess the land in a symbolic sense through his spiritual descendants, his children in the faith. God intends that all of us who believe in Jesus Christ should possess the land through spiritual victory, spiritual power, spiritual abundance, and spiritual fruitfulness. All of these spiritual blessings are the result of a process of sanctification, and they come to us as we allow the Holy Spirit to take more and more control of our lives.

These blessings are already ours by promise because we belong to Jesus Christ. But we have to ask ourselves: "Do I possess the land? Do I own it? Am I experiencing it?" If not, then we must ask the same question that Abram asked of God: "How can I make it truly my own?"

Do you hunger for this land? Do you long to possess what God has promised to you and offers to you? Do you desire not only to be justified but also sanctified for God's use? When Abram asked, "How can I know that I will gain possession of it?" he was not asking out of unbelief. He sincerely wanted to know more and to understand the workings of God's plan for his life.

We see a similar kind of questioning when the angel Gabriel came to the virgin Mary and told her that she was to have a child. Mary asked, "How can I have a child when I am a virgin?" Her question was not prompted by unbelief but by wonder. She wanted to understand the process by which this amazing event would happen.

When Abram asked how he would gain possession of the land, the Lord replied, in effect, "Come along, Abram. I will show you the entire procedure. I will reveal to you the means by which you, through your descendants, will possess the land." And the Lord showed Abram that the first step to possess the land involved death. We read:

> So the LORD said to him, "Bring me a heifer, a goat and a ram, each three years old, along with a dove and a young pigeon."
>
> Abram brought all these to him, cut them in two and arranged the halves opposite each other; the birds, however, he did not cut in half. Then birds of prey came down on the carcasses, but Abram drove them away. (Genesis 15:9–11)

These creatures—the heifer, the goat, the ram, the dove, and the pigeon—picture Christ, our sacrifice. Our deliverance from the enslaving power of sin is based upon the sacrifice of Jesus Christ upon the cross. The perfect life of Christ was poured out for us upon the cross, and His sacrifice is vividly illustrated for us by the sacrifice of these creatures. The animal sacrifices have no power to free us from sin. They are merely pictures and reminders of the fact that, on the cross, something happened that broke the power of sin over our lives. The sacrifice of Jesus on the cross allows the Holy Spirit to enter our lives, produce the character of Christ within us, and sanctify us for God's use.

The heifer symbolizes patience and strength. The goat is a symbol of nourishment and refreshment. The ram is an image of power and might in warfare. The birds speak of gentleness and grace, the Spirit of God at work. Significantly, all of these animals were to be three years old. This reminds us of the public ministry of the Lord Jesus, which lasted three years. All of these qualities were publicly displayed during His earthly life. These animal sacrifices, then, present a symbolic portrait of Jesus Christ in all the dimensions of His character.

Jesus' life and character were made available to us through His death upon the cross. He surrendered His life so that we might live through Him—so that the full list of His character qualities might indwell us and live through us. Some people object to the slaughter of animals in the Old Testament, yet when these sacrifices are properly understood, they are a picture of the most beautiful and selfless act imaginable: the willing sacrifice of our perfect, sinless Lord upon the cross of Calvary.

On the cross, our Lord won the right to own all the kingdoms of the earth. Some day the old hymn will be fulfilled: "Jesus shall reign where'er the sun / Doth his successive journeys run." In a literal sense, Israel, in the land of Palestine, will become the chief of nations. This unique nation, peopled by the descendants of Abraham, shall fully possess the land in accordance with God's promise.

But this principle is equally true in a spiritual sense. On the cross, our Lord won the right to fully possess the kingdom of the heart. We no longer need to struggle to do the best we can, which is never good enough. Through the empowerment of the Spirit, the life of Jesus Christ is available to us in a way that makes us fully acceptable to God.

We begin to possess the land in this spiritual sense when we understand what the Lord Jesus Christ has done for us to make it possible.

## VULTURES OF DOUBT

As Abram sacrifices these animals, we witness a fascinating occurrence. Abram brings the animals before God, slays them, and cuts them in half (except for the birds). Then, as Abram watches, birds of prey—vultures—swoop down from the sky and attack the carcasses. Abram must drive the birds away.

All day long, Abram watches over the sacrifices, waiting and waiting, chasing away the vultures whenever they attack. These birds of prey symbolize doubts sent by Satan, intended to rob the believer of blessing. Satan will try to stir up doubts within us concerning the work of Christ in our lives. Whenever these vultures of doubt descend upon us, we, like Abram, must drive them away.

Next, while Abram watches over the sacrifices, something strange and mysterious takes place:

> As the sun was setting, Abram fell into a deep sleep, and a thick and dreadful darkness came over him. Then the LORD said to him, "Know for certain that your descendants will be strangers in a country not their own, and they will be enslaved and mistreated four hundred years. But I will punish the nation they serve as slaves, and afterward they will come out with great possessions. You, however, will go to your fathers in peace and be buried at a good old age. In the fourth generation your descendants will come back here, for the sin of the Amorites has not yet reached its full measure." (Genesis 15:12–16)

## PICTURE THIS WITH ME:

As the sun touches the western horizon Abram sinks into a deep sleep. While he sleeps, he is overwhelmed by a sense of horror and dread. In the midst of this dark and troubling experience, Abram receives a revelation of the oppression and enslavement of his descendants.

This revelation, as we know, was fulfilled to the letter. Abram's descendants did go down into Egypt (a country not their own), and there they were afflicted and enslaved for four centuries, as recorded here. At last, God sent Moses to lead them out of Egypt. Pharaoh and Egypt were judged, and Israel was brought back into the land of Canaan—exactly as God told Abram.

God also gave a personal word of encouragement to Abram: He would not enter into these times of troubles but would die peacefully at a ripe old age. Only his descendants would suffer these things.

## THE DARKNESS WITHIN

This passage reveals God's great patience with the human race. The Lord tells Abram that Israel must remain in Egypt for four hundred years because "the sin of the Amorites," a godless tribe living in Canaan, "has not yet reached its full measure." In other words, these vicious tribes would be allowed to run the full course of their iniquity and depravity. Why? So that there could be no question of the righteousness of God's judgment.

When the people of Israel at last returned to the promised land, they were commanded to exterminate all of these people, male and female, adults and children. Some skeptics criticize God's command to destroy the idolatrous Amorites and the other Canaanite peoples. They say, "The God of the Old Testament is bloodthirsty and cruel." Some even accuse God of genocide.

But the reality of this picture is quite different from the caricature presented by the skeptics. This passage in Genesis pictures for us a God who waits patiently, giving these rebellious tribes full freedom to do as they please. And what do the Canaanite tribes do with their freedom? They indulged in every foul practice imaginable, including sacrificing living infants to the fires of their demonic idols. Their sexual behavior was polluted beyond description. These Canaanite tribes degenerated into a moral and spiritual cancer that threatened to infect all the nations around, including Israel. That is why God demanded their removal.

The Amorites and other Canaanite tribes are a symbolic picture of the horrible tyranny of the self. They symbolize for us the incomprehensible degeneracy of the human heart apart from God. When we contemplate the cross of Christ, we behold our own enslavement to sin and self. Unfortunately, few of us are willing to gaze upon the horrors that lurk within our own hearts.

We tend to see ourselves as good people. We have received Christ, and we have been granted the gift of eternal life. Oh, we freely admit that we still have our sins and weaknesses. Nothing major—just a fit of temper now and then, an occasional display of jealousy, a touch of stubbornness and willfulness, the occasional word of gossip, and yes, we do have a problem with lust. But these are minor matters. On the whole, we think we are pretty decent folks.

Out of this attitude of self-sufficient pride, we feel justified in looking down our noses at those unregenerate, unwashed people who have not yet come to Christ. If only we could see our sins as God sees them! He does not look upon our fits of anger, jealousy, stubbornness, gossip, and lust as minor. He sees that we are mastered by the self. Ego sits upon the throne of our lives. Our religion is a façade. We pay lip service to the cause of Christ. We have no right to feel superior to anyone.

This is the accurate self-assessment Paul relates to us in Romans 7:24: "What a wretched man I am! Who will rescue me from this body of death?" When this is our honest cry, then we have begun to realize the true horror of sin in our lives. Only then do we become aware of our utter barrenness and powerlessness. Only then do we understand that our worship has become routine and mechanical, and our service to God has become meaningless and self-glorifying.

In fact, I believe this is what Abram experienced when "a thick and dreadful darkness came over him." It's the darkness within each of us—the dreadful reality we all must face in order to truly appreciate the richness of the grace that God has given to us.

## CONFUSION TURNS TO CLARITY

Next we see God's acceptance of the sacrifice Abram has made:

When the sun had set and darkness had fallen, a smoking firepot with a blazing torch appeared and passed between the pieces. On that day the LORD made a covenant with Abram and said, "To your descendants I give this land, from the river of Egypt to the great river, the Euphrates—the land of the Kenites, Kenizzites, Kadmonites, Hittites, Perizzites, Rephaites, Amorites, Canaanites, Girgashites and Jebusites." (Genesis 15:17–21)

Out of Abram's horror and despair comes a miracle of deliverance. When we finally realize that we are enslaved by selfishness, that we are helpless in the grip of our own self-deceived ego and pride, we are finally ready for victory. The moment our hearts are cold and empty, when the light of faith has gone out, when we have reached the depths of a spiritual crisis, God comes to us in a mighty way.

The Lord God Almighty came to Abram in the form of a smoking fire pot with a blazing torch. His presence passed between the pieces of the slaughtered animals. God broke through Abram's darkness and shone His light into Abram's life.

We have seen this same kind of piercing experience in the lives of many of God's saints in the Old and New Testaments. When Jacob met his brother Esau, he turned aside by the brook Peniel, and there the angel of God wrestled with him until he was broken (Genesis 32). At that moment, the blazing light of God broke in upon Jacob's heart.

When the prophet Nathan came to King David and confronted him with his sin of adultery and murder, David was horrified by his sin and confessed it before God. At that moment, the blazing light of God broke in upon King David's heart.

When the newly converted Paul set out to serve God as a preacher and evangelist, he went to Damascus, intending to reach that city for Christ. Not only did the people of Damascus refuse to listen to him, they plotted to assassinate him. So Paul suffered the humiliation of being let down over the city wall in a basket by night. He had to flee the city like a common criminal. Thus the blazing light of God began to break in upon Paul's proud pharisaic heart.

Are you beginning to see yourself in these examples? Perhaps you are suffering a humiliating setback or the exposure of some hidden sin in your life. You have begun to realize that God is speaking to you, and you can no longer shut out His voice. He has put His finger on the moral cancer that is eating away at your soul. The blazing light of God has begun to break in upon your heart. The smoking fire pot and the torch are passing between the sundered pieces of your life. It's time to turn to God and face the light He is shining upon the hidden corners of your life.

And here's the good news: The instant you turn to Him, God is no longer a smoking, blazing furnace in your life. He becomes a lamp of comforting illumination. You are able to see yourself clearly in the glorious light of His love. Your confusion turns to clarity. Your night turns to day. Your fear turns to faith.

Instantly, you know what you have to do and you know how to go about it. Your true enemy is clearly defined. Suddenly, you see the Hittites, the Amorites, the Perizzites, and the Canaanites—all those filthy tribes of sin and self that inhabit the human heart. You see that you have been defending and protecting them, while they have been defiling and polluting you. Bitterness, insensitivity, impatience, envy, self-righteousness, laziness, lust—these are deadly enemies. It's time to drive them out of your heart.

## THE FURNACE OR THE LAMP

But even as you begin to recognize your enemies within, you also begin to see that Jesus Christ is greater than all of them. He is adequate for the enemies you face, whether you are attacked by inner temptations or outward opposition. By His strength, you can stand against your enemies and send them fleeing.

The Lord Jesus Christ is everything you need. He is your wisdom, your righteousness, your strength, and your redemption. When He lives His life through you, then you discover that you are possessing the land. You experience peace and joy within. You find deliverance. Joy, peace, and the grace of God now flood your heart.

This is the Christian life after conversion—the smoking furnace and the shining lamp. This is the story of Israel throughout its history. It's a story of affliction followed by blessing. First Israel is in the furnace, and then the lamp of God's favor shines on the nation again.

Once you set foot upon the promised land of God's power for your life, you discover that the Lord Jesus Christ is always a furnace or a lamp. When self begins to threaten, He is a furnace—burning, scorching, searing. When self is judged, He immediately becomes a lamp, flooding your life with radiance and glory.

Have you found your way to this land of promise? The one thing Abram had to do was hunger for it. "Blessed are those who hunger and thirst for righteousness," said the Lord in His Sermon on the Mount, "for they will be filled" (Matthew 5:6). When we long for God's blessing and His righteousness, then God will keep His promise and satisfy that hunger.

One of the great tragedies of the Christian world is that there are many teachers and preachers in the church who are experts in the doctrines of human depravity and God's grace, but though they know their theology backwards and forwards, though they can cite chapter and verse, they know nothing of this spiritual reality. They can speak for hours on the doctrine of sin, yet they cannot see that sin has enslaved their own lives. Until we descend into the darkness and face the dreadfulness of our own sin, we can never experience the glorious deliverance of God's shining lamp.

My friend, I urge you to begin where Abram began. Like that Old Testament man of faith, go to God and ask, "O Sovereign Lord, how can I know that I will gain possession of the promised land? Reveal to me the true state of my heart. Deliver me from the horror of my sin."

When a Christian discovers the transforming power of a life lived in the strength of God, that life becomes the most revolutionary force the world has ever seen. We in the church desperately need this transforming power. May God transform us and affect our lives so that we will become a revolutionary force in the lives of those around us—in our families, our workplace, our neighborhood, our world.

Let us not be content to live on the edge of the land or merely to pass by it. May God fill us with a hunger for righteousness, and may we never rest until we fully possess the land our Lord has promised to us.

# 8

# IT ALL DEPENDS ON ME

*Genesis 16*

We now come to a series of events that involve a mere handful of people but have profoundly affected all of human history. The choices these people made and the consequences of their actions continue to reverberate down the corridors of time, affecting the lives of millions of people and the fates of nations today. Pick up your morning newspaper or turn on Fox News or CNN. Odds are, you'll learn about the latest tragic consequences resulting from these four-thousand-year-old events.

Let's begin by placing this passage, Genesis 16, in the context of Abram's life. God has given Abram a series of visions. First, as Acts 7:2–3 tells us, God came to Abram in a glorious vision while Abram still lived in Ur in Mesopotamia, and He called Abram to leave his country and "go to the land I will show you."

Next, in Genesis 13, after Lot had parted from Abram, God again spoke to him and told him that the land all around him, north and south, east and west, would belong to him and his descendants. "I will make your offspring like the dust of the earth," God said, "so that if anyone could count the dust, then your offspring could be counted."

Then, in Genesis 15, Abram again experienced a vision, and God said to him, "Look up at the heavens and count the stars—if indeed you can count them. So shall your offspring be."

Now, as we come to Genesis 16, God begins to take what He has shown Abram in visions and translate it into the practical experience of

Abram's life. And what God does in the life of Abram, He does in your life and mine as well. Through His Word, God gives us a vision of truth that we can grasp with our intellects. But these truths have no power or meaning in our lives until they filter down into our everyday experience and begin to affect our actions and change our hearts.

Knowledge must be translated into action. If not, what good is our knowledge?

Abram has been thoroughly instructed through the visions he has received from God. Now he is about to be instructed by sad, tragic experience. He is about to learn the hard way about the destructive power of the self and of his need for the daily power of God's strength and wisdom.

## THE SOLUTION OF THE FLESH

Genesis 16 opens with these words: "Now Sarai, Abram's wife, had borne him no children" (Genesis 16:1a).

Abram has had an amazing series of personal encounters with God. Yet, even after all of these lofty experiences and visions, this was the heartbreaking fact to which Abram returned: For ten years he had been awaiting the fulfillment of God's promise, yet Sarai, his wife, was now almost seventy-five years old. Abram had no son. Despite the renewal and reaffirmation of God's promises, Abram was puzzled and discouraged because of Sarai's barrenness.

Perhaps you can identify with Abram in this or some other area of life. Like Abram, we too are justified by faith. We have accepted the gift of God's righteousness by a simple decision of the will. We know we possess eternal life not because of our own righteousness or our own efforts but by our faith in Jesus Christ.

Immediately after the experience of conversion, we set out to please God. We love Him so much because of what He has done for us that we want to give Him our gratitude and praise. We demonstrate our thankfulness to Him in the only way we know—through good works, through trying to do the best we can. Before long, however, we discover that our zeal and enthusiasm begin to wane. Where is that fire within that we once felt at the thought of serving Him? Where is the joy we once knew?

Something has happened to our love relationship with God. Where once there was an expectation of great fruitfulness and excitement, there is now only barrenness.

In a very real sense, this is the same problem Abram had. God had promised him a life of fruitfulness. So far, he had experienced only barrenness. He could not understand why God's promise was not yet fulfilled. Moreover, as Sarai was becoming advanced in years, it appeared that God's promise would never be fulfilled.

You may be at a similar place in your own walk with God. Years ago, you sensed God speaking to you, promising you a life of fruitfulness. Yet the fulfillment of that promise has been long deferred. When a sense of barrenness haunts the soul, the flesh seeks a solution to the problem, and the solution of the flesh is never God's solution.

## SARAI'S DISASTROUS PROPOSAL

Next, we learn the solution Sarai suggests to Abraham for the unresolved problem of her barrenness:

> Now Sarai, Abram's wife, had borne him no children. But she had an Egyptian maidservant named Hagar; so she said to Abram, "The LORD has kept me from having children. Go, sleep with my maidservant; perhaps I can build a family through her."
>
> Abram agreed to what Sarai said. So after Abram had been living in Canaan ten years, Sarai his wife took her Egyptian maidservant Hagar and gave her to her husband to be his wife. (Genesis 16:1–3)

Sarai's proposal to Abram seems shocking and strange to our twenty-first-century sensibilities and, indeed, to our Christian sense of morality. In our culture and our Christian values system, Abram's wife is suggesting nothing less than adultery.

Yet, in the Middle Eastern culture of four thousand years ago, this solution to the problem of Sarai's barrenness was acceptable, strange as it may seem. It was not considered immoral in the eyes of that community. In fact, many of the Canaanites males of that time would have had more than one wife, and Abram's act would have been considered perfectly proper.

In that cultural context, Sarai's actions seem praiseworthy. She was making a costly sacrifice and suggesting that Abram be permitted to have a child by Hagar, the Egyptian maidservant, in order for the promise of a son to be fulfilled. Sarai evidently reasoned, "God has promised my husband a son, through whom he means to fulfill His promises. Yet God never said that the son must come through me. Perhaps this is how God intended to fulfill this promise all along."

We can only imagine the intense internal struggle that Sarai went through to reach this conclusion. She decided to surrender her own rights as Abram's wife—the right to his sole and undivided affection—and she offered her maid to Abram so that he might have a child by her. Moreover, she took the initiative in suggesting the proposal.

Now, with the benefit of hindsight, we can clearly see that this proposal was an act of folly. It produced nothing but sorrow and heartache. The text goes on to tell us: "He slept with Hagar, and she conceived" (Genesis 16:4a).

The child Abram and Hagar conceived together would become the father of all the Arab tribes and nations. The enmity between the people of Israel and the Arab peoples began with this foolish proposal forty centuries ago, and it continues to trouble the world to this day. If you ever needed a picture of the lasting effects of sin, you find it in this story. Abram, Sarai, and Hagar committed an act in an attempt to help God fulfill His promise, and it turned out to be the worst thing they could have possibly done.

What was wrong with Sarai's proposal? How could she have known the centuries of heartache that would follow? How can we blame her or Abram for what they did?

We need to examine this story closely and carefully in order to understand what Sarai and Abram did wrong. And we need to discern the lesson in this story for our lives. If we do not learn the lesson of Abram and Sarai, then we shall find our Christian lives continually plagued with barrenness, and we shall miss the secret of victory and fruitfulness for our lives.

## "IT ALL DEPENDS ON ME."

The most basic problem with Sarai's plan was that it grew from a mindset that says, "God has told me what He wants. The rest depends on me. God has shown me the goal. It's up to me to figure out how to reach that goal. God isn't getting the job done by himself. He needs me to do it." This mindset produced incalculable sorrow and conflict.

God had a plan for fulfilling His promise, and His plan was for a child to be born to Sarai, not Hagar. The child God promised to Abram was Isaac, who was to be born to his wife, Sarai. But Sarai and Abram substituted their Plan B in place of God's Plan A, and the result was a child named Ishmael, born to Sarai's Egyptian maidservant, Hagar.

The tragic fact is that many Christians still operate by the same mindset as Sarai: "It may be God's plan, but it all depends on me." Many of us seem to think the reason God's work is not going forward as it should is that we have not put forth the right effort. We are not helping God along as we should. We are barren because we have not really put ourselves into this effort. Let's hold more committee meetings, hold a bigger fundraising drive, and devise more outreach programs. Let's get going, people—it all depends on us!

One example of how this kind of thinking operates in the church involves the Great Commission, which the resurrected Lord gave to us near the end of Mark's gospel: "Go into all the world and preach the good news to all creation" (Mark 16:15). This is the goal God has set for us, and so we think that meeting that goal depends on us: We must plan the strategy. We must set the budget. We must determine where we will send preachers, teachers, and missionaries, and what they should do. It all depends on us.

And many times, we do get results of a sort. We hold our meetings, put on our programs, apply our pressure and persuasion, and a few people come to Christ. But, oh, the results are disappointing! Why? Because we have gotten Ishmael instead of Isaac!

We read in Scripture that we should have elders in every church, because it is God's plan to govern His church through elders. So we hold an election and choose the wealthiest businessmen and the most popular individuals or the ones with the most imposing personalities. Then these elders run the church as they would a secular board of directors. The decisions they make seem sound from a business perspective, but from a spiritual perspective, these elders are stumbling in the dark. They were not chosen for their spiritual qualifications, and they operate in ignorance of the Spirit's leading.

The problem is that we have not bothered to find out how God makes known to us the elders of His choosing and how He proposes to declare His will through them. So we have a church that is barren and spiritually dead, torn by strife and division, because worldly elders cannot agree on competing goals and strategies. God gave us an Isaac plan for the church, but we have chosen Ishmael.

The plan Sarai proposed shows clearly what results when we think that God's plan depends on us. Sarai's plan seemed so noble, so selfless and self-sacrificing. And her plan did indeed bear fruit. Hagar bore Abram a child, just as Sarai planned. But the child was Ishmael, not Isaac. Ishmael was the fruit of the flesh, not the work of the Spirit.

## DOING GOD'S WORK GOD'S WAY

Before we lay too much blame on Sarai, we should note that at the end of verse 2, "Abram agreed to what Sarai said." Abram is more to blame than Sarai. Abram's wife saw his deep discouragement over not having a son. She knew his lack of an heir was troubling to his faith, especially since it involved a seemingly unfulfilled promise from God. So Sarai probably blamed herself for her barrenness. Wanting to find some way to pull her husband out of his discouragement, she proposed this plan to Abram.

But Abram knew that this was not God's plan. I think there's a definite reason why the next verse tells us that this event occurs "after

Abram had been living in Canaan ten years." I believe this fact is significant because it tells us that Abram has been learning every day for ten years that God is sufficient for every need. During that decade, Abram should have learned that God knows what He is doing, He is capable of administering His plans without help from anyone, and He operates on His own sovereign timetable.

Instead of accepting Sarai's plan, Abram should have used that moment as a teaching opportunity. He should have told his wife, "God's plan does not depend on us. He does not need our help in order to keep His promises. I know you mean well, Sarai, but we cannot rush God's plan along. Now is the time to stretch our faith and wait upon the Lord." When Abram, who knew better, listened to his wife and did what he knew was wrong, it was the story of Adam and Eve all over again.

Abram made a number of huge mistakes. First, he listened to the counsel of someone who was not as spiritually mature as he was. Sarai had not experienced the visions and other profound spiritual experiences that Abram had. Abram had reached level of spiritual growth and maturity that Sarai could not claim to possess.

I have observed that some Christians seek advice in a helter-skelter fashion, taking opinion polls of all their friends, even those who are spiritually immature. This is a major mistake and can produce disastrous results. Often what these Christians are doing is sifting through advice until they hear what they want to hear. They are not looking for insight and wisdom. They want permission from other Christians to do what they know is wrong. If you truly want to make sound spiritual decisions, seek insight from Christians who are more mature in the faith than you are.

Abram's second mistake was that he agreed to do something that was consistent with his own will, not God's will. Abram longed to have a son. He knew that God had promised him a son. There is nothing wrong with Abram's desire to be a father. But that strong desire inclined him to accept a scheme that was outside of God's plan for his life.

A third mistake Abram made was that he convinced himself he

was doing God's will and helping to fulfill God's promise, yet he never stopped to discover God's way. This is the heart of the problem.

Hudson Taylor once said, "God's work, done in God's way, will never lack God's supply." And the history of the organization he founded, China Inland Mission, proves that to be true.

All through the Scriptures, we see example after example of the folly of trying to do God's will without being committed to God's way. Young Moses knew he was God's chosen instrument for delivering the people of Israel from slavery. Once, when he saw an Egyptian beating an Israelite, he thought, "Here's my opportunity! God sent me here to free the slaves, and I'll begin with this man who is being beaten." So he killed the Egyptian and hid his body in the sand. As a result of his hasty action, Moses was forced to flee into the desert, where he remained for forty years. There he learned the secret of yielding himself to the control of God's Spirit. He had to learn to do God's work in God's way.

So did Abram. And so do we.

## THE MORAL OF THE STORY

We have seen the plan that Sarai proposed and that Abram accepted. Now let's look at the consequences that ensued:

> He slept with Hagar, and she conceived.
>
> When she knew she was pregnant, she began to despise her mistress. Then Sarai said to Abram, "*You* are responsible for the wrong I am suffering. I put my servant in your arms, and now that she knows she is pregnant, she despises me. May the LORD judge between you and me."
>
> "Your servant is in your hands," Abram said. "Do with her whatever you think best." Then Sarai mistreated Hagar; so she fled from her. (Genesis 16:4–6)

The immediate results of acting in the flesh are always the same: We become petty and petulant, displaying enmity, strife, jealousy, anger, selfishness, and other ugly emotions that always lie just beneath the surface of the fallen human heart.

First, we see the fleshly behavior of Hagar. She treats her mistress with contempt. When Abram slept with Hagar, he created a rivalry between his wife, Sarai, and the servant Hagar. As a result, Hagar became insolent and impertinent. She taunted Sarai about her barrenness.

Next, we see the fleshly behavior of Sarai. She becomes irrational and unreasonable. Sarai says to Abram, "You are responsible for the wrong I am suffering." Remember, it was Sarai who urged this plan on Abram, yet when he carried it out, she threw it back in his face, crying, "It's all your fault!"

When Sarai said, "May the Lord judge between you and me," she was using an ancient expression of anger, used elsewhere in the Old Testament (see Genesis 31:53). It means, "May the Lord keep us from murdering each other in our sleep while we are furious with each other!" This is a statement of wild, unreasoning rage.

Next, we see the fleshly behavior of Abram, exhibited in an attitude of cowardice and irresponsibility. Abram said to Sarai, "Your servant is in your hands. Do with her whatever you think best." Here, Abram dodges responsibility. "It's your problem," he says, in effect. "You deal with it."

The next result is cruelty and rebellion. "Then Sarai mistreated Hagar," we read, "so she fled from her." The whole household was in an uproar. Everyone was blaming everyone else. No one in this triangle was willing to face the evil in his or her own heart. This is the sad and tangled result of trying to help God by doing His will in our own way.

We don't have to guess at the moral to this story: Nothing is too hard for God, so let God do His will His way. If we try to help Him and hurry His will along, we will make a mess of things.

## A SPRING IN THE DESERT

In the last section of the chapter, we see the provision of grace that God makes for Hagar and her son, Ishmael:

The angel of the LORD found Hagar near a spring in the

desert; it was the spring that is beside the road to Shur. And he said, "Hagar, servant of Sarai, where have you come from, and where are you going?"

"I'm running away from my mistress Sarai," she answered.

Then the angel of the LORD told her, "Go back to your mistress and submit to her." The angel added, "I will so increase your descendants that they will be too numerous to count."

The angel of the LORD also said to her:

"You are now with child
and you will have a son.
You shall name him Ishmael,
for the LORD has heard of your misery.
He will be a wild donkey of a man;
his hand will be against everyone
and everyone's hand against him,
and he will live in hostility
toward all his brothers."

She gave this name to the LORD who spoke to her: "You are the God who sees me," for she said, "I have now seen the One who sees me." That is why the well was called Beer Lahai Roi; it is still there, between Kadesh and Bered.

So Hagar bore Abram a son, and Abram gave the name Ishmael to the son she had borne. Abram was eighty-six years old when Hagar bore him Ishmael. (Genesis 16:7–16)

The angel of the Lord finds Hagar beside a desert spring. Who is this angel of the Lord? This is the first place in Scripture where we find this phrase used. The Hebrew word for "angel" literally means "messenger." As we compare this appearance with other appearances in Scripture of the angel of the Lord, it becomes clear that this is probably an appearance of the pre-incarnate Christ, God the Son. (For other instances where the phrase "the angel of the Lord" refers to God, see Genesis 22:11–12; 16:10–13; 48:15; Exodus 3:2–14; Judges 13:14–23; and Zechariah 12:8.)

I'm convinced that the Son of God appeared to this woman in distress. There in the desert, He said four important things to her.

First, He asked her a question: "Where have you come from, and where are you going?" These are profound questions. Whenever anyone asks you, "Where have you come from, and where are you going?" you are forced to examine the course of your life, the choices you have made in the past, and the direction you have charted for the future. Hagar can answer the first question easily enough: "I'm running away from my mistress Sarai." But she has no answer for the second question, because she has no idea where she is going. Indeed, where can she go? The question forces her to recognize her utter helplessness.

Second, He gives her instructions: "Go back to your mistress and submit to her." He points her to the only way to experience the grace and blessing of God. She has wandered into the desert, and if she continues going that way, she and her child will die. Whenever God's children wander from His will, His instructions to us are always, "Return and submit." Hagar realizes that she must follow these instructions or die.

Third, He gives her a promise of blessing. I suspect that the angel of the Lord gave this promise to Hagar after she agreed to obey His instructions. Blessing always follows obedience. The blessing He gives her is, "I will so increase your descendants that they will be too numerous to count."

Fourth, He gives Hagar a prophecy regarding her soon-to-be-born child: "He will be a wild donkey of a man; his hand will be against everyone and everyone's hand will be against him, and he will live in hostility toward all his brothers." Hagar's son will be unruly and troublesome, someone who is almost impossible to get along with.

Paul explains the spiritual significance of this story in his letter to the Galatians. He writes:

> Tell me, you who want to be under the law, are you not aware of what the law says? For it is written that Abraham had two sons, one by the slave woman and the other by the free woman. His son by the slave woman was born in the ordinary

way; but his son by the free woman was born as the result of a promise. . . . Now you, brothers, like Isaac, are children of promise. At that time the son born in the ordinary way persecuted the son born by the power of the Spirit. It is the same now. (Galatians 4:21–23, 28–29)

Paul tells us that Hagar is a symbolic picture of the law, and Ishmael, her son, symbolizes those who try to gain favor in God's sight through observing religious rules and rituals. As we shall later see, Ishmael, the son of Hagar, grows to become a bully and a persecutor of Sarai's son, Isaac. In many churches, we see the very principle that Paul writes of here: Legalistic people who try to earn their salvation by strict adherence to burdensome religious laws become tormentors and persecutors of those who live under both the freedom and the control of the Holy Spirit.

Remember the Lord's promise to Hagar: "I will so increase your descendants that they will be too numerous to count." This promise, referring to Ishmael and his descendants, has both a literal and a spiritual application. In a literal sense, the Ishmaelites were a number of tribes, descended from Ishmael, who collectively became known as the Arab peoples. As the promise to Hagar stated, these people did become too numerous to count. In a spiritual sense, as Paul makes clear, the Ishmaelites are all people, including those in Christian churches, who live according to rigid religious laws and rituals and impose their legalistic views on others. The spiritual children of Isaac are those who live according to the indwelling power of God's Spirit, by faith in Jesus the Messiah.

After receiving this fourfold pronouncement from the angel of the Lord (the pre-incarnate Son of God), Hagar glimpses the truly omniscient and powerful nature of God. Having received this visitation from God, she names Him "The God Who Sees Me," for she says, "I have now seen the One who sees me."

This was a profound and gripping event for Hagar. Her life had just been invaded by the God who knows her, understands her heart, and comforts her in her suffering. Hagar probably told many people about her experience, because the desert spring where she had this encounter with God became widely known as Beer Lahai Roi, "The Well of Him Who Lives and Sees Me."

## BETWEEN THE SANCTUARY AND THE STORM

If you have ever found God to be the one who sees into your life, the one who understands your circumstances, then perhaps you have a place you think of as your own Beer Lahai Roi. Maybe there is some physical location or some point in your life that you recognize as the place where God met you and spoke to you, perhaps in a fourfold way:

You may have felt God confronting you with the question: "Where have you come from, and where are you going?" And He may have given you clear instructions regarding your life: "Return and submit." You may have felt God giving you a clear sense of His blessing. You may have even felt that He had prophesied regarding His provision for your future. That moment or place is your spring in the desert. For you, it is the place you can call "The Well of Him Who Lives and Sees Me."

Genesis tells us that Hagar's spring in the desert was located "between Kadesh and Bered." These names are significant. In the Hebrew language, *kadesh* meant "sanctuary." *Bered* meant "hail storm," and this word was often used to signify God's judgment, which was sometimes sent in the form of a punishing stormy blast (see Psalm 148:8; Job 38:22–23). So Hagar's well was a spring of grace, providing life and refreshment in the desert between sanctuary and the storm.

When we stray from the place of God's blessing toward the certainty of judgment, God meets us on the way, at the well of grace, saying, "Stop and consider where you have been and where you are going. I don't want you to cause further harm to yourself and others. I don't want to see you destroyed by your own willfulness and sin. I appeal to you to return to the sanctuary of my love and submit to my will for your life. If you proceed on to the hailstorm of judgment, you may never receive another chance to return."

That is God's message to us at the well of grace when we wander into the wilderness of disobedience.

Hagar returned to the tent of Abram and Sarai. There, Ishmael was born. We read nothing about Abram's story for thirteen years. When the next chapter opens, Abram is ninety-nine years old. This means that Abram spent thirteen years living in an atmosphere of strife, bitterness, and jealousy. It was God's way of teaching Abram, as Jesus taught His disciples, "Apart from me you can do nothing" (John 15:5).

God's plan does not depend on us. It all depends on Him. We need to constantly recommit ourselves to total dependence on the God who knows us. He truly knows our circumstances, our problems, our hurts, and our potential. He is able to work through us to accomplish all that He desires in us if we will do God's will in God's way.

# 9

# THE CIRCUMCISED LIFE

*Genesis 17*

I will never forget an incident that occurred during my ministry as a pastor. A young man came to my office carrying a thick Bible under his arm. He had recently come to Christ and was serious about his faith. He had been reading through the Bible, and he took everything he read with utter seriousness.

Looking at me earnestly, he said, "Pastor Stedman, would you circumcise me?"

After I had picked myself up from the floor, I sat down with him and explained why physical circumcision is no longer required of God's followers. Then I explained to him why circumcision was ordained by God and what it meant. As we are about to see in this section of Genesis, circumcision is an eloquent symbol when it was properly understood.

At this point in the narrative, Abram is a believer and follower of the one true God, sojourning in the land of promise. Though he is a genuine believer, he is not yet a circumcised believer, and there is a vital difference between a believer who is circumcised and one who is not. It's important to understand at the outset that the most fundamental issue for our lives is not the physical rite of circumcision but the spiritual state of having a circumcised heart. The profound distinction between a circumcised and an uncircumcised heart is the issue to which the Spirit of God directs our attention in Genesis 17.

## LEANNESS FOR THEIR SOULS

When we last saw Abram in Genesis 16, he was attempting to hurry God along in fulfilling His promise. Seeing that his wife, Sarai, was advanced in age, he decided to take direct action and solve a problem that was (in his mind) too hard for God. At Sarai's suggestion, Abram took her Egyptian maidservant, Hagar, for a wife (she was, in today's terms, a surrogate mother). The child born to Abram and Hagar was Ishmael, father of the Arab peoples, and a thorn in Israel's side to this day.

Now, as we come to Genesis 17, thirteen years have elapsed. For Abram, they were undoubtedly years of misery. The presence of Ishmael in Abram's household produced endless conflict and rebellion. Those thirteen years must have been corrosive to Abram's soul, yet those years were lovingly planned by God to teach Abram the folly of acting on his own.

Perhaps you have had a similar experience. At some time in your life, you may have wanted your own way instead of God's way. So He allowed you to do as you pleased, and the results were disastrous. You got what you wanted, according to your own headstrong will, but you learned the hard way that getting what you want can make you miserable. And misery is a powerful teacher. You discover the folly of acting apart from God.

It is like the Lord's story of the prodigal son. The son goes to his father and demands half of his inheritance. It's a foolish demand, an insulting demand—for what son is entitled to an inheritance while his father still lives? But the father gave him what he asked for, and after the son had wasted it all on a wild and sinful lifestyle, he repented of his folly. His misery had taught him a lesson that no fatherly lectures ever could have achieved.

So it is with us. When we demand our own way, God often lets us have what we demand in order to teach us a valuable life lesson. As the psalmist tells us, "He gave them their request, but sent leanness into their souls" (Psalm 106:15 KJV).

## BE BLAMELESS

After thirteen years of heartache, a new aspect of God's grace opened up in Abram's life. Three new developments arise in Genesis 17. The first is a new revelation of God:

> When Abram was ninety-nine years old, the LORD appeared to him and said, "I am God Almighty; walk before me and be blameless. I will confirm my covenant between me and you and will greatly increase your numbers." (Genesis 17:1–2)

After thirteen years of silence, God appears to Abram in a new revelation and with a new name—God Almighty. In the Hebrew, His name is *El Shaddai*, which means "the God who is sufficient"—that is, the God who knows what He is doing and is able to meet all of our needs.

This moment of revelation suggests that Abram has learned something from his recent bitter experience. God tells him, in effect, "You have been learning for thirteen years the total inadequacy of your own efforts, through Ishmael. Now learn a new thing about me. I am El Shaddai, God almighty and God all-sufficient. I am able to do everything I desire to do, whenever I desire to do it, and I do not need you to hurry my plans along."

Abram's life is about to be revolutionized and transformed by the revelation of El Shaddai. If we would place our complete trust in the almighty and all-sufficient One, our lives would be transformed as well.

Along with this revelation comes a new demand from God: "Walk before me and be blameless." In the King James Version, the word "blameless" is translated "perfect." The root meaning of the word is "wholehearted." So God is saying to Abram, "Because I am God Almighty, the all-sufficient El Shaddai, I demand that you walk before me and be perfect and wholehearted. I am able to make you blameless."

Once, when I was a boy, I was looking through the iron bars of a gate at a beautiful estate. Beyond the gate were stately trees, a neatly manicured lawn, and flower-bordered walking paths. Peering through that gate with my arms dangling through the bars, I gazed at that lush landscape with envy, wondering what it would be like to be rich enough to afford such an estate.

Suddenly, before I saw him or had a chance to react, a boy about my own age ran up from the other side of the gate, grabbed both of my arms, and jerked me forward. My chest and face crashed painfully against the bars. I received a bump on my head that taught me the foolishness of trying to be on two sides of a fence at once.

This is a principle God often tries to teach us in the New Testament. We constantly try to serve two masters—to please the Lord and the self at the same time. We are happy to serve Christ as long as we can also serve ourselves. But God now says to Abram, and to us, "I will no longer permit you to be divided in your loyalty. I am all-sufficient. You don't need anything or anyone but me. So walk before me, and be wholehearted, perfect, and blameless. Be totally on my side, without divided allegiance, appropriating what I am. Be completely mine."

This is what it means to be a circumcised believer. This is what it means to live a circumcised life.

## THE CIRCUMCISED BELIEVER

For us as Christians today, four thousand years after Abraham, one of the most crucial issues of our lives is the condition of our hearts: Are they circumcised or not? To have a circumcised heart as a follower of Christ means that we have granted Jesus total lordship over our lives. What does that mean?

When you became a Christian, you gave your life to Christ, recognizing His right to be Lord of your life. At that point, you did not understand fully what that would involve. But you did understand, at least to some degree, that His willingness to save you involved His right to control your life. You were not your own anymore. You had been bought with a price—the price of His death on the cross.

So, you began this journey called the Christian life. You knew that you had undergone a profound change. You became involved in Christian fellowship, Christian worship, prayer, and Bible study. But though you knew that, as a Christian, you were essentially a changed person, there were many areas of your life left unchanged.

There were sins, habits, and attitudes left over from the old you, and you held on to them, hid them, and rationalized them to yourself. You made decisions on the basis of your own will, your own feelings, and your own desires, regardless of God's will for your life. You were a genuine believer, and you wanted to please God, but you also wanted to please the self and be friends with the world. You had not come to the point of fully surrendering all of those dark corners of your life to the bright searchlight of His lordship and control.

Then the Holy Spirit begins to put on the pressure. He says, "It's time to surrender that habit to me," or, "It's time to let go of your bitterness and resentment and start forgiving and loving those who have hurt you," or, "It's time to stop resisting me and start yielding to this new direction to which I'm calling you." He is asserting the lordship of Christ in your life. Either gently or forcefully, depending on how much persuasion you require, He is cutting the ties that bind you to the world and the self within you.

That is what God is saying to Abram in these words in Genesis 17: "I am God Almighty; walk before me and be blameless."

## CHANGED HEARTS, NEW NAMES

At this point, God wants to underscore the importance of what has taken place here. Not only has Abram been transformed from an uncircumcised to a circumcised believer, but God also has revealed himself in a totally new way to Abram. Therefore, God gives new names to both Abram and Sarai:

> Abram fell facedown, and God said to him, "As for me, this is my covenant with you: You will be the father of many nations. No longer will you be called Abram; your name will be Abraham, for I have made you a father of many nations. . . . God also said to Abraham, "As for Sarai your wife, you are no longer to call her Sarai; her name will be Sarah. I will bless her

and will surely give you a son by her. I will bless her so that she will be the mother of nations; kings of peoples will come from her." (Genesis 17:3–5, 15–16)

In the Scriptures, when a man or woman undergoes a profound spiritual transformation, God often highlights that change by giving that person a new name, a new identity. So Simon becomes Peter the Rock; Saul becomes the apostle Paul; and Abram and Sarai become Abraham and Sarah. This is God's way of saying, "You are no longer the person you used to be. You are no longer a prisoner of your past. You are a totally new you." As Paul wrote, speaking out of his experience, "Therefore, if anyone is in Christ, he is a new creation; the old has gone, the new has come!" (2 Corinthians 5:17).

So God now says to Abraham, "Look, Abram, your old name means 'exalted father.' Your trouble all along has been that you have been seeking your own exaltation. This must change. You must stop trying to advance and please yourself. Your name will now be 'the father of a multitude,' for great fruitfulness shall be evident in your life. Because you have learned that I am El Shaddai, your name shall no longer be 'exalted father' but 'fruitful father,' for you will be the father of a multitude."

God dealt with Sarai in the same way. The name Sarai means "contentious." This speaks volumes about the home life of Abram and Sarai. In Proverbs 21:9, Solomon writes, "Better to live on a corner of the roof than share a house with a quarrelsome wife." Having had a thousand wives, Solomon spoke with authority. For Abram, Sarai was clearly a quarrelsome wife.

Yet, in the New Testament, Peter commends Sarah as a role model for all women to follow (see 1 Peter 3:4–6)—a woman who possessed "the unfading beauty of a gentle and quiet spirit, which is of great worth in God's sight." It's important to note, however, that Peter does not call her by her old name, Sarai, but by her new name, Sarah ("princess"). Nowhere in the New Testament is she ever referred to as Sarai. She is cited as an example of faith, obedience, and godly womanhood in the

New Testament letters of Romans, Galatians, Hebrews, and 1 Peter, and in every instance she is referred to as Sarah, never Sarai.

Clearly, Sarah was not always a woman of "a gentle and quiet spirit." That was not her natural disposition. By nature, she had a difficult and argumentative personality. But she, like Abraham, had learned the lessons God wanted to teach her through the trying and painful experiences of her life. She was taught by hardship and taught by grace, and through the years she let go of the need to defend herself at every occasion. She ceased to be Sarai, the contentious one, and she became Sarah, the princess, a woman of honor, with a gentle and quiet spirit, which is precious in God's sight.

## A SIGN IN THE FLESH

Now we come to the great sign and covenant of circumcision. Let's look at the entire passage so that we can see the context of this physical sign of God's ownership of His people:

"I will make you very fruitful; I will make nations of you, and kings will come from you. I will establish my covenant as an everlasting covenant between me and you and your descendants after you for the generations to come, to be your God and the God of your descendants after you. The whole land of Canaan, where you are now an alien, I will give as an everlasting possession to you and your descendants after you; and I will be their God."

Then God said to Abraham, "As for you, you must keep my covenant, you and your descendants after you for the generations to come. This is my covenant with you and your descendants after you, the covenant you are to keep: Every male among you shall be circumcised. You are to undergo circumcision, and it will be the sign of the covenant between me and you. For the generations to come every male among you who is eight days old must be circumcised, including those born in your household or bought with money from a foreigner—those who are not your offspring. Whether born in your household or bought with your money, they must be circumcised. My covenant in your flesh is to be an everlasting covenant. Any uncircumcised male, who has not been circumcised in the flesh, will be cut off from his people; he has broken my covenant."

God also said to Abraham, "As for Sarai your wife, you are no longer to call her Sarai; her name will be Sarah. I will bless her and will surely give you a son by her. I will bless her so that she will be the mother of nations; kings of peoples will come from her."

Abraham fell facedown; he laughed and said to himself, "Will a son be born to a man a hundred years old? Will Sarah bear a child at the age of ninety?" And Abraham said to God, "If only Ishmael might live under your blessing!"

Then God said, "Yes, but your wife Sarah will bear you a son, and you will call him Isaac. I will establish my covenant with him as an everlasting covenant for his descendants after him. And as for Ishmael, I have heard you: I will surely bless him; I will make him fruitful and will greatly increase his numbers. He will be the father of twelve rulers, and I will make him into a great nation. But my covenant I will establish with Isaac, whom Sarah will bear to you by this time next year." When he had finished speaking with Abraham, God went up from him.

On that very day Abraham took his son Ishmael and all those born in his household or bought with his money, every male in his household, and circumcised them, as God told him. Abraham was ninety-nine years old when he was circumcised, and his son Ishmael was thirteen; Abraham and his son Ishmael were both circumcised on that same day. And every male in Abraham's household, including those born in his household or bought from a foreigner, was circumcised with him. (Genesis 17:6–27)

Clearly, this is a strange command that God has given to Abraham. He has ordered the removal of the foreskin of the male procreative organ—literally carving into human flesh the sign of God's lordship. This is the great sign of the Jewish people, intended by God to mark them as His special possession. This physical sign was intended to indicate that God's people were to be physically separate from the people of other nations.

The foreskin, that loose cap of flesh that covers the tip of the male organ, symbolizes the flesh of our fallen humanity. The apostle Paul explains it this way: "In him you were also circumcised, in the putting off of the sinful nature [literally, the flesh], not with a circumcision done by the hands of men but with the circumcision done by Christ" (Colossians 2:11).

By removing the foreskin, the Jews symbolized the removal of the flesh, the sinful nature that was our inheritance from the Fall. Though Abraham and the rest of the Old Testament Hebrews did not fully understand the symbolic significance of circumcision, this rite looked forward in time to the crucifixion of the Messiah, the Lord Jesus, when He removed our sin from us and took it upon himself.

This visible symbol of God's ownership, this mark that was made in the most private and personal portion of a man's body, was no small matter to the Jews. It was the Jewish mark of identity. The Jews call themselves the circumcised. They called those in the Gentile, pagan world the uncircumcised.

One of the hallmarks of pagan society in those days was open, flagrant sexual degeneracy. Even the religion of the pagans was sexually corrupt. The temples of the Romans, Greeks, and other Gentile nations were filled with images of a polluted sexual nature. So the idea of dividing the righteous from the unrighteous on the basis of a mark in the flesh of the male sexual organ makes a good deal of rational sense. To the Jews, the circumcised were those who were morally virtuous and religiously enlightened; the uncircumcised were those who were sexually corrupt and religiously ignorant.

Circumcision was originally intended as a sign of humility and a seal of God's intention to use His people to bless the nations. Over the centuries, however, this mark in the flesh became perverted by some into a source of pride. There arose various sects within the Jewish community, such as the Pharisees and Sadducees, who viewed circumcision as a mark of superiority and God's favoritism. Some of the circumcised began to look upon the uncircumcised as Gentile dogs.

Though the true meaning of circumcision was distorted by some, its significance has been etched into the pages of Scripture for all time. Moreover, what was a literal and physical sign to Abraham has deep spiritual significance to us as New Testament believers. In the New Testament, we are no longer commanded to circumcise the flesh. Instead, we are commanded to circumcise the heart.

The heart is the symbol of the soul, the seat of the mind, emotions, and will, the foundation of our entire personality. Every believer in Christ is to bear upon his or her heart the sign of the lordship of Jesus Christ. Our total personality is to be at His disposal and under His control. We are to live circumcised lives. We are to walk before Him and be blameless, giving not part or half but all of our loyalty and devotion to Him.

That is what it means to be circumcised in the heart. Everything we think, everything we plan, everything we do belongs totally to Christ. Everything we are is His to use as He wills. As Paul wrote to the Philippians: "For it is we who are the circumcision, we who worship by the Spirit of God, who glory in Christ Jesus, and who put no confidence in the flesh" (Philippians 3:3).

As heart-circumcised believers, we do not rely upon ourselves but depend totally upon God. Every thought, every plan, every intention is brought into captivity to Christ. That is the circumcised life.

Today, God calls us to an exclusive relationship with Him. He tells us, as He once said to Abram, "I am God Almighty; walk before me and be blameless." If we walk before Him with circumcised hearts, He will confirm His covenant with us. He will lead us into a life of fruitfulness and blessing, a life that is well-pleasing to Him. This life is available to all who place their trust in El Shaddai, the all-sufficient God.

# 10

# WHEN GOD COMES TO DINNER

*Genesis 18:1–15*

A story is told of a man who attended a Sunday morning church service. The ushers noticed that he sat down while wearing his hat. One of the ushers went to him and whispered, "Sir, you neglected to remove your hat."

"Thank you," the man replied, "but I prefer to keep my hat on." And he kept his hat on throughout the service. The people behind him had to squeeze together in order to see. One parishioner tapped him on the shoulder and pointed to the hat. The man turned and smiled, and left the hat firmly in place atop his head.

Up on the platform, the preacher also noticed the man with the hat. In fact, he found the hat quite distracting throughout the service. A couple of times, he was so distracted that he lost his place while preaching the sermon.

Following the service, the preacher greeted people as they filed out the door. The man with the hat put out his hand and said, "Fine sermon, pastor."

"Er, thank you," the preacher said. Then he added, "You're welcome in our church. But in the future I hope you'll respect the decorum of our church by removing your hat."

The man smiled. "Thank you, pastor," he said. 'The fact is, I'm not a visitor to this church. I have been attending every Sunday for three years. But in all that time, no one has ever spoken to me. After going unnoticed for three years, I decided to keep my hat on and see what happened. As a result, I've had the pleasure of speaking with the ushers, with members of the congregation, and with you. Because of this hat, people have taken the time to notice me and make me feel welcome."

From that day forward, the people in the church made it their business to notice strangers and make them feel welcome.

As we come to Genesis 18, we see the recently renamed Abraham facing one of the first tests of his newly circumcised life. It begins with a test of his willingness to show hospitality to strangers. This story will unfold in three acts:

> Act I: God in Disguise
> Act II: Abraham in Haste
> Act III: Sarah in Doubt

Now let's examine each act of this powerful and instructive drama.

## ACT I: GOD IN DISGUISE

The chapter opens at the great trees of Mamre, the same place where Abraham was when word came to him that his nephew Lot had been taken prisoner by the kings from the east (see Genesis 14:3). It's a homey scene, a demonstration of what we might call kitchen-sink religion or faith in overalls, a combination of grace and groceries. These opening verses focus on the unexpected appearance of three strangers, one of whom is the Lord himself, appearing in disguise:

> The LORD appeared to Abraham near the great trees of Mamre while he was sitting at the entrance to his tent in the heat of the day. Abraham looked up and saw three men standing nearby. When he saw them, he hurried from the entrance of his tent to meet them and bowed low to the ground.
>
> He said, "If I have found favor in your eyes, my lord, do not pass your servant by. Let a little water be brought, and then you may all wash your feet and rest under this tree. Let me get

you something to eat, so you can be refreshed and then go on your way—now that you have come to your servant."

"Very well," they answered, "do as you say." (Genesis 18:1–5)

The Scriptures tell us clearly who has come to Abraham: "The LORD appeared to Abraham near the great trees of Mamre." The identity of the visitor: the Lord, Yahweh himself, accompanied by two angels—the same two angels who will later appear in connection with the destruction of Sodom. These are the same two angels who visit Lot to warn him of God's impending judgment upon the cities of the plain.

Because there are three men here, some Bible commentators have taken this to be a representation of the Trinity—Father, Son, and Holy Spirit. But a careful look at the context indicates that this is what we might regard as a pre-incarnate appearance of the second person of the Trinity, the Lord Jesus Christ. It's one of those mysterious appearances of Christ before He came to earth as a baby in Bethlehem.

In the heat of the day, Abraham sat in the doorway of his tent, looking out on the blazing countryside, and he saw three figures approaching. It was the Son of God in human disguise, accompanied by two angels. Abraham didn't recognize the Lord. Instead, he merely saw three human travelers, weary and thirsty as they come in from the desert.

In accordance with the custom of his culture, Abram greeted them with the deferential words, "If I have found favor in your eyes, my lord, do not pass your servant by." The phrase "my lord" was a greeting of common courtesy, not a recognition that one of these three men was in fact the Lord Yahweh. Abraham's offer of rest and refreshments shows that he had no idea whom he was entertaining.

This encounter was a test of Abraham's heart. The Lord wanted to reveal whether or not Abraham was truly a circumcised believer. So God appeared in such a commonplace guise that Abraham was not aware of his identity. I've often thought that a similar test should be used in Bible schools and seminaries to determine whether the students are genuinely mature in Christ or merely proficient in theological knowledge. A written test can reveal the mastery of information but says little about an individual's true spiritual state. It's quite possible to graduate from seminary with doctorates in divinity and theology but without any spiritual maturity.

Though human beings have never devised a test to reveal the true state of the heart, God continually tests us. His testing does not come when we are well-prepared and ready. If I tell you, "Here comes a test of your ability to keep your temper," you'd be consciously prepared to maintain your cool, no matter what happened.

But God wants to test us in real-life situations, when we are off guard. He doesn't want to see our religious act. He wants to see the real you, the real me. He wants to see how we respond when the phone rings and our plans are upset and our schedule is disrupted by a plea for help. Will we demonstrate spiritual maturity or the old sin nature? Will we demonstrate the fruit of the Spirit—love, joy, peace, patience, kindness, goodness, faithfulness, meekness, and self-control? Or will we demonstrate the irritability, impatience, selfishness, and pettiness of the flesh?

When trials and troubles are few, it's easy to say, "Here I am, Lord. I give my life to you. But that is not the true test of our hearts. The test comes when a situation arises unexpectedly, forcing us to face the question: Am I truly yielded and committed to God? Am I a willing instrument in His hands? Or am I still ruled by selfishness and my own stubborn will?

These are the true tests of the heart. These tests always come to us as Abraham's test came to him—without warning, in the heat of the day.

## ACT II: ABRAHAM IN HASTE

Now let's see how Abraham fared in the test that God gave him:

> So Abraham hurried into the tent to Sarah. "Quick," he said, "get three seahs of fine flour and knead it and bake some bread."

Then he ran to the herd and selected a choice, tender calf and gave it to a servant, who hurried to prepare it. He then brought some curds and milk and the calf that had been prepared, and set these before them. While they ate, he stood near them under a tree. (Genesis 18:6–8)

## ABRAHAM PASSED THE TEST

Notice the action words in this passage: Abraham hurried into the tent. He told Sarah to quickly get flour and bake bread. He gave the finest calf of the herd to a servant, who hurried to prepare it. These words indicate Abraham's eager spirit and his prompt response to the need before him. We see that Abraham not only involved his servants and his wife Sarah but also hastened to show hospitality to his three guests.

When I read that Abraham personally selected a tender calf from his herd, I'm reminded of an experience I had while traveling with Dr. H. A. Ironside. After Dr. Ironside had spoken at a church service, a dear old man came up to him and said, "Oh, Doctor, that was a wonderful message! It was just like Abraham's calf, tender and good." Dr. Ironside always thought that was one of the finest compliments he had ever received.

Abraham and Sarah quickly prepared a wonderful meal. The curds mentioned in the text were like cottage cheese, probably served as a fruit salad with figs and grapes stirred in. Milk was kept cool and fresh by lowering it down the well in an earthen container, so Abraham probably served cups of cool, extra-rich milk to his guests. Then he served fire-roasted veal, the most tender and mouth-watering meat of all. And Sarah set out baskets of fresh, hot bread.

As the three guests basked in the gracious hospitality of Abraham and Sarah, Abraham visited with them. This is a beautiful picture of the fellowship that is enjoyed by the circumcised heart in the presence of Christ. When we willingly, eagerly become His instruments to meet the human need all around us, we have intimate fellowship with Him.

This Old Testament meal is a vivid image of the New Testament truth expressed in the book of Revelation, where the Lord says: "Here I am! I stand at the door and knock. If anyone hears my voice and opens the door, I will come in and eat with him, and he with me" (Revelation 3:20).

The Lord does not say, "Come, knock on my door." No, He is the one who knocks on the door of your heart and mine. He wants to know if we will eagerly invite Him in and offer Him a welcoming meal—the best we have to offer. If we make Him welcome as Abraham did, we will enter into an experience of intimate fellowship with the heart of our Lord Jesus Christ.

When Jesus comes in to have fellowship with us, He doesn't come in merely to bless us and increase our enjoyment. He comes in to fulfill His long-standing desire to be what He came into the world to be—a Savior who seeks and saves that which was lost, who shows us how to love so that we can, in turn, show that same love to others. He ministers to our needs so that we may minister to the needs of those around us. The love of Christ flows not only to us but also through us.

That is the true test of our faith: Do we love others as He has loved us? In Matthew 25:31–46, the Lord describes a scene of judgment. At the end of history, He will divide the nations into two groups. Both groups think they belong to Him. One group, the Lord claims as His own. But to the other group, He says, "Depart from me, you who are cursed, into the eternal fire prepared for the devil and his angels. For I was hungry and you gave me nothing to eat, I was thirsty and you gave me nothing to drink, I was a stranger and you did not invite me in, I needed clothes and you did not clothe me, I was sick and in prison and you did not look after me."

Those whom Jesus sends away are stunned. They thought they had lived good lives, following all the proper religious rites and rituals. They are baffled by the Lord's statement that they left Him hungry, thirsty, homeless, unclothed, sick, and lonely. So Jesus explains, "I tell you the truth, whatever you did not do for one of the least of these, you did not do for me."

You see, we face the same tests that Abraham faced. The Lord Jesus comes to us in disguise. He comes to us in the form of needy, homeless, sick, and imprisoned people. These are the people who inconvenience us and interrupt our meals; the people who sit on the sidewalk, so that we must walk around them; the people who have drug habits or AIDS. And Jesus wants to know if we truly love these people. Because if we do not love them, we do not love Him. This is the true test of our faith. James says: "Religion that God our Father accepts as pure and faultless is this: to look after orphans and widows in their distress and to keep oneself from being polluted by the world" (James 1:27).

A faith that does not truly reach our hearts and move our hands and feet into loving action toward others is not a faith worth having. It is not a true, saving faith. The proof that our hearts are yielded to Christ is our willingness to respond to Him by reaching out to meet the human need around us. That is the test of a circumcised heart.

Abraham revealed his circumcised heart in his eager response to the three strangers. He didn't offer his hospitality because he wanted something in return. He was not trying to impress anyone. He was not trying to win recognition or prove how pious he was. He did not know if these three men were paupers or kings, yet he treated them royally nonetheless. That is the evidence of a heart filled with grace and love, a heart that is selfless and circumcised.

I once heard a Christian speaker at a men's conference talking about the growing attitude of callous indifference in the world today. He said, "A friend and I were walking through a busy city street the other day. We came upon a man who was drunk or sick, lying in the gutter. I was appalled to see people simply walked over him or step around him and go on their way. And I was even more appalled when my friend and I came back from lunch and the poor man was still there!"

The point was clear. We all find it shocking and disturbing to see people ignoring the suffering of their fellow human beings. But while we are incensed over the indifference of others, are we behaving any better? When Jesus comes to us disguised as someone who is hungry or homeless or sick or in prison, do we demonstrate that we have circumcised hearts?

These tests come to us every day. How do we respond? Do we pass the test? Do we hurry to meet those needs and to show the love of Christ to a world in need? These are the questions that confront us in the story of Abraham and the three strangers.

## ACT III: SARAH IN DOUBT

In the third and final act of this three-act drama, we see Sarah in doubt:

"Where is your wife Sarah?" they asked him.

"There, in the tent," he said.

Then the LORD said, "I will surely return to you about this time next year, and Sarah your wife will have a son."

Now Sarah was listening at the entrance to the tent, which was behind him. Abraham and Sarah were already old and well advanced in years, and Sarah was past the age of childbearing. So Sarah laughed to herself as she thought, "After I am worn out and my master is old, will I now have this pleasure?"

Then the LORD said to Abraham, "Why did Sarah laugh and say, 'Will I really have a child, now that I am old?' Is anything too hard for the LORD? I will return to you at the appointed time next year and Sarah will have a son."

Sarah was afraid, so she lied and said, "I did not laugh."

But he said, "Yes, you did laugh." (Genesis 18:9–15)

Here Abraham receives his first hint of the true identity of his three guests. They ask, Where is your wife Sarah?" Only the Lord would know of her recent name change, yet these three men know her name.

If this question didn't convince Abraham that he was being visited by the Lord, then the next statement would surely establish His identity: "I will surely return to you about this time next year, and Sarah your wife will have a son." This same promise had been made to Abraham before, and the one who made that promise was the Lord.

This scene reminds me of the incident in Luke 24:13–35, following the resurrection of Jesus Christ. There, two of His disciples were walking along the road to the village of Emmaus when they were joined by a stranger—the Lord in disguise. The two men walked and talked with Him while on the road and even shared a meal with Him, but it was not until they saw Him in the familiar act of breaking bread that they realized who this stranger truly was: the Lord himself.

In a similar way, Abraham recognizes the Lord when he hears those familiar words of the promise of a son. As those words were spoken, Sarah was eavesdropping. She heard the question and the promise, and she realized that God was reaffirming the promise of a son. She looked down at her ninety-year-old body and could not repress her cynical laughter over this absurd promise from the Lord.

The passage does not say that she laughed loudly. It says that Sarah "laughed to herself." But the Lord knew her thoughts. So He said to Abraham, "Why did Sarah laugh and say, 'Will I really have a child, now that I am old?' Is anything too hard for the Lord?" Moreover, the Lord added something to this promise that He had never said before: He set a date when this promise would be fulfilled. He said, "I will return to you at the appointed time next year and Sarah will have a son."

After hearing this, Sarah was afraid. She saw that her heart was an open book before the Lord. She realized that every unrighteous thought was known to God. Even so, she tried to cover up the truth by lying and denying that she had laughed. But God knows when we are living in denial of the truth. So He told Sarah sternly, "Yes, you did laugh."

And that is the end of the account.

## POWER TO BELIEVE AND TO CONCEIVE

It seems odd that this account should end so abruptly. Sarah denied that she laughed, God confronted her with the truth that she had, in fact, laughed—and the subject is dropped. What are we to make of this abrupt transition?

In Genesis 17:17, when God again reaffirmed His promise of a son to Abraham, we read that Abraham fell on his face, laughed, and said, "Will a son be born to a man a hundred years old? Will Sarah bear a child at the age of ninety?"

But Abraham's laughter was not like Sarah's. Abraham's laughter was that of a man who was deliriously joyful over all that God had promised him. It was the laughter of faith, the laughter of delight in the amazing miracle God was going to do through Abraham's time-worn body and that of his aging wife. That is why the apostle Paul observed:

> Without weakening in his faith, he faced the fact that his body was as good as dead—since he was about a hundred years old—and that Sarah's womb was also dead. Yet he did not waver through unbelief regarding the promise of God, but was strengthened in his faith and gave glory to God, being fully persuaded that God had power to do what he had promised. This is why "it was credited to him as righteousness." (Romans 4:19–22)

By contrast, Sarah's laughter is cynical and unbelieving. If this were the whole story of Sarah's life, she would not be a role model of faith. But the New Testament book of Hebrews gives us the rest of Sarah's story. There, in Hebrews 11, the roll call of heroes of the faith, we read these words about Sarah: "By faith even Sarah herself received ability to conceive, even beyond the proper time of life, since she considered Him faithful who had promised" (Hebrews 11:11 NASB).

Here's what must have happened: After the three guests left, Sarah pondered what she had heard, and especially the question God had asked, "Is anything too hard for the Lord?" As Sarah thought about it, she realized that she had received a promise from the Creator, the Almighty One who had summoned the entire universe into existence with a mere word. And the answer to that question was inescapable: No. Nothing is too hard for the Creator of heaven and earth. If He promised it, then His promise would be fulfilled.

In that moment of realization, Sarah received power to believe and to conceive. Even though she was ninety, she could receive the Lord's seemingly impossible promise. She realized that God, who had made that promise, was faithful. Nothing was too hard for Him.

What a beautiful lesson on the nature of faith! Authentic faith looks beyond all the improbabilities and impossibilities and rests upon the character of the One whose promises are sure. Do not be misled by the popular delusion that says that faith is nothing more than unfounded belief or wishful thinking. Faith must have a promise to rest upon. Faith must have a Person to rely upon. Anything else is presumption and folly.

When God has given His word, you can trust that word in spite of any circumstances, trials, or opposition. Is anything too hard for the Lord? Absolutely not! Sarah learned to place her trust in the Lord of impossibilities—and so should we.

## "BUT GOD . . ."

I was once invited to Asia to speak at a series of conferences for pastors. My ministry would begin in Taiwan, where I would speak through interpreters to more than three hundred pastors from all over the island. In spite of the strong Christian witness on the island, I could sense the spiritual oppression of the surrounding pagan culture. After Taiwan, I would speak at conferences in Vietnam, Hong Kong, Singapore, and the Philippines. I felt completely inadequate and unequal to the task.

Unlike Sarah, I didn't laugh at my impossibilities; I trembled before them. So I went to the Lord and confessed my fears and doubts. Opening His Word, I asked for a message of peace and assurance. I came upon these words in Psalm 18:

> You, O LORD, keep my lamp burning;
> my God turns my darkness into light.
> With your help I can advance against a troop;
> with my God I can scale a wall. (Psalm 18:28–29)

I thought of the darkness of the land, of all those pastors, of the language barrier and cultural barrier—and I knew that these were the walls God had called me to scale. As I claimed that promise from the Psalms, my heart felt light. My confidence surged. I plunged into that ministry, and the Lord kept my lamp burning and turned my darkness into light. At the end of the series of conferences, I looked back and saw that God had enabled me to advance against a troop of difficulties—and God gave me the victory over them all.

What is your impossibility today? What is the obstacle or circumstance that is so unthinkable that you either laugh in unbelief or tremble in fear?

Is it impossible for you to let go of some sin or self-destructive habit? Is it impossible for you to control your lusts or anger or dishonest impulses? Is it impossible for you to resolve that broken relationship? Is it impossible for you to forgive what someone did to you or said about you? Is it impossible for that friend you've been praying for to open her heart to the Lord? Is it impossible to think that your wayward child or spouse will ever return to Christ?

What seems impossible with us is never too hard for the Lord. Don't give in to cynicism and unbelief. Our faith is not in our circumstances or in wishful thinking. Our faith is in the One who promises that nothing is impossible.

If you have ever read the Bible through, you may have noticed a phrase that appears repeatedly throughout the Old and New Testaments: "But God . . ." Here are a few examples: " 'You would surely have sent me away empty-handed. But God has seen my hardship' " (Genesis 31:42). " 'You intended to harm me, but God intended it for good' " (Genesis 50:20). "Day after day Saul searched for him, but God did not give David into his hands" (1 Samuel 23:14). "My heart may fail, but God is the strength of my heart" (Psalm 73:26). "You killed the author of life, but God raised him from the dead" (Acts 3:15).

Again and again, when human resources have come to an end, when despair and pessimism have overshadowed us, the Spirit writes in luminous letters, "But God . . ." The same God reigns in our world. Is anything too hard for the Lord? No! Whenever we face an impossible challenge or obstacle, we must remember those two words: "But God . . ."

His power is limitless. His character is dependable. His promises are sure. Whatever He says, He will do.

11

# HOW PRAYER WORKS

*Genesis 18:16–33*

The ancient city of Sodom was a fortress of worldly power and strength. In fact, the name Sodom is probably akin to the Arabic word *sadama*, which means "to fortify or strengthen." For many years, unbelieving historians considered Sodom to be a mythical place, one of many supposed myths in the Bible.

Then, in 1976, Dr. Giovanni Pettinato, a noted linguistic archaeologist and author of *Ebla: A New Look at History,* announced an astonishing discovery. Among the fifteen thousand cuneiform tablets discovered in the newly excavated ruins of the ancient city of Ebla in modern-day Syria, Dr. Pettinato had found an inscription with the names of all five cities of the plain mentioned in Genesis 10:19 and Genesis 14:2. The cities were listed in the same order as in Genesis: Sodom, Gomorrah, Admah, Zeboiim, and Bela. Genesis 14:3 tells us that these cities of the plain were located near "the Salt Sea," which we know today as the Dead Sea.

A number of ancient ruins have been excavated near the Dead Sea. Significantly, stones and other artifacts uncovered at these sites show clear evidence of intense fire and chemical traces of sulfur (brimstone). These ruined cities all abruptly ceased to be inhabited around the end of the Early Bronze Age, which is precisely the period of history encompassed by this portion of the book of Genesis.

As we saw previously, Abraham has been visited by three strangers—the Lord and two of His mighty angels. Their visit served as a test of Abraham's changed and circumcised heart. Once Abraham had passed the test, the two angels proceeded toward these ancient and wicked cities of the plain.

Against this strange, dark background of idolatry and human sin, the Lord will give us a profound and valuable lesson in the true nature of prayer.

## GOD REVEALS HIS SECRETS

Our study in how to pray begins with God's consideration of the grievous sin of the cities of Sodom and Gomorrah, which He contrasts with His beautiful plan of blessing for Abraham and his descendants:

> When the men got up to leave, they looked down toward Sodom, and Abraham walked along with them to see them on their way. Then the LORD are said, "Shall I hide from Abraham what I am about to do? Abraham will surely become a great and powerful nation, and all nations on earth will be blessed through him. For I have chosen him, so that he will direct his children and his household after him to keep the way of the LORD by doing what is right and just, so that the LORD will bring about for Abraham what he has promised him." (Genesis 18:16–21)

Abraham accompanied his three guests as they left his encampment and headed east toward the valley of the Jordan. The Lord, the two angels, and Abraham came to a promontory at the edge of a steep slope leading down toward the valley of the Dead Sea. The doomed and unsuspecting cities lay far below, their spires gleaming in the afternoon sun. To this day, you can visit the site where, according to tradition, Abraham intervened with God for the city of Sodom—a high promontory called Capharbarucha (today known as Beni Naim), a high place about four miles east of Hebron, with a commanding view of the plains around the Dead Sea.

This incident reveals a crucial and often-ignored truth about prayer: Authentic prayer is always initiated by God, not by humanity. We tend to think of prayer as a process whereby we go to God and ask Him to bless our plans. But that is not so. God always proposes genuine prayer. True prayer is not where we ask God to become a partner in our plans but when He enlists us in a partnership of carrying out His program. Unless we base our prayers on His promise and His Word, we are not praying according to His will. We should not expect God to answer any prayer that is not initiated by Him.

Some people think praying in faith means crawling out on a slender limb, then pleading with God, "Please don't let it break!" That's not prayer. That's presumption. If God makes it clear that He wants you out on a limb, fine—you'll be perfectly safe there. If not, stay off of that limb!

An authentic prayer of faith acts on previous knowledge of what God wants. It is always founded upon God's promise. It begins with a proposal God makes, or a conviction He gives, or a warning He utters. But the prayer of presumption is a self-willed prayer. It is a prayer that seeks God's blessing upon human-conceived plans. Such prayers are doomed at the outset.

When God proposes something, as He does here concerning the destruction of Sodom and Gomorrah, he usually enlists a human being as His partner. Genesis shows us a scene in which God asks himself, "Shall I hide from Abraham what I am about to do?" Then God lists the reasons why He should include Abraham as a partner in His plan.

Those reasons might be called the rights of friendship. Here is where Abraham earned the title by which he is known in Scripture: "the friend of God" (see 2 Chronicles 20:7; Isaiah 41:8; and James 2:23). Here God says, in effect, "I won't keep Abraham in the dark because of what I am about to do to Sodom and Gomorrah. I will tell him because by grace I have favored him and called him to be the father of many descendants and a blessing to all the nations of the earth; and I have chosen him so that he might instruct his household to keep my ways. Because I have taught him to walk rightly before me, I will reveal to him my secrets."

Perhaps you already see a parallel to your Christian life. The parallel is this: Every believer in Jesus Christ stands in exactly the same relation-ship with God that Abraham experienced. Like Abraham, we have been given a favored position before God, and we have received this position by His grace, not through our own merit or effort. We have been called into the family of God and have become children of the living God by grace through faith in Jesus Christ.

Furthermore, we are continually being taught by grace how to walk righteously and justly before God. As we learn these lessons, we become the people to whom God reveals His secrets. I think many Christians believe that simply because they have accepted Jesus Christ as their Lord and Savior, all God has is now open to them. But it's not enough to merely have a favored position before Him. We must also learn to walk before God in righteousness and justice. Only then does God begin to share His secrets with us.

Perhaps the reason some people get more out of the Bible than oth-ers is that they have learned this two-way relationship. God truly loves to reveal His secrets to His obedient people.

## THE SINS OF SODOM

God's proposal not only enlists the partnership of people but also demonstrates His impartial and careful justice:

> Then the LORD said, "The outcry against Sodom and Gomorrah is so great and their sin so grievous that I will go down and see if what they have done is as bad as the outcry that has reached me. If not, I will know." (Genesis 18:20–21)

Clearly, God does not need to physically, personally visit a city in order to know what is going on. Here, the Lord uses Abraham's own language to express the truth that reflects His nature. He speaks as though a great outcry has been coming to His throne in heaven from these wicked cities.

When I read this passage, I can't help but think that every sin com-mitted by human beings is like a hideous wailing cry from the earth, echoing to the heavens. What kind of a cry must God be hearing at this very moment at the surging tide of violence, greed, sexual depravity, pornography, child abuse, and cruel indifference that floods our society? It pours forth from our television screens and cinemas and the Internet. It destroys marriages and families. It ruins the lives of children and adults alike. It even ruins Christian homes, destroys Christian witness, and divides Christian churches.

The great outcry of human sin rises to heaven—and God hears and sees it all. It is no mere metaphor to say that God is walking our streets, observing what human beings do to one another, and He takes note of everything, missing nothing. Even our thoughts are open and naked before Him.

The Lord is a just judge. Before God pronounces His verdict on the cities of the plain, He carefully examines the evidence and investigates the charges. So He tells Abraham what He plans to do, concluding with the ominous words: "I will know."

Though the Lord has not specifically said that he would destroy those cities, Abraham knew what God meant when He said, "I will know." Abraham knew about the rampant and unbridled sin that was practiced openly in those cities. He knew about the arrogance and greed of those cities and of the fact that the people of those cities had no concern for the poor and needy among them.

Many Christians mistakenly assume that the sin of Sodom was one specific form of sin—namely, homosexuality. Perhaps this is why some churchgoers view the gay community with judgment and hatred while at the same time excusing their own heterosexual sins, their own adultery, fornication, lust, and addiction to pornography. But the wickedness of Sodom went far beyond the sexual depravity of its people. As the prophet Ezekiel warns, the people of Sodom were guilty of many other sins, including sins that commonly infect the church:

> "Now this was the sin of your sister Sodom: She and her daughters were arrogant, overfed and unconcerned; they did not help the poor and needy. They were haughty and did detestable things before me. Therefore I did away with them as you have seen." (Ezekiel 16:49–50)

The people of Sodom were arrogant—they considered themselves better than other people. They were overfed—that is, greedy and gluttonous. They were unconcerned, and they left the poor and needy to die in the streets. They were haughty toward God and did detestable things—lying, stealing, murdering, abusing children, and indulging their perverted lusts—without any regard for God's moral law. Can you and I honestly say that we are completely innocent of all the sins of which Sodom was guilty?

## THE PRAYER OF ABRAHAM

Next, the Lord's two angels turn toward Sodom. Abraham, knowing what is about to take place, begins to implore the Lord for mercy:

> The men turned away and went toward Sodom, but Abraham remained standing before the LORD. Then Abraham approached him and said: "Will you sweep away the righteous with the wicked? What if there are fifty righteous people in the city? Will you really sweep it away and not spare the place for the sake of the fifty righteous people in it? Far be it from you to do such a thing—to kill the righteous with the wicked, treating the righteous and the wicked alike. Far be it from you! Will not the Judge of all the earth do right?"
>
> The LORD said, "If I find fifty righteous people in the city of Sodom, I will spare the whole place for their sake."
>
> Then Abraham spoke up again: "Now that I have been so bold as to speak to the Lord, though I am nothing but dust and ashes, what if the number of the righteous is five less than fifty? Will you destroy the whole city because of five people?"
>
> "If I find forty-five there," he said, "I will not destroy it."
>
> Once again he spoke to him, "What if only forty are found there?"
>
> He said, "For the sake of forty, I will not do it."
>
> Then he said, "May the Lord not be angry, but let me speak. What if only thirty can be found there?"

He answered, "I will not do it if I find thirty there."

Abraham said, "Now that I have been so bold as to speak to the Lord, what if only twenty can be found there?"

He said, "For the sake of twenty, I will not destroy it."

Then he said, "May the Lord not be angry, but let me speak just once more. What if only ten can be found there?"

He answered, "For the sake of ten, I will not destroy it." (Genesis 18:22–32)

This is a strange and remarkable account. It almost seems as though Abraham is trying to back God into a corner by lowering the ante a little more with each question.

How would you and I have prayed for Sodom if we had been in Abraham's sandals? Would we have asked God to spare that city? Or would we have asked Him to judge that city and wipe it off the map? How many times have you seen a television news story about some shocking exhibition of human depravity and said to God, "Lord, why do you tolerate such filth and degradation? Why do you allow this obscenity and blasphemy to go on? Why don't you wipe those people off the face of the earth?"

Of course, such questions seem to assume that we are the good people and the people doing those vile and degraded acts are the bad people. We easily forget that, as Solomon tells us:

> There is not a righteous man on earth
> who does what is right and never sins. (Ecclesiastes
> 7:20)

And we forget the wisdom of the psalmist, who reminds us:

> All have turned aside,
> they have together become corrupt;
> there is no one who does good,
> not even one. (Psalm 14:3)

As measured by God's moral standard, there are no good people.

You and I are on the same moral plane with those sinners we would so gladly ask God to sweep out of existence. There is no punishment they deserve that we do not deserve as well. The fact that we are saved by God's grace does not make us morally superior to any other human being. In fact, it should fill our hearts with compassion for those who are lost in their sins. Truly, we must acknowledge, "There, but for the grace of God, go I."

Abraham, the friend of God, the man with the circumcised heart, understands both his own sinful nature and the goodness of the grace of God. There is no spiritual arrogance or self-righteousness in him. He does not feel superior to the people of Sodom. When he saw the two angels turn their faces toward the doomed cities of the plain, he immediately began pleading with the Lord. He prayed that God would have mercy on the city of Sodom.

## ABRAHAM ACKNOWLEDGES GOD'S MERCY

The form of Abraham's prayer is endlessly fascinating. Few of us would ever think to pray as Abraham does here. In fact, at first glance, Abraham's prayer seems almost like an attempt to manipulate God. But a closer look reveals that this is not so.

Notice first that Abraham begins by recognizing the mercy of God. He says, "Will you sweep away the righteous with the wicked? What if there are fifty righteous people in the city? Will you really sweep it away and not spare the place for the sake of the fifty righteous people in it? . . . Will not the Judge of all the earth do right?"

Some people read this passage and think that Abraham is trying to shame God into sparing the city by making God feel guilty. Some seem to think that Abraham is saying, in effect, "Lord, you should be ashamed of yourself! What are you thinking? Don't you know there are innocent people in that city? If there are, say, fifty righteous people in that city, wouldn't it be right and just to spare the wicked for the sake of the righteous? Since you are the judge of all the earth, shouldn't you do the right thing?"

But God does not need anyone to remind Him to do what is right and just. God is the author of all morality and virtue, all justice and righteousness. He does not need Abraham to instruct him in the right thing to do, and Abraham knows it. So what is Abraham's point? He is basing his appeal on his knowledge of God's righteous, just, and merciful nature. Abraham knows full well that God would never destroy the righteous along with the wicked. So Abraham now goes a step further and asks God to spare the wicked for the sake of the righteous. By this reasoning, Abraham reveals the basis of God's mercy in every age of history.

A friend once told me that he and another man were walking past a church. The bulletin board in front of the church announced the title of next Sunday's sermon: "If I Were God." The man who was walking with my friend said, "When I think of this world, with all of its sin and depravity, its cruelty and suffering, I know exactly what I would do if I were God. I would lean over the battlements of heaven, take a deep breath, and blow this sorry planet out of existence!"

Have you ever felt that way? Have you ever wondered why God waits so long and puts up with so much human rebellion and depravity? Do you ever wonder why He didn't long ago put an end to the human race? We find the answer to these questions in Abraham's prayer: God spares the wicked of this world for the sake of the righteous.

Of course, as we noted earlier, the righteous are not better people than the unrighteous. All have sinned, all fall short of God's standard of moral perfection. The only difference between the righteous and the unrighteous is that the righteous have accepted God's grace while the unrighteous have rejected it.

Those who have received the righteousness of God as a gift of His grace have become what Jesus called "the salt of the earth" (Matthew 5:13). Salt seasons food and adds a dash of flavor and zest to life. Salt also preserves food from corruption. Since ancient times, salt has been used to preserve dried meat and fish, so that food that would normally spoil within hours can be safely stored for weeks or months. The righteous people of God lend a flavor of God to society and help preserve society against corruption and destruction.

Because of the merciful character of God, He has patiently refrained from destroying the earth so long as there are righteous people—"the salt of the earth"—living in it. And so it is with the city of Sodom. Abraham, acknowledging God's mercy, asks God to spare the city of Sodom for the sake of fifty righteous people. Of course, Abraham's appeal raises a thorny question: Are there truly fifty righteous people in Sodom? Knowing that city as he does, Abraham clearly doubts that there are.

So we come to the next feature of Abraham's prayer.

## ABRAHAM ACKNOWLEDGES HIS OWN UNWORTHINESS

The second part of Abraham's appeal to God focuses on his own awareness of his unworthy state. Abraham prays: "Now that I have been so bold as to speak to the Lord, though I am nothing but dust and ashes, what if the number of the righteous is five less than fifty?" In other words, "Lord, I haven't any right to ask this of you. Who am I? A mere man, which you created of dust and ashes. Even so, I can't help expressing the agony of my heart. Would you spare the city if there were only forty-five righteous people?"

Again, people sometimes misread Abraham's words, thinking that he is trying to manipulate and cajole God by putting on an "I'm not worthy" act, a kind of verbal sackcloth and ashes to impress God with his humility. But God knows Abraham's heart. He would not be fooled by phony words meant only to impress. God receives Abraham's prayer and replies, "If I find forty-five there, I will not destroy it." Because of God's reply, we can be sure that Abraham's words were sincere and from the heart.

Abraham's genuine meekness before God is the opposite of the pride and presumption with which many people approach God. I have heard certain preachers and faith healers address God as if He were a magic genie from a bottle, obliged to perform miracles upon command. God does not take orders from human beings, and any human being who seeks to make demands on God reveals only the awful pride of his or her own heart. That is not true prayer.

But when God's people come to Him in genuine humility, He delights to hear their prayers. Abraham approached God saying, in effect, "Lord, who am I to ask anything of you? Yet, because you are gracious and merciful, you have permitted me to come before your throne of grace with this request." That is the prayerful attitude God honors.

## ABRAHAM INTERCEDES
## ON BEHALF OF THE LOST

The third part of Abraham's appeal to God focuses on the welfare and protection of other people. He is concerned for the lives of the righteous remnant in Sodom. So he continues his dialogue with God, each time reducing the number of potentially righteous people in that city: forty, thirty, twenty, and finally ten.

Why does Abraham stop at ten? The answer is not clear. Abraham was surely aware that there were fewer than ten people in Lot's family. The account in Genesis 19 lists six individuals: Lot, his wife, his two daughters, and the two men to whom his daughters were engaged. Abraham clearly had Lot and his family in mind as he pleaded for mercy for Sodom. Perhaps Abraham hoped that Lot would have won his own family to the Lord, plus a few other friends. He may have been hoping against hope that Lot was able to have at least some influence on a few people in that wicked city. Perhaps it never occurred to Abraham that his nephew's witness for God would bear no fruit whatsoever.

In his prayer, Abraham never directly asked God to spare Lot and his family. Yet, out of compassion for the lost souls of Sodom, Abraham tried to save the whole city for the sake of Lot and his family. Abraham certainly had no use for the sin of Sodom. The immorality and callous indifference of the people of Sodom surely disgusted this righteous friend of God with the circumcised heart.

But Abraham was also aware of his own sinfulness. He knew that the only righteousness he possessed was the unmerited righteousness of God, which was his by grace alone. So Abraham had compassion for those who were lost in ignorance and sin.

Abraham's compassion for the lost is a mirror reflection of God's love for this lost world. Though God is deeply concerned about the welfare of the righteous, he is also compassionate toward those foolish human beings who harm themselves and others through ignorance and sin. Abraham, like God, seeks the slightest opening to show mercy toward lost human souls.

## THE PURPOSE OF PRAYER

In the concluding verse of this chapter, there is an interesting and subtle turn of phrase that speaks volumes about the purpose of prayer: "When the LORD had finished speaking with Abraham, he left, and Abraham returned home" (Genesis 18:33).

We think of prayer as a process by which we talk to God. But this verse makes clear that the opposite is true: Prayer is the conversation God has with us. The verse does not say, "When Abraham had finished speaking with the Lord." It says, "When the Lord had finished speaking with Abraham." Abraham did not initiate the conversation, nor did Abraham conclude the conversation. God initiated it, and God brought it to a close.

Some commentators, reflecting on this passage, conclude that Abraham's faith failed him when he reached the number ten. They conclude that Abraham did not have sufficient faith to ask God to save Sodom for the sake of any fewer than ten righteous people. Some suggest that, had Abraham's faith been greater, God might have spared the city of Sodom. I think this is highly unlikely.

Suppose Abraham had asked God to spare the city for the sake of five righteous people. In Genesis 19, we find that only three people got out of the city alive. That is a tiny remnant indeed out of the city of thousands.

Even more importantly, we must remember that it was God, not Abraham, who initiated the conversation. God led Abraham through this prayer, and when Abraham had responded fully as God desired, the Lord concluded the dialogue and went His way. It was not Abraham but God who set the limits of the conversation.

These facts fully agree with what the New Testament tells us about prayer. Paul tells us, "We do not know what we ought to pray for, but the Spirit himself intercedes for us with groans that words cannot express" (Romans 8:26b). These inexpressible thoughts and feelings, too deep for words, are there within our hearts. The Holy Spirit understands those thoughts and feelings, and He expresses them on our behalf. True prayer, therefore, is far more than merely talking to God. It is God talking through people to God.

Where did Abraham get his deep compassion for the lost? It came from God. The Lord moved Abraham to reflect His heart of mercy and compassion. Through prayer, Abraham was able to feel and know the heart of God. That, after all, is one of the principal reasons for prayer.

When we approach the subject of prayer, we tread on the edges of a mystery. There is much about prayer we can't understand. Yet certain principles about prayer become clear through this account.

First, prayer enables us to experience the joy of partnership with the Lord, our Creator. It's like the joy a little boy feels when he picks up his toy hammer and toy saw and says to his mother, "I'm going to help Daddy build a house!" He full of the pride of partnership with his daddy, the grownup he most admires in the world. So he goes outside and helps Daddy by handing him nails and tools, and though Daddy could do the job faster without his little boy's dubious help, he enjoys his son's company and is grateful for these golden moments with his boy.

That's what prayer is like. The Creator of the universe hardly needs our help, but He is a loving Father, and He rejoices to work in partnership with us. In the process, He deepens our sense of partnership and fellowship with Him. That's why the apostle Paul says that we are "God's fellow workers" (1 Corinthians 3:9). When we truly belong to Him, we want to work with Him and share in His plan for human history.

I once heard of a man pray, "Lord, let my heart be broken by the things that break the heart of God." That is a hunger for partnership with God. That is the heart's cry of a believer who truly wants to be used by God to further His work in the world.

## TAKING ON THE CHARACTER OF GOD

Prayer also opens up the human spirit to the Spirit of God. It enables us to take on the character of God. Abraham was never more like God than at the moment he was praying for Sodom. His prayer did not save the city. It was never intended to. But Abraham's prayer enabled him to reflect the mercy and compassion of God. The Lord invites us to pray so that we might take on something of His character.

The apostle Paul said this about prayer: "Do not be anxious about anything, but in everything, by prayer and petition, with thanksgiving, present your requests to God" (Philippians 4:6). Immediately after these words, Paul, under the inspiration of the Holy Spirit, makes a promise. Notice, the promise is not that God will fulfill all your requests and do everything you ask. Rather, the promise is: "And the peace of God, which transcends all understanding, will guard your hearts and your minds in Christ Jesus" (Philippians 4:7).

This is God's pledge that even amid trials and circumstances we cannot solve by human reason, He will give us a peace and serenity far beyond human understanding. God's peace will encompass and guard our hearts and minds. Our circumstances may not change as a result of our time in prayer, but we will be changed. The problem or crisis we've prayed about—the chronic illness, the shattered relationship, the financial struggle—may still be there. But something will be changed within us: The inexplicable peace of God will displace our anxious thoughts. Instead of worrying about our problems, we will face the future with a serene and confident faith.

Instead of viewing our problems from a horizontal, human perspective, we will begin to see them from a vertical, divine perspective. Prayer enables us to take on the character and perspective of God. As we begin to see our lives and our problems from His infinite point of view instead of our own finite point of view, we experience peace. We increase our faith and grow in character.

## FOCUSING GOD'S POWER

Just as a magnifying glass focuses the light of the sun, turning solar rays into intense heat and power, so prayer serves as a lens to focus the power of God on a single place or person. In the next chapter of Genesis we will encounter this statement: "So when God destroyed the cities of the plain, he remembered Abraham, and he brought Lot out of the catastrophe that overthrew the cities where Lot had lived" (Genesis 19:29).

I don't understand how this works, but somehow the prayer that Abraham prayed became the key to Lot's salvation from the doom that came upon Sodom. Abraham never mentioned Lot by name in his prayer. Yet God remembered Abraham and saved Lot from the catastrophic judgment that destroyed the cities of the plain. I don't know why this prayer made such a difference, but it did.

God still uses your prayers and mine in this same way. In other words, you can plan your program, think through all the details, set up all the committees, line up all the resources, rehearse every part, and cover the entire enterprise with prayer—and when the time comes to present the results of all that labor, it falls utterly flat. You look at the results and say, "What a disaster! What a failure! Lord, we prayed and we worked and we thought you were blessing this enterprise! Yet it ended in complete collapse! What went wrong? Why didn't you answer our prayers?"

Perhaps nothing went wrong. It may well be that God answered your prayers and blessed the enterprise exactly as He intended from the beginning. It may well be that your project, had it succeeded as you intended, would have benefited no one. But it may have succeeded precisely as He intended. Perhaps God brought someone safely into a relationship with Him, even though your project seemed to end in catastrophe. You may never know, this side of eternity, all the good things that were accomplished by the seemingly failed efforts and unanswered prayers of your life. Those apparent failures may have been grand successes according to God's eternal plan, and those unanswered prayers may have been answered beyond your wildest dreams.

Our prayers may not always be answered according to our expectations or our timetable. But prayer always focuses the power of God.

## THE TIMING OF GOD

Finally, prayer affects the timing of God. Here is a ministry that transcends human understanding, but it is absolutely true. In some paradoxical manner that defies rational explanation, our prayers can defer God's judgment and accelerate God's blessing. Does this mean that we can change God's mind or alter His plans through prayer? Certainly not! When God declares that He will act, no amount of prayer will change His mind. But God is pleased to work in partnership with human beings, and He allows us, through prayer, to affect the timing of his plans.

There is a fascinating incident in the first chapter of the book of Acts. There the disciples meet together with the risen Lord Jesus and ask, "Lord, are you at this time going to restore the kingdom to Israel?" Jesus replies, "It is not for you to know the times or dates the Father has set by his own authority. But you will receive power when the Holy Spirit comes on you; and you will be my witnesses in Jerusalem, and in all Judea and Samaria, and to the ends of the earth" (Acts 1:6–7).

God the Father, in His sovereign authority, has fixed the times and dates of His eternal plan. Yet He imparts to us power to serve as His witnesses and ambassadors throughout the world. He gives us responsibility, authority, and tasks to carry out within the broad outline of His eternal plan. By our actions and our prayers, we can affect events within that plan, but the ultimate times and dates are known only to Him.

We see how prayer affects God's timing in the story of Jonah's mission to the city of Nineveh. When Jonah arrived in that wicked city, he announced that God's judgment would fall upon Nineveh and the city would be overthrown in forty days. When the people of Nineveh heard Jonah's message, they repented of their sin and turned to God. As a result, the destruction of Nineveh was postponed. Decades passed, and eventually the people of Nineveh forgot God and turned back to their former wickedness. After waiting patiently for nearly a hundred years, God carried out His judgment against that city. Jonah could not change God's mind or His plan, but he did affect God's timing.

Hezekiah was a king of the kingdom of Judah. The book of 2 Kings records that he became ill with a severe illness. Painful boils ate away at his flesh. Finally, God sent the prophet Isaiah to him to announce, "Put your house in order, because you are going to die; you will not recover." At that word, Hezekiah turned his face to the wall and cried out to God, pleading with Him to spare his life.

God heard the prayer of Hezekiah. The Lord stopped Isaiah as he was still walking through the king's courtyard and sent the prophet back to the king with this message: "I have heard your prayer and seen your tears; I will heal you and add fifteen years to your life." And the Lord healed Hezekiah and extended his life (see 2 Kings 20:1–11).

God is just, but He is also merciful, and we can avail ourselves of His mercy through prayer. Peter speaks of this truth in his second letter:

> The Lord is not slow in keeping his promise, as some understand slowness. He is patient with you, not wanting anyone to perish, but everyone to come to repentance.
>
> But the day of the Lord will come like a thief. The heavens will disappear with a roar; the elements will be destroyed by fire, and the earth and everything in it will be laid bare. Since everything will be destroyed in this way, what kind of people ought you to be? You ought to live holy and godly lives as you look forward to the day of God and speed its coming. (2 Peter 3:9–12a)

What a profound and amazing truth this is! God's plan will surely come to pass. The earth and all of human history shall one day come to an end. Meanwhile, you and I are partners with Him in His great eternal plan. We look forward to the culmination of human history, but by living godly lives we can speed the coming of that day. We can hasten the day when the earth will be delivered from its suffering and the oppression of sin and Satan. When that day comes, a golden age will break forth, and righteousness will encompass the world, as in those expectant, triumphant words near the end of the book of Revelation, "Amen. Come, Lord Jesus!"

# 12

# THE WASTED YEARS

*Genesis 19*

Earlier, in Genesis 14, we read the account of a fierce battle in which the armies of Sodom, Gomorrah, and the other cities of the plain fought against the invading armies of the kings from the east. The invaders routed the forces of the cities of the plain, sending them fleeing through the Valley of Siddim, which Genesis tells us "was full of tar pits." Many of the retreating soldiers fell into those tar pits and died.

Now, as we come to Genesis 19, those tar pits in the Valley of Siddim, near the Dead Sea, take on a new significance. Many Bible scholars and archaeologists suggest that Sodom and the other cities of the plain were destroyed by a catastrophic combination of forces—an intense lightning storm combined with the highly combustible petroleum-rich tar that was so abundant in the Valley of Siddim.

The ancients wrote of the strong odor of sulfur that hung over the tar pits. The fumes emanating from those pits could have been ignited by a great lightning storm, producing explosions and raging flames that would have destroyed the cities of the plain as effectively as an atomic bomb. This explanation would account for the events we now come to in Genesis.

When last we saw Abraham, he was interceding on behalf of the city of Sodom, where his nephew Lot lived. The two angels who accompanied the Lord on His visit to Abraham have gone down into the valley to carry out His judgment on the cities there. Abraham and the

Lord remained behind, conversing together on the high promontory overlooking the plain. When the Lord concluded their conversation, He left, and Abraham returned home to his tent.

Now we pick up the story as the two angels come into Sodom in the evening hours. They enter in the guise of ordinary men. They do not have any features that distinguish them as supernatural beings. The first person they encounter in the city of Sodom is Abraham's nephew, Lot.

In this account, we will discover two distinct views of Lot. First, we will see Lot in the city of Sodom. Second, we will see how much of Sodom was in Lot.

## LOT IN SODOM

Let's look at the encounter between the two angels and Lot:

> The two angels arrived at Sodom in the evening, and Lot was sitting in the gateway of the city. When he saw them, he got up to meet them and bowed down with his face to the ground. "My lords," he said, "please turn aside to your servant's house. You can wash your feet and spend the night and then go on your way early in the morning."
>
> "No," they answered, "we will spend the night in the square."
>
> But he insisted so strongly that they did go with him and entered his house. He prepared a meal for them, baking bread without yeast, and they ate. (Genesis 19:1–3)

Note the wording at the beginning of this account, "Lot was sitting in the gateway of the city." This is a Middle Eastern expression that needs to be explained. This phrase does not mean that Lot was passing the time of day at the city gate, watching the people come and go. Rather, this is a technical phrase that means that Lot was the chief magistrate of the city of Sodom. His job was not only to give an official welcome to visitors of the city but also to investigate the nature of any strangers who might arrive and to administer justice concerning any disputes within the city. He carried out duties that were much like those of a mayor or a justice of the peace.

So this account opens by revealing to us that Lot, who years earlier had "pitched his tents near Sodom" (Genesis 13:12), had now moved into Sodom, had risen in the Sodomite society, and had become a person of distinction and authority in that city. Isn't that fascinating? Here is a classic rags-to-riches story—an immigrant boy from a foreign land who came to the big city and made a name for himself.

Years earlier, after Abraham and Lot returned to Canaan from Egypt, Abraham's herdsmen and Lot's herdsmen had quarreled over pasture rights. To settle the conflict, Abraham had given Lot the right to choose any grazing land he wished. Lot had chosen the choicest pastures, and that was the beginning of his downfall. He had looked out over the well-watered plain by the Jordan River, toward the city of Zoar—one of the cities of the plain. The plain reminded him of the lush "garden of the LORD" or the beautiful land of Egypt, and so Lot chose to settle there (Genesis 13:10).

The phrase "the garden of the Lord" is used in Scripture to suggest a place of divine fellowship. The original garden of the Lord was the garden of Eden, where Adam and God walked together in fellowship and companionship. And Isaiah spoke of the garden of the Lord as a place of comfort and gladness in the presence of God:

> The LORD will surely comfort Zion and will look with compassion on all her ruins; he will make her deserts like Eden, her wastelands like the garden of the LORD. Joy and gladness will be found in her, thanksgiving and the sound of singing. (Isaiah 51:3)

Isn't it fascinating that, when Lot looked out upon the plain of the Jordan River, he was reminded of two places: "the garden of the LORD" and a rich but pagan land, Egypt.

Lot's uncle, Abraham, had learned an important lesson in Egypt: He had to choose between loving God and loving the world. Abraham chose God. But Lot did not want to choose between God and the world. He wanted to have God plus the world. He thought the plain of the River Jordan was a place where he could have both. He thought he could have the garden of the Lord plus the riches of Egypt. He thought he could worship God while still having all the luxuries and cultural advantages of a pagan, godless city.

So, as Genesis 13:11 tells us, "Lot chose for himself the whole plain of the Jordan." Lot followed his selfish, ambitious desires. He lived for a while on the plain but then moved into the city, where he became wealthy and respected. Lot became a man of great political influence in Sodomite society.

In so doing, Lot lost sight of a basic spiritual principle that is found throughout God's Word and throughout human existence: No one can serve two masters. You can't have both the garden of the Lord and Egypt. You can't have both God and the world. Everyone must choose—and if you do not choose God with all your heart, you choose the world by default.

Our Lord expressed this principle in His Sermon on the Mount: "But seek first his kingdom and his righteousness, and all these things will be given to you as well" (Matthew 6:33). In other words, if we seek first the Lord and His kingdom and His righteousness, all our material needs will be met. Lot's error was that he sought material things first. His first priority was to gain riches and status, to make a good living and advance his family's standing in the community, to become a person of wealth, power, fame, and influence. He achieved all that, and lost sight of God's kingdom and God's righteousness.

## SODOM IN LOT

Lot's downfall was gradual, so gradual he was not even aware that he had fallen. He began by pitching his tent near Sodom. At the beginning, Lot was not in the city, he was not of the city, he was simply near it. He was still living in his tent. He was still a sojourner and a pilgrim in the land. But he wanted to be close to the city so that he could take advantage of the wealth and cultural pursuits to be found there.

Later, in Genesis 14, we find that Lot has moved into the city and has become a leader of Sodomite society. Finally, in Genesis 19, we see that he has become the mayor and magistrate of the city of Sodom.

There is a clear progression in the life of Lot. Though he still considers himself a follower of the one true God, it is obvious that he has made some compromises to achieve his high position in the pagan culture of Sodom. He meant to do the right thing. He probably thought that, as a follower of the Lord, he could influence the culture for good. He may have even thought he could win some of the people to faith in the Lord Jehovah.

But Lot's motives were tainted by the love of the world. Like so many Christians today, he thought he could add God to his worldly ambitions, his lust for wealth and power, his desire for self-advancement. So he became an influential leader, the mayor of the town. But as the Scriptures make clear, he had no moral influence on the city of Sodom. He did not win any converts. His witness for God was nil.

Tragically, there was more of Sodom in Lot than there was Lot in Sodom. The city infected the man far more than the man affected the city.

I would like to sit down with Lot and ask this civic leader four questions. I think these four questions will reveal how much there is of Sodom in Lot. The rest of the chapter will reveal the answers to these questions.

Question 1: "Lot, you have become a successful man, as the world measures success. You started as a nobody, a stranger and a foreigner. You've achieved both wealth and honor in Sodom. So I ask you: How has your success affected your relationship with God? Have you found that garden of the Lord, that place of fellowship with God that you once saw?"

Question 2: "Have you been successful in influencing the city of Sodom toward God and away from evil?"

Question 3: "How much wealth have you accumulated in Sodom?"

Question 4: "What influence has the city of Sodom had on your family?"

Lot is not unlike many people in the church today—people whose first priority is the world but who think they can have it all, the world plus God. So the answers to these questions will provide insight not only into the life and values of an ancient man named Lot but also into your life and mine.

## QUESTION 1: LOT'S RELATIONSHIP WITH GOD

Let's examine the answer to the first question: "Lot, how has your success affected your relationship with God?" As we pick up the story, the two angels, disguised as men, are staying with Lot as guests in his house. We read:

> Before they had gone to bed, all the men from every part of the city of Sodom—both young and old—surrounded the house. They called to Lot, "Where are the men who came to you tonight? Bring them out to us so that we can have sex with them."
>
> Lot went outside to meet them and shut the door behind him and said, "No, my friends. Don't do this wicked thing. Look, I have two daughters who have never slept with a man. Let me bring them out to you, and you can do what you like with them. But don't do anything to these men, for they have come under the protection of my roof."
>
> "Get out of our way," they replied. And they said, "This fellow came here as an alien, and now he wants to play the judge! We'll treat you worse than them." They kept bringing pressure on Lot and moved forward to break down the door.
>
> But the men inside reached out and pulled Lot back into the house and shut the door. Then they struck the men who were at the door of the house, young and old, with blindness so that they could not find the door. (Genesis 19:4–11)

Notice the corrosive environment of Sodom. Verse 4 tells us that all of the men of the city, both young and old, surrounded the house. "Where are the men who came to you tonight?" they say. "Bring them out to us so that we can have sex with them." The men of Sodom had come to commit homosexual rape upon these two strangers. Not only was homosexual promiscuity rampant and even the dominant form of sexual behavior in that city, but also the city of Sodom was so corrupt and depraved that the entire population approved of the violent act of rape against guests within the city walls. Clearly, Sodom was not just an immoral place. It was truly a lawless, violent, and corrupt society.

Did Lot approve of the evils that were commonplace in Sodom? No. As the apostle Peter observed:

> [God] rescued Lot, a righteous man, who was distressed by the filthy lives of lawless men (for that righteous man, living among them day after day, was tormented in his righteous soul by the lawless deeds he saw and heard). (2 Peter 2:7b–8)

Lot knew right from wrong. He had tasted the sweetness of fellowship with God, and his soul was continually vexed by the ugliness and the horrors of Sodomite society. But Lot had made his choice. He had chosen Sodom, with its luxuries and wealth, its power and advancement. He had chosen a life of material gain and worldly ambition first and God second. The result was that he had become a powerful and successful man, but he did not have peace or rest. Instead, he spent his days continually "distressed by the filthy lives of lawless men."

So if we can ask Lot, "How has your success affected your relationship with God?" his honest answer would be tragic: "My relationship with the Lord has been stunted and blighted by the wickedness and horrors of this city."

## QUESTION 2: LOT'S INFLUENCE ON SODOM

Lot undoubtedly intended to have a positive influence on his culture. Perhaps he told himself that by becoming the mayor and chief magistrate of the city, he would be able to tame that lawless place. He had a position of great influence, but how many citizens of Sodom did he influence for God? Answer: None. He was the civil court judge of that city, but did the citizens of Sodom respect and obey the law? Not at all.

So how much real influence did Lot have on the city of Sodom? The inescapable answer: None. Again we read:

> The two men said to Lot, "Do you have anyone else here—sons-in-law, sons or daughters, or anyone else in the city who belongs to you? Get them out of here, because we are going to destroy this place. The outcry to the LORD against its people is so great that he has sent us to destroy it."
>
> So Lot went out and spoke to his sons-in-law, who were pledged to marry his daughters. He said, "Hurry and get out of this place, because the LORD is about to destroy the city!" But his sons-in-law thought he was joking. (Genesis 19:12–14)

What a tragic scene! Lot didn't even have any influence with his sons-in-law. Though Lot's political power in Sodom was great, his spiritual influence was nonexistent. If he had intended to have an influence for God in that city, he had failed miserably.

Remember, Abraham pleaded with God for mercy for the city, and God had promised to spare the city for the sake of only ten righteous people. But there weren't ten righteous people in the entire city. In fact, there weren't even five or six. The young men who were engaged to his two daughters were scoffers and unbelievers like the rest of the men of that city.

Question 2 was, "Lot, have you been successful in influencing the city of Sodom toward God and away from evil?" The answer: No. He had failed to be even an influence for God in his own family.

## QUESTION 3: LOT'S WEALTH

What of Lot's ambition? He had gone to Sodom with the intention of amassing wealth and power. In the end, what did he have to show for his lifetime of ambition and achievement? The next section gives us the answer:

> With the coming of dawn, the angels urged Lot, saying, "Hurry! Take your wife and your two daughters who are here, or you will be swept away when the city is punished."

When he hesitated, the men grasped his hand and the hands of his wife and of his two daughters and led them safely out of the city, for the LORD was merciful to them. As soon as they had brought them out, one of them said, "Flee for your lives! Don't look back, and don't stop anywhere in the plain! Flee to the mountains or you will be swept away!"

But Lot said to them, "No, my lords, please! Your servant has found favor in your eyes, and you have shown great kindness to me in sparing my life. But I can't flee to the mountains; this disaster will overtake me, and I'll die. Look, here is a town near enough to run to, and it is small. Let me flee to it—it is very small, isn't it? Then my life will be spared."

He said to him, "Very well, I will grant this request too; I will not overthrow the town you speak of. But flee there quickly, because I cannot do anything until you reach it." (That is why the town was called Zoar.)

By the time Lot reached Zoar, the sun had risen over the land. Then the LORD rained down burning sulfur on Sodom and Gomorrah—from the LORD out of the heavens. Thus he overthrew those cities and the entire plain, including all those living in the cities—and also the vegetation in the land. But Lot's wife looked back, and she became a pillar of salt.

Early the next morning Abraham got up and returned to the place where he had stood before the LORD. He looked down toward Sodom and Gomorrah, toward all the land of the plain, and he saw dense smoke rising from the land, like smoke from a furnace.

So when God destroyed the cities of the plain, he remembered Abraham, and he brought Lot out of the catastrophe that overthrew the cities where Lot had lived. (Genesis 19:15–29)

What did Lot have to show for all of his ambition and effort in Sodom? Nothing. Not a single thing. All of his influence and fame disappeared. All of his wealth and possessions were consumed by the fires of judgment.

If you ever go to the Holy Land, I suggest you visit the shore of the Dead Sea. Look out over that lifeless, brackish waste. It's the lowest and most desolate spot on the face of the earth, thirteen hundred feet below sea level. Nothing lives in the caustic brine of that sea. The waves of the aptly named Dead Sea lap upon a beach of gritty salt crystals. Hardly anything grows in the desolate valley around that forsaken sea. All that remains of Sodom and her sister cities are buried ruins—archaeological sites that are of interest only to those who study the dead past.

The plain around the Dead Sea, where God's judgment fell in a blast of fire and fury, symbolizes all that remained of Lot's former life. The catastrophe that befell the cities of the plain left him as empty and desolate as that ruined landscape. The man who wanted it all and had it all suddenly lost it all.

And not only did Lot lose everything, but so did his wife. The heart of Lot's wife was knit to the pleasures of the city. She ignored the warnings of the two angels. When God poured out the fire of judgment upon the cities of the plains, Genesis tells us, "Lot's wife looked back, and she became a pillar of salt." The Lord Jesus gave us a brief commentary on this tragic event in Luke's Gospel: "Remember Lot's wife! Whoever tries to keep his life will lose it, and whoever loses his life will preserve it" (Luke 17:32–33).

Lot's wife couldn't let go of her past life in Sodom. Wishing to preserve some treasured memory of her old worldly life, she looked back, and she lost her life. This, the Lord says, is a sobering lesson for us all.

What a tragic story for everyone concerned, but above all, for Lot himself. He was the one who made the choices that placed his family in the center of that moral and spiritual cesspool. Lot was not a wicked man. He was a good man who wanted to do right. But he chose his own way, and in the end he lost his peace, his influence, his wife, and his wealth.

Yet even while the angels were urging Lot to flee to the hills for his life and not look back, the city of Sodom had such a grip on his soul that he still longed for a city, even a little one. He begged the angels to send him to the little town of Zoar, whose name means "small."

## QUESTION 4: LOT'S FAMILY

We come now to the last and most terrible question: "Lot, what influence has the city of Sodom had on your family?" When Lot chose to turn his back on the life of a pilgrim, life in a tent, and moved himself and his family into the city of Sodom, what happened to his children? As we are about to see, the evil lifestyle and corrupt values of Sodom had completely infected the thinking of his daughters:

> Lot and his two daughters left Zoar and settled in the mountains, for he was afraid to stay in Zoar. He and his two daughters lived in a cave. One day the older daughter said to the younger, "Our father is old, and there is no man around here to lie with us, as is the custom all over the earth. Let's get our father to drink wine and then lie with him and preserve our family line through our father."
>
> That night they got their father to drink wine, and the older daughter went in and lay with him. He was not aware of it when she lay down or when she got up.
>
> The next day the older daughter said to the younger, "Last night I lay with my father. Let's get him to drink wine again tonight, and you go in and lie with him so we can preserve our family line through our father." So they got their father to drink wine that night also, and the younger daughter went and lay with him. Again he was not aware of it when she lay down or when she got up.
>
> So both of Lot's daughters became pregnant by their father. The older daughter had a son, and she named him Moab; he is the father of the Moabites of today. The younger daughter also had a son, and she named him Ben-Ammi; he is the father of the Ammonites of today. (Genesis 19:30–38)

Lot's two daughters were virgins in body but debauched in mind. They had long since grown accustomed to obscenity and sexual depravity of Sodom. So, in that cave on the mountainside, they seized the thinnest excuse to engage in a foul orgy of drunkenness and incest.

In the end, Lot had nothing but heartbreak and shame to show for his years in Sodom. The two daughters who had escaped the fiery judgment of Sodom took a big piece of Sodom with them—a vile and perverted view of sex.

Lot, the man who wanted both the garden of the Lord and Egypt, who tried to have the best of both worlds, lost everything. He became for all time the symbolic picture of the Christian who is saved, as Paul said, "but only as one escaping through the flames" (1 Corinthians 3:15). Though he has eternity ahead, he has nothing to look back on but wasted years, tinged with shame and regret.

Here the narrative of Lot ends. Abraham's nephew disappears from the Genesis record at this point. There are a number of important lessons to be learned from the tragic experience of Lot. Let's focus on two of those lessons.

First, the hour of greatest danger is when you first begin to choose. Young Christians especially feel the tug of the world and its pleasures. They want to be popular, to have what everyone else has, to do what everyone else does. They want to be accepted by their worldly friends, but they want to be Christians as well.

Many of them try to do what Lot did. They try to have the best of both worlds. They compromise. Yes, they try to live as pilgrims, at least at first, but they pitch their tents near Sodom. They put popularity, pride, and selfish ambition first. They allow the corrupt values of the surrounding culture to seep into their souls. Eventually, though they still call themselves Christians, they begin to live worldly lives. They may attend church on Sundays, but they live like worldlings the rest of the week.

The Scriptures teach and experience shows that you can't have it both ways. No one can serve two masters. No one can walk down two diverging paths at the same time. You must make God and His righteousness your first priority, or you will lose everything, as Lot did. The hour of choosing is now, during your youth, while you are setting the direction for your life.

Second, when you try to have the best of both worlds, you destroy others besides yourself. What was Lot's most painful regret when he awoke in that mountain cave and learned what had taken place while he was drunk? Do you think he was grieving his lost wealth at that moment? Hardly! Without question, he was horrified over the realization of how his choice to live in Sodom had brought about his own disgrace, the death of his wife, and the utter depravity of his daughters.

By his choices, Lot had destroyed his own family.

Don't think for a moment that your family is immune from the effects of your choices. As a parent, you are being observed by your children. They see your outward respectability, your desire to do good. But they also know whether you have made God your first priority or have begun to compromise with Sodom, with the world around you. Your children may not end up doing anything as degraded and vile as Lot's daughters did, but they may have already begun to lose interest in the Bible, in Christian fellowship, in an intimate relationship with God. They may have already begun to compromise with the world and its corrosive values.

In one Christian home after another, the tragic story of Lot is being replayed again and again. Who can deny that the world in which we live has become a modern-day Sodom? If we do not put God first in our personal lives and in our families, we risk suffering the same sense of loss, sorrow, and regret that Lot experienced in that mountain cave when he awoke and asked himself, "What have I done to my family?"

It does not have to be so.

Early on the morning following the destruction of Sodom and the other cities of the plain, Abraham awoke and went to the high promontory where he had prayed before the Lord. From that high place, he looked down toward Sodom and Gomorrah, and he saw dense clouds of smoke billowing up from the land, like smoke from a furnace. Abraham and his family were safe because he had chosen to put God first in his life. He had chosen the tent and the altar.

In the end, Abraham gained the whole land—all that Lot possessed and more besides. A day is coming when Abraham shall inherit the earth, according to the Scriptures, because he spent his life in quest of the city that has foundations, whose architect and builder is God.

# 13

# OLD NATURES NEVER DIE

*Genesis 20*

Robert Robinson grew up wild on the streets of London in the eighteenth century. He had seen friends die violently and young, and he always assumed he was destined for an early grave. One day, when he was seventeen, Robinson and his rowdy friends were harassing a drunken gypsy woman. They gave her gin and demanded that she tell their fortunes.

"You!" the old woman said, pointing her finger at Robinson. "You will live a long life. You'll have children and grandchildren, and you'll live to see them grow up."

Her words startled the young man. Robinson decided then and there that if he was going to live that long, he'd have to change his ways. So he went to hear the Methodist evangelist George Whitefield. The text of Whitefield's sermon was Jesus' stinging rebuke to the Pharisees: "You brood of vipers! Who warned you to flee from the coming wrath?" (Matthew 3:7).

Robinson did not give his life to Christ that night. In fact, he felt his sins were so grievous and terrible that God would never accept him. For three years, he suffered with a deep dread of God's punishment.

It wasn't until sometime after his twentieth birthday that Robert Robinson finally made peace with God and received Jesus as the Savior and Lord of his life. With a heart on fire for God, he became a Methodist minister and began preaching the gospel all around London. In

1757, two years after his conversion, he wrote a hymn that is still sung in churches today:

*Come, Thou Fount of every blessing,*
*Tune my heart to sing Thy grace*
*Streams of mercy, never ceasing,*
*Call for songs of loudest praise.*

The most memorable stanza of that hymn expresses a fear that every Christian has felt at one time or another:

*Prone to wander, Lord, I feel it,*
*Prone to leave the God I love*
*Take my heart, O take and seal it*
*Seal it for thy courts above.*

Prone to wander! This was the anxious cry of Robert Robinson's heart. And for a time, years after writing those words, he did wander away from his faith and from the God he loved.

One day, he happened to be sharing a coach with a young woman. As they rolled along the streets of London, the woman hummed a refrain from a hymn. "Excuse me, miss," Robinson said, "do you know the words to that song?"

"Yes, I do," she said—and she sang the refrain: "Prone to wander, Lord, I feel it, / Prone to leave the God I love." Then she said, "Do you know the song?"

"Know it?" Robinson said. "I wrote it! But that was so long ago. I would give a thousand worlds, if I possessed them, to have that same love for God that I had then."

History records that his coach ride with that young woman was a turning point in Robinson's life. He later went back to the pulpit and declared his faith in Jesus Christ with a renewed passion and confidence. Many years later, in June 1790, Robert Robinson passed from this life and into the presence of the God he loved.

There are many examples in Scripture of believers who relapsed into sin and wandered from a godly way of life: King David, who sinned grievously with Bathsheba; Samson who was led astray by Delilah; Judas Iscariot, who followed the Lord then betrayed Him; Demas, whom Paul said "loved this world" and deserted the ministry (2 Timothy 4:10). Some of these wanderers eventually returned to a right relationship with God—but some did not.

Now, as we come to Genesis 20, we must add one more name to our list of those who suffered a spiritual relapse: Abraham.

## ABRAHAM AMONG THE PHILISTINES

Immediately after the destruction of Sodom and Gomorrah, God presents us with a vital lesson in the life of faith. We last saw Abraham in a literal mountaintop experience with God, standing on a high promontory overlooking the Valley of the Dead Sea, looking out over the smoking ruins of the wicked cities of the plain. Though he is grieved by the great loss of life in those cities, this is nevertheless a high point in Abraham's life. He has grown deep in his spiritual maturity and close in his friendship with God.

Many Christians have the mistaken notion that the Christian life involves becoming gradually more and more righteous and godly until at last we become worthy of friendship with Christ. Ultimately, we become wise, saintly believers like Abraham who never again have to worry about succumbing to folly and sin. But that is not what the Christian life is like. No human being ever reaches a point in this life where he or she is beyond the reach of temptation, sin, and spiritual error.

As we're about to see, even wise old Abraham, the friend of God, is vulnerable. Abraham is about to suffer a spiritual relapse. As the chapter opens, we read:

> Now Abraham moved on from there into the region of
> the Negev and lived between Kadesh and Shur. For a while he
> stayed in Gerar, and there Abraham said of his wife Sarah, "She
> is my sister." Then Abimelech king of Gerar sent for Sarah and
> took her. (Genesis 20:1–2)

Abraham is understandably upset over the destruction of the cities of the plains. Perhaps he is troubled and traumatized over the large-scale death and devastation he has witnessed. Feeling he must go someplace to clear his thoughts and erase the images from his mind, he moves to Gerar, the seacoast country on the southwest side of Palestine, on the way to Egypt. There he comes among the people who will later be known as the Philistines, the very enemies of Israel from whom would come Goliath, the giant slain by young David.

Living at the borders of Israel, the Philistines symbolically represent those moral but unregenerate churchgoers who live in proximity to the truth of God but who never invite Jesus Christ into their lives as Lord and Savior. Outwardly, these churchgoers practice a form of the Christian religion. Inwardly, they belong to the world.

The world is full of religious people. Thousands of them meet in churches across our land. They listen to sermons, hear the reading of God's Word, and sing the hymns, yet they do not know what it means to be born again. They do not know what it is to have the life of Christ dwelling in them. They think the church is a place where they can learn ethical and moral principles in order to advance the highest good of society. They consider themselves Christians and would feel insulted at the suggestion that they are not true Christians in the scriptural sense.

The Philistines, too, were a highly religious people. The king of the Philistines was named Abimelech, which means "my father is king." This suggests an authority no higher than man. Again we see a symbolic suggestion of the worldly church of our era—the liberalized and secularized institutional church that sees ultimate church authority as residing not with God but with church councils, synods, assemblies, and ecclesiastical offices. These secularized religionists are the Philistines of our day, having an outward form of godliness and religion but denying its true authority, who is Jesus Christ alone (see 2 Timothy 3:5).

## ABRAHAM'S LIE

What Abraham does among the Philistines is amazing and

troubling. He falls into a behavior pattern of deception, exactly as he had done thirty years earlier in Egypt: He lies about his wife. He says that Sarah is his sister. Why did Abraham lie about her? He lied because Sarah was a lovely woman who attracted the attention of every man who saw her.

At this point, you may be thinking, "Hold it right there! In Genesis 17, we saw that Sarah was ninety years old! How could a woman in her nineties be so beautiful and desirable that she would catch the eye of every lusty male she passed?"

But remember that when Abraham told this same lie in Egypt thirty years earlier (Genesis 12:10–20), Sarah, this exotic beauty who was then named Sarai, was already well into her sixties. Abraham eventually lived to be 175 years old and Sarah lived to be about 127. So it is only reasonable to assume that God granted them both a more youthful appearance to match their youthful strength and vigor. Sarah had reached an age which, to us, means wrinkles, white hair, and advanced osteoporosis. But she was still a stunning and desirable woman.

Because of Sarah's beauty, Abraham again felt he had to protect himself with a lie. Abraham, who has just had a mountaintop experience with God, now displays a yellow streak of cowardice a mile wide. By protecting himself with this lie, he is exposing his beloved wife to extreme danger—the danger that she will be taken as the bride of some other man. And just as had happened before in Egypt, it happens again: "Then Abimelech king of Gerar sent for Sarah and took her."

Now Abraham is once again in deep trouble, and Sarah's honor is again in jeopardy. But God is not going to permit Abraham's cowardly sin to stand:

> But God came to Abimelech in a dream one night and said to him, "You are as good as dead because of the woman you have taken; she is a married woman."
>
> Now Abimelech had not gone near her, so he said, "Lord, will you destroy an innocent nation? Did he not say to me, 'She is my sister,' and didn't she also say, 'He is my brother'? I have done this with a clear conscience and clean hands."

Then God said to him in the dream, "Yes, I know you did this with a clear conscience, and so I have kept you from sinning against me. That is why I did not let you touch her. Now return the man's wife, for he is a prophet, and he will pray for you and you will live. But if you do not return her, you may be sure that you and all yours will die." (Genesis 20:3–7)

The king was on the verge of committing a grievous moral transgression—the sin of adultery—when God stopped him. This event shows clearly how God views the sin of taking another man's wife. Even this pagan king understands the seriousness of this sin. When God tells Abimelech what he is about to do, Abimelech acknowledges the wicked nature of this sin without argument. Even the ancient pagans recognized how terrible it was to take another man's wife. If only our own culture retained such a clear sense of right and wrong!

Abimelech protested that he couldn't know what he was doing because he had been deceived. He was therefore innocent of any wrongdoing.

Notice, however, that Abimelech's integrity and his ignorance were no protection against moral responsiblity for sin. Though he displayed a higher moral standard than Abraham, and though he sought to do right, he was still on the verge of falling to sin, and God would have held him accountable.

Abimelech represents the unhappy state of all those who do not know Jesus Christ as Lord and Savior. They do not have the inner voice of God's Spirit to protect and restrain them from evil. Had it not been for the direct intervention of God through Abimelech's dream, this man would have plunged unknowingly into sin. For Abraham's sake, God restrained Abimelech.

As we see at the end of this account, God not only came to Abimelech in a dream but also struck Abimelech with a deadly disease that prevented him from taking Sarah as his wife. This disease, which must have seemed like a terrible affliction, was God's mercy and kindness, preventing Abimelech from incurring an even greater burden of sin and guilt by committing adultery with Sarah.

Events that seem like obstacles, afflictions, or even tragedies often turn out to be a gift of mercy from God. He sometimes prevents us from succumbing to evil, and does so in ways that seem harsh to us. But the truth is that, had God not allowed some harsh event in our lives, the outcome would have been far more destructive and tragic.

## ABRAHAM'S RELAPSE DRAWS ABIMELECH'S REPROACH

In the next section, we see the result of Abraham's moral relapse as he suffers the reproach of Abimelech:

> Early the next morning Abimelech summoned all his officials, and when he told them all that had happened, they were very much afraid. Then Abimelech called Abraham in and said, "What have you done to us? How have I wronged you that you have brought such great guilt upon me and my kingdom? You have done things to me that should not be done." And Abimelech asked Abraham, "What was your reason for doing this?"
>
> Abraham replied, "I said to myself, 'There is surely no fear of God in this place, and they will kill me because of my wife.' Besides, she really is my sister, the daughter of my father though not of my mother; and she became my wife. And when God had me wander from my father's household, I said to her, 'This is how you can show your love to me: Everywhere we go, say of me, "He is my brother." ' " (Genesis 20:8–13)

Abimelech has every right to feel enraged and offended. He has done nothing to harm Abraham, yet Abraham placed Abimelech and his kingdom in great jeopardy through his cowardly deception. So Abimelech demands to know, "Abraham, how could you have done such a thing?" And Abraham is forced to confess that he deceived the king because he was still, at heart, a fearful man who did not trust God to protect him.

Old natures never die. There was still a lot of Abram in Abraham.

After thirty years, he was still capable of relapsing into his old, dishonest ways. He still displayed a cowardly streak, hiding behind his wife, subjecting her to dishonor and disgrace in order to save his own skin.

This old nature, which is our tragic inheritance from Adam, is depraved and incapable of fulfilling God's intention for our lives. Sometimes the old nature is able to put on a false façade of integrity or righteousness, and that façade can fool many people. But a simulated righteousness does not stand up to tests of temptation and pressure. A purely outward show of righteousness that does not come from a godly and righteous heart is good for nothing but self-praise and prideful attention getting. The old nature, which the Bible calls the flesh, can never please God.

That's why, when God comes into the human heart through Jesus Christ, He never tries to clean up the old nature. He writes off the flesh as worthless and proceeds to slay the old nature while giving us a new nature, a Christ nature. When we become Christians, we must renounce the old self and stop feeding it, defending it, and trying to make it look good. We must accept all that Jesus Christ wants to be through us, for only His nature is perfect and pleasing to God.

## TURNING HARM INTO HEALING, BLUNDERS INTO BLESSING

This story concludes in a surprising way. King Abimelech had every right to be enraged with Abraham. Yet by his actions, the king appears to reward Abraham:

> Then Abimelech brought sheep and cattle and male and female slaves and gave them to Abraham, and he returned Sarah his wife to him. And Abimelech said, "My land is before you; live wherever you like."
>
> To Sarah he said, "I am giving your brother a thousand shekels of silver. This is to cover the offense against you before all who are with you; you are completely vindicated."
>
> Then Abraham prayed to God, and God healed Abimelech, his wife and his slave girls so they could have children

again, for the LORD had closed up every womb in Abimelech's household because of Abraham's wife Sarah. (Genesis
20:14–18)

God healed Abimelech and blessed Abraham. This scene points up
the difference between a genuine Christian and a moral non-Christian.
In terms of his actions, Abimelech was far more noble than Abraham.
In other words, Abimelech's old Adamic nature behaved in a more righ-
teous way than Abraham's old nature. But both men failed to please
God.

Perhaps you have noticed that some non-Christians can appear
more cultured, refined, and pleasant to live with than some Christians.
The Christian who is living in his old nature by the will of the flesh is
quarrelsome, irritable, self-centered, and hard to live with. But neither
the cultured and pleasant non-Christian nor the crotchety Christian is
capable of pleasing God through the works of the old nature.

Abraham had something Abimelech didn't have. He had a life that
was from God—a regenerate heart, a new nature. When he repented,
he was forgiven. God turned his failure into fullness and blessed him
and caused him to be the instrument through which Abimelech was
restored. It was only when Abraham prayed for Abimelech that Abimelech was healed.

Here we see a profound lesson regarding the grace of God. When
we slip back into the flesh and sin against God, we tend to say, "There I
go again, yielding to the old nature. Won't I ever learn?" But even when
we are ready to give up on ourselves, God says to us, "I'm not finished
with you. I'm going to restore you."

Remember when our Lord was in the Garden of Gethsemane? The
temple soldiers and priests came to take Him by force, and rash, impet-
uous Peter grabbed a sword and struck off the ear of the high priest's
servant. The Lord reached down, picked up the ear, replaced it, and
healed the servant (see John 18:10; Luke 22:51). I have often thought
this incident describes what we often do: In our effort to defend our
Lord, we go around lopping off people's ears. But the Lord graciously

reaches out and brings healing where we have clumsily, impetuously brought harm.

That is what the Lord did for Abraham and what he so often does for us. He corrects our mistakes and turns our harm into healing, our blunders into blessing. This is a lesson we must learn. We have not been called to improve our old nature but to allow God to give us a new nature. By our old nature, we can never please God. We must lay hold of all that Christ can be through us. Only His life is acceptable to God. As we allow Christ and His nature to live through us, we will demonstrate His grace and truth before the watching world.

# 14

# ISHMAEL MUST GO!

*Genesis 21:1–14*

Augustine of Hippo (AD 354–430) was a brilliant pagan scholar and an unruly hedonist throughout his young life. At the age of thirty-two, he was reading this passage in Paul's letter to the Romans:

> Let us behave decently, as in the daytime, not in orgies and drunkenness, not in sexual immorality and debauchery, not in dissension and jealousy. Rather, clothe yourselves with the Lord Jesus Christ, and do not think about how to gratify the desires of the sinful nature. (Romans 13:13–14)

Instantly, he knew that God was calling him to give up his fleshly life and make Jesus Christ his Lord and Savior. Years later, in *The Confessions*, he wrote that long after his conversion, his life continued to be a daily struggle to deny the flesh and walk in the Spirit. Even as he prayed for strength to live a godly life, the flesh continued to tug at him. His prayers, he said, were tainted with a touch of his fleshly insincerity: *Da mihi castitatem et continentiam*, he prayed in Latin, *sed noli modo*. "Give me chastity and self-control—but not yet."

In the Christian life, we either live for the self or live for Christ. We either live by the flesh or live by the Spirit. Whenever we depend on Christ, we triumph. Whenever we rely on the flesh, we fail. The Lord allows us to experience both the triumphs of the Spirit and the failures of the flesh so that we will learn the difference, and learn not to depend on the self.

As we gradually learn to live in total dependence on Christ alone, we will experience more and more times of victory, joy, and fruitfulness in our lives. Over time, we will look back and see that we have grown in our character and Christlikeness. The fruit of the Spirit—love, joy, peace, gentleness, goodness, patience, meekness, and self-control—will become increasingly present in our lives. There may be occasional set-backs and relapses, but the trend of our lives will be upward, toward increasing conformity with the image of Christ.

This is the place to which we come in the life of Abraham.

At the beginning, God promised him a son who would bring joy to his heart. This son would be the first of a long line of descendants who would eventually outnumber the stars in the sky. But the promised joy came after years of delay. Abraham went though many trials and failures, all of which taught him important lessons about himself and about his relationship with God.

Now, Abraham has begun to walk so consistently in the Spirit that the continual fruit of love, joy, and peace have begun to truly charac-terize his life. In the midst of this high point in Abraham's spiritual life, the child of promise is born—Isaac, the long-prophesied son of Abraham's old age. With the birth of Isaac, Abraham's joy is complete.

## THE FLESH VERSUS THE SPIRIT

At the beginning of Genesis 21 we read:

> Now the LORD was gracious to Sarah as he had said, and the LORD did for Sarah what he had promised. Sarah became pregnant and bore a son to Abraham in his old age, at the very time God had promised him. Abraham gave the name Isaac to the son Sarah bore him. When his son Isaac was eight days old, Abraham circumcised him, as God commanded him. Abraham was a hundred years old when his son Isaac was born to him.
>
> Sarah said, "God has brought me laughter, and everyone who hears about this will laugh with me." And she added,

"Who would have said to Abraham that Sarah would nurse children? Yet I have borne him a son in his old age." (Genesis 21:1–7)

## THIS IS THE JOY OF FULFILLMENT!

At last we have two sons of Abraham living side by side, Isaac and Ishmael. We don't need to wonder what this means in the life of faith, because Paul tells us in the letter to the Galatians. He says that Isaac pictures that which is born of the Spirit, while Ishmael is a picture of that which is born of the flesh (see Galatians 4:28).

Isaac is the result of a life controlled by the Spirit. What does a Spirit-controlled life look like? Later in the same letter, Paul tells us that "the fruit of the Spirit is love, joy, peace, patience, kindness, goodness, faithfulness, gentleness and self-control" (Galatians 5:22–23). These are the offspring produced by the life that is lived under the control of God's spirit. This fruit that the Spirit produces in our lives is our Isaac.

By contrast, Ishmael stands for the works of the flesh, the acts of our old sinful nature. In Galatians, Paul describes the Ishmael-like works of the flesh this way:

> The acts of the sinful nature are obvious: sexual immorality, impurity and debauchery; idolatry and witchcraft; hatred, discord, jealousy, fits of rage, selfish ambition, dissensions, factions and envy; drunkenness, orgies, and the like. I warn you, as I did before, that those who live like this will not inherit the kingdom of God. (Galatians 5:19–21)

There is a striking contrast between Isaac and Ishmael, between that which is born of the Spirit and that which is born of the flesh: While Ishmael's birth was natural, Isaac's birth was supernatural. Isaac was not born until Abraham and Sarah had reached an advanced age. Sarah was ninety years old, and Abraham was a hundred. His birth took place some thirty years after God had first promised to give Abraham a son. The apostle Paul refers to this fact when he writes: "Without weakening in his faith, he faced the fact that his body was as good as dead—since he was about a hundred years old—and that Sarah's womb was also dead" (Romans 4:19).

Now we see why God waited so long to fulfill His promise to Abraham. He was waiting until the ticking biological clock of Sarah's womb had run down. He wanted to leave no doubt as to the reason for Isaac's birth. That birth was a supernatural demonstration of God's power. All the credit for the miracle of Isaac's birth went to God alone.

This is what God now says to us about the fruit of the Spirit in our lives. This fruit can never come about by the flesh. It is never the result of self-effort or positive thinking. Love, joy, and peace are gifts from God, and we cannot produce them in ourselves. We can produce nothing but Ishmael. God alone produces Isaac in our lives.

## CIRCUMCISION AND THE NEW LIFE

Eight days after Isaac was born, Abraham circumcised him. He placed upon Isaac the sign of God's ownership. In this way, Abraham showed that his son Isaac was dedicated to God.

When a Christian is dedicated to God, we see a parallel sign of God's ownership—the fruit of the Spirit, which provides evidence that God is at work in that human life. What is the function of the fruit of the Spirit? Why does God enable these qualities of love, joy, peace, gentleness, goodness, patience, meekness, and self-control shine forth from our lives? Is it for our private enjoyment? No, God produces the fruit of the Spirit in our lives so that we can share this fruit with others. We grow in Christlikeness so that we can bless others.

When I was a boy in Minnesota, a neighbor lady lived nearby. She had a large family and was regarded by the entire community as an eccentric, a religious fanatic. She would often take her Bible out into the fields and spend all day sitting in a haystack, reading the Bible. She neglected her own household. Her children ran wild and were always dirty and unruly. Her house was a mess. Her husband constantly complained that she didn't lift a finger, inside the house or out on the farm.

Yet every Sunday, she came to church, stood up in the meeting, and testified about the wonderful experience she had sitting in the haystack, reading God's Word. She spoke of the joy and ecstasy she felt as she enjoyed fellowship with God. I have no doubt that she truly did have those joyful emotional experiences while she was out in that haystack, but I don't believe her joy came from the Lord. It was an uncircumcised emotion.

The Lord Jesus didn't save us so that we could spend the entire day sitting in a haystack, having an emotional high while reading the Bible. He didn't save us so that we could neglect our work, our families, and our important relationships. The Lord saved us so that we could be devoted to His purpose. And one of the basic truths about the Christian life is that it's not a series of haystack experiences. It's not one ecstatic emotional high after another. The Christian life involves work, duty, discipline, and yes, cleaning up after dirty kids.

God gave us His Word to show us how to live. He intended that we should live for Him and live for others, not just for ourselves. True, circumcised, godly joy comes from serving God and serving others. The fruit of the Spirit and a life devoted to servanthood—these are the true marks of God's ownership.

## THE BIRTH OF LAUGHTER

Isaac's name means "laughter." The birth of Isaac brought the laughter of joy and true satisfaction into the household of Abraham and Sarah. I wish we could have seen Sarah, a woman of ninety, holding that newborn infant in her arms. If she had seemed beautiful before, imagine her face radiant with the delight of holding that little bundle of blessing close to her heart.

This is a picture of the joy that Christ brings into every human heart that welcomes Him. Words are inadequate to convey the emotions we feel when we fully realize what it means to belong to Christ. As the hymn writer George W. Robinson (1838–1877) once wrote:

*Heav'n above is softer blue,*
*Earth around is sweeter green!*
*Something lives in every hue*

*Christless eyes have never seen;*
*Birds with gladder songs o'erflow,*
*Flowers with deeper beauties shine,*
*Since I know, as I now know,*
*I am His, and He is mine.*

These words, as beautiful as they are, convey just a taste of the joy of having Christ dwelling in our hearts. A true Isaac experience is beyond words. Have you discovered the secret of walking in the Spirit? Is the fruit of the Spirit expressed through your life? Have you truly had an Isaac experience? The day you put away all self-centeredness and begin to live as God intended you to live, you'll know the joy and yes, the laughter, of true Christ-centered love and peace.

The story of Isaac and Ishmael continues:

> The child grew and was weaned, and on the day Isaac was weaned Abraham held a great feast. But Sarah saw that the son whom Hagar the Egyptian had borne to Abraham was mocking, and she said to Abraham, "Get rid of that slave woman and her son, for that slave woman's son will never share in the inheritance with my son Isaac."
>
> The matter distressed Abraham greatly because it concerned his son. But God said to him, "Do not be so distressed about the boy and your maidservant. Listen to whatever Sarah tells you, because it is through Isaac that your offspring will be reckoned. I will make the son of the maidservant into a nation also, because he is your offspring."
>
> Early the next morning Abraham took some food and a skin of water and gave them to Hagar. He set them on her shoulders and then sent her off with the boy. She went on her way and wandered in the desert of Beersheba. (Genesis 21:8–14)

Here again, this story has symbolic significance for our Christian lives. As we've seen, Isaac represents the fullness of the fruit of the

Spirit. Ishmael, by contrast, represents those self-willed sins and habits that we are reluctant to surrender. Notice how perfectly this principle is reflected in this story. Isaac, the long-promised and long-awaited son, has been born, yet Abraham remains attached to Ishmael, the son who was born of the flesh.

## WHAT IS YOUR ISHMAEL?

Most Christians have an Ishmael in their lives. Though they have committed their lives to Christ and want to live for Him, they have some habit or sin that they cling to or some feeling of resentment or bitterness that they refuse to let go of. That is their Ishmael. God may allow them to cling to their Ishmael for a time, but eventually He speaks to them and says, "These have to go."

Sometimes the Ishmael we cling to seems good and righteous. For some of us, our Ishmael may even be a Christian doctrine we hold dear—an idea that has brought nothing but division and separation between us and other Christians. It may be our pride over our Bible knowledge; God may be saying, "Your spiritual pride is your Ishmael; it has to go." Your Ishmael may be your insistence on a particular mode of baptism or your insistence on a certain partisan political viewpoint. You are so sure you're right, and perhaps you are. It's not your viewpoint that is your Ishmael so much as the way you express it, argue it, justify it, delight in it, and criticize others who don't share your views. That is your Ishmael, and Ishmael must go.

The story of Abraham and his reluctance over Ishmael is instructive for our lives. Notice, first of all, how distressed Abraham was. He went through an agonizing reappraisal when the word came from the Lord that Ishmael had to go. Abraham loved the boy. True, he had often grieved over Ishmael's arrogance and hasty ways, but Abraham still didn't want to give the boy up.

The passage does not directly tell us this, but I think Abraham was angry with God for bringing the matter up. He may well have said to God, as we so often say, "Why bring this up, Lord? Can't you leave well enough alone? Just let me continue on the way I've been going. Everything will be all right."

The agony of Abraham's heart showed that this was no trivial matter. He clung to his son in the flesh, just as we often cling to the Ishmaels in our lives. Sending Ishmael away was going to cost Abraham dearly.

I once received a phone call from a lady who attended a Bible class I was teaching. She said, "I've been thinking about what you said in class—that we need to turn away from those things in our lives that hinder us. I have something like that in my own life. I don't want to let go of it, and I don't know what to do about it."

She told me what this thing was. Clearly, it was the Ishmael in her life.

"I've heard testimonies," she said, "from other Christians who have had problems with smoking or alcohol or pornography or sexual promiscuity. Some say that after they became Christians, God took away their desire to do those things. I've prayed and prayed, asking God to take this desire away from me, but the temptation won't leave me alone. It's always there. What should I do?"

"Well," I said, "it's true that God does sometimes deliver Christians by taking away their desire for a certain sin. But I think that kind of deliverance is rather uncommon. In most cases, I think God leaves the desire within us and tells us to obey anyway. It may cost us a good deal of heartache and anguish to let go of that sin, but God wants to know if we love Him enough to sacrifice our self-willed sin on the altar."

I told her the story of Abraham and his reluctance to say goodbye to Ishmael and of the anguish he felt. But Abraham obeyed. This woman realized that she would have to accept the pain of obedience and send her Ishmael away, just as Abraham did.

In a sense, Abraham's grief over sending Ishmael away was a delayed judgment or consequence for Abraham's earlier sin of trying to hurry God's plan along. Ishmael was fourteen years old by this time, and Abraham had known from the beginning that Ishmael was not God's choice. Ishmael had come from Abraham's deliberate, self-indulgent choice. Since God had not chosen Ishmael, the boy could not be Abraham's heir. Yet God permitted him to stay until Isaac was born.

God never takes away an Ishmael until he has given an Isaac. Because this is so, we should be slow to judge others for their habits. We may see Ishmaels in other people's lives, and we may say, "You need to get rid of that habit." But it may well be that God has not spoken to them yet about that habit. He hasn't taken away that Ishmael because he is not yet given an Isaac. God never tells us to give up some self-indulgence until He first gives us some fruit of the Spirit to take its place and satisfy that longing of the heart. But when God gives us that gift of grace and blessing, then the self-indulgence has to go.

When the Spirit of the Lord speaks to us about a matter, we tend to think of God as harsh and demanding. In reality, He has been patient, forbearing, and tender toward us. Just as God allowed Ishmael to live in Abraham's household for fourteen years, He is often just as patient with us, if not more so.

When you first became a Christian, there were some aspects of your life that needed to change instantly. But there were also some areas that God permitted to go on unchanged. As you grew and matured in the faith, the fruit of the Spirit began to appear in your life, and you began to see that these behaviors and attitudes needed to go. They were the Ishmaels in your life.

A prominent Christian leader was once offered a highly visible position as the head of a media ministry. It was a great opportunity, and it would be the capstone of this man's career. But there were some people who knew him well, and they had some deep concerns about this opportunity. They had been praying for him a long time because they knew that there were some Ishmaels in his life.

One day, one of these friends sat down with this man and confronted him with some of the problem areas in his life—the Ishmaels that had to go. "You have a problem with pride," the friend told him. "You've always wanted to be the big shot, running everything your own way. You need to allow others to step in, to offer their views, and to hold you accountable. Another problem: You have a bad temper. People are afraid to tell you the truth because they don't know if you'll take it well or if you'll blow up."

The friend listed several other problem areas in this man's life. He concluded, "Now that this new ministry opportunity has come your way, these habits need to be dealt with. They have to go." Although it was hard for this man to hear these words, he realized that his friend had loved him enough to tell him the truth. He recognized the voice of his friend as the voice of God's Spirit speaking to him. That day, he began dealing with these issues. He let go of his Ishmaels.

It's painful to let Ishmael go. God knows this, and He is patient with us. But when He says, "This has to go," then let it go.

When God speaks, we must listen—and we must act. If you are going to walk in the power of the Spirit, you must let go of the flesh. You cannot obey two masters. One must go.

God told Abraham that Ishmael could never share in the inheritance with Isaac. Abraham apparently thought that the blessing of God and the inheritance of the promise could somehow be divided between the two sons. God had to destroy that false notion. Ishmael was Abraham's son by the flesh. The inheritance belonged to Abraham's son by the Spirit.

This is what Jesus meant when He said, "Flesh gives birth to flesh, but the Spirit gives birth to spirit" (John 3:6). When the time comes for us to stand before our Lord at the judgment seat of Christ, our lives will be divided into two classifications. Some actions of our lives will be classed as wood, hay, and stubble, acts of the flesh. Others will be classed as gold, silver and precious stones, imperishable acts of the Spirit (see 1 Corinthians 3:10–15).

The Lord says to us, as he said to Abraham, "Ishmael must go." If you refuse to examine and remove that which is born of the flesh, then you must face this choice as Abraham did. Ishmael must go.

I once read an article about Dr. Donald Barnhouse, the famed preacher and radio Bible teacher. He said, "Early in my ministry I had the idea that I must strike out against all error wherever I saw it. I'd hit Christian Science, Unitarianism, Romanism, and if error was in some fundamental leader with whom I was in ninety-five percent agreement, I swung hard at the five percent."

In those early days, Dr. Barnhouse was a highly controversial figure. He could be mercilessly sharp and dogmatic. But God dealt with this issue in his life. In the article, Dr. Barnhouse said that there came a time when the Spirit of God convicted him of his need to show love and mercy to others. His stubborn, unbending zeal for the truth was his Ishmael, and it had to go. So he made a decision to be more tolerant of the views of others.

He wrote, "Some time ago, I published a New Year's resolution expressing regret that I had had differences with men who are truly born again. The results of that resolution were astounding. In the years which followed its publication, my ministry has been transformed. I need to know all who have been redeemed by Christ, for I will never know my Lord fully until I see Him in every individual life whom He has redeemed and saved by the outpouring of His life for us all upon the cross. This is true fellowship."

It was wonderful to see Dr. Barnhouse so graciously and publicly say goodbye to his Ishmael. The closing years of his life were characterized by the sweetness of the fruit of the Spirit. A man who had once been known for his harshness and his criticism of others became even more famous for his Christlike love and grace.

When God told Abraham that Ishmael had to go, Abraham obeyed. Early in the morning, he arose, took bread and a skin of water, and sent Hagar and Ishmael out of his camp. It grieved him dearly to do so. It broke his heart. But Abraham obeyed God so that he might have the fullness of the life of the Spirit.

What is your Ishmael? It's time to stop clinging, defending, and justifying the thing in your life that was born of the flesh. Whatever is Ishmael in your life is a threat to the inheritance and the life of the Spirit. Send it away. Say goodbye to your Ishmael. Be fully and completely yielded to the Spirit of God, and you will find the joy and satisfaction of Isaac.

# 15

# THIS THIRSTY WORLD

*Genesis 21:14–34*

We have been walking alongside Abraham through all the great experiences of his life, both his triumphs and his failures, his highs and his lows. Throughout this journey, we have seen again and again how the events of Abraham's life symbolize the stages and events which take place in our own spiritual progress as Christians.

At the beginning of the account, Abraham obeyed God's call, left his home in Ur of the Chaldeans, and journeyed to the land of Canaan. This event mirrors the journey of every individual who responds to God's call, leaves his old life, and begins a new pilgrimage with Christ. Was Abraham's arrival in Canaan the end of his story? Absolutely not! It was the beginning of the story of God's work in Abraham's life. In the same way, when we come to Christ, it is just the beginning of God's work in our lives.

When we present the gospel of Jesus Christ to other people, we tend to present the moment of conversion as a solution to the great problems of life. And it is. When we commit our lives to Jesus Christ, we receive power to conquer sin, forgiveness to conquer guilt, and eternal life to conquer death.

But in another sense, the moment of conversion is when our real problems begin. That's when the young Christian begins encountering opposition without and within. Old sins, old habits, and old temptations that were simply a way of life before now become enemies in an agonizing struggle. Our preconversion mindset must be painfully peeled away like layers of an onion. The old sin nature repeatedly asserts itself and makes war against the spirit.

There's an old saying, "You can take the boy out of the country, but you can't take the country out of the boy." That is God's problem with Abraham, and God has the same problem with every individual who comes to Christ. He called Abraham out of Ur, and then it took decades of patient work to get Ur out of Abraham.

In the same way, many Christians come to Christ in a single moment of decision. But it takes decades to bring the old self under submission. In the course of that journey, every Christian experiences times of joy and blessing along with times of heartache and failure. The flesh fights back. It invents a thousand and one excuses for itself. We try and try to kill it, but the flesh dies hard.

But God never gives up on us. He never gives up on His plan for our future. He never lets us stop short of His goal for our lives, which is perfection—perfect conformity to the image of Christ.

## THE SIGNIFICANCE OF THE WELL

In the closing section of Genesis 21, the story of Abraham divides into three strands: the journey of Hagar and Ishmael in the wilderness; the covenant between Abraham and Abimelech; and Abraham and his family at the well, enjoying the fullness of God. It's important to note that a well is a central feature in each of these three strands of the story. It would be easy to overlook the well as an unimportant detail in Abraham's life, but nothing is unimportant in the Word of God. As the apostle Paul noted, the events of the Old Testament "were written for our instruction" (1 Corinthians 10:11).

By interpreting Scripture with Scripture, it's easy to understand the significance of this well. Throughout Scripture, we see the symbol of a well or spring as a picture of the Word of God. The water in the well is the refreshing, life-giving Spirit of Christ. He is the ultimate source of refreshment for the thirsty soul. It's because of Him that the psalmist says, "My cup overflows" (Psalm 23:5).

Remember the words the Lord spoke to the woman of Samaria as she came to Jacob's well to draw water: "Everyone who drinks this water will be thirsty again, but whoever drinks the water I give him will never thirst. Indeed, the water I give him will become in him a spring of water welling up to eternal life" (John 4:13–14). Jesus, the living Word of God, is the well that never runs dry.

The presence of the well in each of these three story strands is profoundly significant. Once we understand that the well represents Christ, the well becomes the Rosetta Stone that unlocks the meaning of this passage of Scripture. In these three vignettes, we will see how the well that symbolizes Christ appears in various ways, suggesting three unique facets of Christ's role in our lives.

## THE WELL OF PROMISE

The first of these three strands presents what we might call the Well of Promise. The passage begins:

> Early the next morning Abraham took some food and a skin of water and gave them to Hagar. He set them on her shoulders and then sent her off with the boy. She went on her way and wandered in the desert of Beersheba.
>
> When the water in the skin was gone, she put the boy under one of the bushes. Then she went off and sat down nearby, about a bowshot away, for she thought, "I cannot watch the boy die." And as she sat there nearby, she began to sob.
>
> God heard the boy crying, and the angel of God called to Hagar from heaven and said to her, "What is the matter, Hagar? Do not be afraid; God has heard the boy crying as he lies there. Lift the boy up and take him by the hand, for I will make him into a great nation."
>
> Then God opened her eyes and she saw a well of water. So she went and filled the skin with water and gave the boy a drink.
>
> God was with the boy as he grew up. He lived in the desert and became an archer. While he was living in the Desert

of Paran, his mother got a wife for him from Egypt. (Genesis 21:14–21)

There is much more to this passage than a mere description of historical events. In Galatians, the apostle Paul tells us how to interpret the story of Hagar and Ishmael. He begins by contrasting the two women, Hagar and Sarah:

> These things may be taken figuratively, for the women represent two covenants. One covenant is from Mount Sinai and bears children who are to be slaves: This is Hagar. Now Hagar stands for Mount Sinai in Arabia and corresponds to the present city of Jerusalem, because she is in slavery with her children. But the Jerusalem that is above is free, and she is our mother. (Galatians 4:24–26)

Hagar, Paul says, is a symbolic picture of Mount Sinai, from which the law of Moses was given. She and her son Ishmael represent the nation of Israel that rejected Christ yet retained God's promises and His preserving care. Elsewhere, Paul tells us that after the nation rejected Christ, Israel experienced a spiritual blindness that would last until all the Gentiles who would believe had come in (see Romans 11:25). Here in the Old Testament, two thousand years before the birth of Christ, these same events were symbolically foretold in the life of Abraham. The New Testament confirms what the Old Testament portrays, proving that both Testaments come from the hand of God.

Like Ishmael, the nation of Israel has wandered in the wilderness of the world ever since the people said as they gathered before Pilate, "We don't want this man to be our king" (Luke 19:14). In AD 70, during the great Jewish revolt against Roman oppression, Roman legions under Titus ransacked and destroyed the city of Jerusalem, including Herod's temple. The center of Jewish worship was destroyed, and the people of Israel were driven out among the nations. They wandered like Ishmael in the desert for centuries, with only their traditions and the Old Testament Scriptures binding them together.

Even though the state of Israel was restored in 1948, the Jewish people still have no great temple in which to worship. To this day, most of the Jewish people still live outside of Israel's borders. In a spiritual sense, they have been wandering since the rejection of Christ, and they are perishing with thirst.

But a day is coming, as the New Testament tells us, when their eyes will be opened, just as Hagar's eyes were opened in the desert. When God opened her eyes, the first thing she saw was a well. And that well, remember, represents Jesus Christ, the promised Messiah, the son of God. It may be that we are nearing the hour when Israel will have its eyes opened and behold Christ once again in its own Scriptures.

As New Testament Christians, we look at the Old Testament Scriptures, and it seems so clear to us that images of Christ appear repeatedly across its pages. For example, the Lord's birth is prophesied in Isaiah 9:6–7. His ministry of teaching and healing is foretold in Isaiah 35:3–6. The messianic prophecies in Psalm 22, Isaiah 53, and Isaiah 69:19–20 portray the rejection and crucifixion of Christ with such clarity and detail that it's hard to believe they were written centuries before the event. The resurrection is declared in Psalm 16:10–11. The Lord's ascension into heaven is foreshadowed in Psalm 16:11 and Psalm 110:1. And we have only scratched the surface of the vast body of Old Testament prophecies that point clearly to Jesus as the promised Messiah.

Why, then, do so few Jewish people believe in Christ when the Old Testament is rich in messianic prophecies that so clearly portray Him? The answer of the apostle Paul: "Israel has experienced a hardening in part" (Romans 11:25). In other words, while not all Jews refuse to believe, many of them have failed to understand the testimony of their own Scriptures. So even though the Jewish people longed for and expected the Messiah who was foretold, when He came, they did not believe He was truly the Messiah.

But God says that a day will come at last when their eyes will be opened, and they will see that Jesus is indeed Yeshua Ha'Mashiach, Jesus the Messiah. When their eyes are opened, they will turn to the Lord and be refreshed. Like Hagar when her eyes were opened, they will go to the well and receive the Living Water. God will be with them, and like Ishmael, they will become a great nation once more. Jesus, the Well of Promise, will be their Lord and King.

All of this is portrayed in this little vignette in Genesis 21.

## THE WELL OF CONTENTION

In the second of these three strands of the story, the well appears in a different form, which we could call the Well of Contention. We read:

> At that time Abimelech and Phicol the commander of his forces said to Abraham, "God is with you in everything you do. Now swear to me here before God that you will not deal falsely with me or my children or my descendants. Show to me and the country where you are living as an alien the same kindness I have shown to you."
>
> Abraham said, "I swear it."
>
> Then Abraham complained to Abimelech about a well of water that Abimelech's servants had seized. But Abimelech said, "I don't know who has done this. You did not tell me, and I heard about it only today."
>
> So Abraham brought sheep and cattle and gave them to Abimelech, and the two men made a treaty. Abraham set apart seven ewe lambs from the flock, and Abimelech asked Abraham, "What is the meaning of these seven ewe lambs you have set apart by themselves?"
>
> He replied, "Accept these seven lambs from my hand as a witness that I dug this well."
>
> So that place was called Beersheba, because the two men swore an oath there.
>
> After the treaty had been made at Beersheba, Abimelech and Phicol the commander of his forces returned to the land of the Philistines. (Genesis 21:22–32)

This is a strange account. We have previously met Abimelech, king of the Philistines, in Genesis 20, when Abraham told Sarah to lie and Abimelech unknowingly took Sarah as his wife. The name of Abimelech's commander, the general of the Philistine army, is Phicol, which means "the voice of all." Throughout the Scriptures the Philistine nation symbolizes unregenerate human beings seeking to reach God through their own religious efforts. Phicol exercises authority as if he were the voice of all the Philistines.

In light of the ecumenical movement of our day—a global movement that seeks to blend all human religions into one super-religion that claims to speak for all—this exchange between Abraham and Abimelech takes on a profound significance. Applying the symbols of this Old Testament story to our lives, we can translate the dialogue between Abraham and Abimelech this way:

Abimelech: "I don't understand you Jehovah worshipers! It's obvious that God is with you, yet you are a mystery to me. You have a remarkable ability to cause trouble for people. We Philistines are just as religious as you are, but you and we have totally different approaches to life. We are city dwellers, but you are pilgrims in the land, living in tents while talking about a future city that has foundations which cannot be seen. I'm worried that this city you talk about might someday be a threat to my nation and my descendants. I want you to make a promise that is binding on you and your descendants. Swear to me that you will always show kindness to us."

Abraham: "Very well. I will give you the promise you ask for. But there is one matter that bothers me."

Abimelech: "Oh? What is that?"

Abraham: "Do you see this well? It represents the coming Messiah to me and my people. This is our place of refreshment, where our souls meet God. Your men have been trying to take this well away from me."

Abimelech: "Oh, we would never do that! I only heard about this situation for the first time today. We never meant to take this well away from you."

Abraham: "Here are seven little ewe lambs. Take them as a perpetual reminder that this well means life or death to me. This well is my source of refreshment, strength, and wisdom. I dug this well myself, and I will not give it up."

In this story, the well has become a well of contention and dispute. Let's see what this story means for our individual Christian lives and for the Christian church.

First, we need to define our terms when we speak of the Christian church. When the world speaks of the church, it refers to an institution, a religious organization. But when the Scriptures speak of the church, they refer to the body of Christ, the mystical fellowship of all true followers of Christ. The body of Christ is not an institution or an organization. In fact, the institutional church is made up of both authentic Christians and false Christians.

The institutional church—the religious organization that the world calls the church—is often in conflict with genuine believers regarding the well of God. This well is the Lord Jesus Christ and the Scriptures that speak of Him. There are many institutional church denominations, church leaders, theologians, and preachers who do not believe the Scriptures and do not regard the Lord Jesus as the promised Messiah and the Son of God.

There are voices within the institutional church that reject the virgin birth, the miracles of Jesus, His atoning death, and His resurrection. They do not believe that the Bible is the infallible word of God. Instead, they teach that Jesus was merely a good human teacher and that the Bible is a patchwork of ancient stories and teachings that have much to say to us but should not be viewed as God's revelation of himself to the human race. In short, they do not hold the well of God in high esteem.

But those who authentically believe in Christ and His Word are like Abraham. They say, "This well means everything to me. It means life or death to me. It's the source of my refreshment, my strength, and my wisdom. I will never give it up."

Those non-Christian Christians of the institutional church do not understand our devotion as biblical Christians to this well of living water. They view born-again believers as strange, fanatical, and profoundly ignorant. This has always been the ground of struggle and disagreement with worldly religious groups. These worldly religious groups are the Philistines of our time.

## THE GOOD NEWS OF FREEDOM

The story of Abraham and Abimelech gives us guidance in how to respond to the worldly religious groups of our day. In saying that these religious groups are worldly, I'm not saying their intentions are necessarily evil. While these groups do not believe that Jesus is Lord or that the Bible is truth, they do want to improve the world through social programs and political policies. As Bible-believing Christians, we recognize that there is great suffering and injustice in the world, and we believe God calls us to alleviate suffering and oppose injustice wherever we find it. But does this mean we should ally ourselves with the programs and policies of these worldly religious groups?

Let's take a lesson from Abraham. Abimelech said to him, in effect, "Abraham, you don't think as we do. You have a different objective." I'm amazed at the insight of this pagan man. He demonstrated a remarkable understanding of Abraham's life and outlook. "You are a pilgrim, a stranger passing through our land," Abimelech continued. "Please promise that you won't get involved in our business."

And Abraham replied, in effect, "I'll be glad to stay out of your business."

I believe this is the position Christians must take today. I'm not saying that the social programs and policies advocated by the worldly religious institutions are wrong. I'm not saying that we, as Christians, should not be intensely engaged in alleviating suffering and opposing injustice. We should. The Lord was constantly meeting human needs and standing against oppression, and so should we.

By His words and His example, Jesus taught us to reach out to people in need. If we preach only the spiritual side of the gospel and fail to live out the compassionate side of the gospel, then we become like the Levite and the Pharisee in the parable of the good Samaritan (see Luke 10:33), passing by human suffering with a shrug of indifference. At the beginning of His earthly ministry, Jesus proclaimed His mission on earth, quoting a passage from Isaiah 61:

"The Spirit of the Lord is on me,
    because he has anointed me
    to preach good news to the poor.
He has sent me to proclaim freedom for the prisoners
    and recovery of sight for the blind,
    to release the oppressed,
    to proclaim the year of the Lord's favor." (Luke
    4:18–19)

Now His mission is our mission. We are His hands and feet in the world. How do we help the poor, the prisoners, the blind, and the oppressed? We start by reaching out and doing whatever we can. If we can visit a lonely person in a hospital or a convalescent home, we do that. If we can volunteer our time to a ministry to prisoners or a Christian homeless shelter, we do that. Whatever we can do to show the love of Jesus Christ to those who have a need or a burden, we do that. And when we show the love of Jesus, we will have opportunities to share the good news of Jesus.

And the good news of eternal life through Jesus Christ must always be the centerpiece of our ministry. If we want to lift up the poor, or free the prisoners, or open the eyes of the blind, or release the oppressed, we must begin with the good news of Jesus Christ. Everywhere the church has proclaimed His gospel, liberation followed. It is Christ who sets captives free, and whom He sets free is free indeed!

Our Lord told us that we are the salt of the earth—if we do not lose our saltiness. We are to preserve and season the lives of those around us (see Matthew 5:13; Mark 9:50; Luke 14:34). We are to allow God to use us in His program for transforming lives through the sharing of His Word. When we give ourselves to the proclamation of the good news of Jesus Christ to our friends and neighbors—to the least and the last and the lost, to the grocery checker and the barber and the postman and the next-door neighbor—we create an atmosphere where every kind of freedom can flourish.

The gospel sets people free from addictions and destructive habits.

It sets people free from the selfishness and lawlessness that put them behind prison bars. It sets people free from the poor choices that trap them in poverty and destructive relationships. The gospel of Jesus Christ compelled the British politician William Wilberforce (1759–1833) to spend his life in a relentless effort to abolish the slave trade and free the slaves—a fight he won in the last year of his life. The gospel compelled the Quakers, the Free Methodists, and other evangelical revivalists to fight against slavery in America.

The spiritual freedom that Christ brings always produces social and political freedom. Those who try to bring about social and political justice without laying a foundation of freedom in Christ are doomed to fail. No amount of political action and organizing will ever succeed in setting people free until the gospel of Jesus Christ has planted the seeds of freedom in human hearts.

## THE WELL OF COMMUNION

Next, we see that Abraham's Well of Contention in Beersheba has become a Well of Communion. We read: "Abraham planted a tamarisk tree in Beersheba, and there he called upon the name of the Lord, the Eternal God. And Abraham stayed in the land of the Philistines for a long time" (Genesis 21:33–34).

Abraham planted a shade tree and lived beside his well, and that well became a Well of Communion. There he called upon the Lord and enjoyed fellowship and communion with the eternal God.

Why does the Spirit of God include this final vignette? God gives us this insight because it shows us what is taking place in Abraham's heart and life. The tree reminds us of the imagery of the Psalm 1, which tells us that those who belong to God are like "a tree planted by streams of water, which yields its fruit in season and whose leaf does not wither" (Psalm 1:3). This is an image of a fruitful life that yields blessing to everyone around.

Shaded by the tamarisk tree, Abraham calls on the name of Yahweh, the everlasting God. I am increasingly convinced that if the church desires to do anything to help this poor, blind, struggling world, it needs to daily call upon the everlasting God for wisdom, guidance, and power. Continual fellowship with God produces a joy in our hearts that shines forth from our faces. When the worldlings all around us see the life of the everlasting Lord reflected in our lives, they will want what we have, and we will have an opportunity to share the good news with them.

I once gave a radio talk on the subject of God's all-sufficient grace for times of trial and suffering. The next day, I received a brief letter from a man who had heard my talk. His letter consisted of just one sentence: "Dear Mr. Stedman—if it is true that God gives us grace to bear all our trials, then why are there so many long-faced Christians?" It was a good question, and my reply was almost as brief as his question.

I wrote: "If it is true that the soap companies have provided all the soap that this world needs, then why are there so many dirty people in the world?" The answer, of course, is that many people neglect to use the soap—and many Christians neglect to accept the grace God offers. Any Christian who is chronically long-faced and dour is missing out on the grace and peace of God.

Abraham found the joy of fellowship with the eternal God. Thus he became a source of blessing even to the pagan Philistines. As a friend of God and a channel of grace, Abraham did more to advance the cause of social justice and freedom among the Philistines than any political policies and social welfare programs could have achieved.

The world is searching for men and women who have convictions that flow from a living fellowship with the eternal God. God calls us to discharge our duties as citizens and to do all we can to meet the needs of the hurting people around us. But above all, we must give ourselves to the first priority and supreme task of the church of Jesus Christ—the task of declaring of the good news of our risen Lord. Through the sharing of His gospel, men, women, and children will be saved, prisoners will be set free, and lives will be transformed.

There are thirsty souls all around us. We have the living water that can satisfy their thirst forever. Let God use you to open their eyes and point the way to the Well that never runs dry.

# 16

# LIFE'S HARDEST TRIAL

*Genesis 22:1–19*

Every night, Martin Luther would gather his family and read a story from the Bible for family devotions. One night, he read the account in which God commanded Abraham to sacrifice his son Isaac. When Luther had finished reading the story from Genesis 22, his wife, Katharina, said, "I don't believe it! How could God ask Abraham to do such a thing to his son? God would certainly not treat His Son like that!"

"But, Katie," Luther replied, "He did."

It's true. This remarkable Old Testament story of a father's willingness to offer up his son parallels the sacrifice by the Father of His only Son Jesus in the New Testament. In this story, the cross of Christ reaches back through time to stab deep into the heart of Abraham. As we take a close look at the symbolic features of this Old Testament story, we will see aspects that foreshadow every feature of the New Testament account of the passion of Christ. In the story of Abraham and Isaac, as in the story of the crucifixion, we find a Gethsemane, a Calvary, and a resurrection.

This is one of the most famous accounts in the entire Bible, and it is easy to understand why. Here, Abraham undergoes the most intense and painful trial of faith anyone could imagine. No one could watch Abraham binding his dear son to the altar without feeling his heartbreak. As we identify with the pain of Abraham, we gain at least a little insight into what it cost God the Father to offer up His Son on the cross.

## THE TEST ON MOUNT MORIAH

In the opening verses of Genesis 22, we read:

> Some time later God tested Abraham. He said to him,
> "Abraham!"
>
> "Here I am," he replied.
>
> Then God said, "Take your son, your only son, Isaac,
> whom you love, and go to the region of Moriah. Sacrifice him
> there as a burnt offering on one of the mountains I will tell
> you about."
>
> Early the next morning Abraham got up and saddled his
> donkey. He took with him two of his servants and his son
> Isaac. When he had cut enough wood for the burnt offering,
> he set out for the place God had told him about. On the third
> day Abraham looked up and saw the place in the distance.
> (Genesis 22:1–4)

About twenty years have elapsed since the end of Genesis 21. We
last saw Abraham in a tent in the wilderness by the well of Beersheba.
There he worshiped at an altar he built, calling on the name of the
everlasting God. For twenty years, Abraham experienced blessed fellowship with God. His son Isaac has been with him—the delight of
Abraham's heart. True to his name, Isaac has brought laughter to the
tent of Abraham and Sarah.

Suddenly, like a meteor striking out of a clear blue sky, this strange
command from God comes to Abraham. The old man can hardly
believe his ears. God says, "Take your son, your only son, Isaac, whom
you love, and go to the region of Moriah. Sacrifice him there as a burnt
offering on one of the mountains I will tell you about." No more shocking and horrifying command has ever been issued from God to man.

Every detail of the story is significant, beginning with the location.
Mount Moriah, the site of the sacrifice, is the ground King David purchased (see 1 Chronicles 21) and upon which the temple of Solomon
was later built (see 2 Chronicles 3). That temple was later destroyed by

the Babylonians. A second temple was built on Mount Moriah, and it was destroyed in AD 70 by the Romans. Today the Dome of the Rock, the golden-domed Islamic shrine that dominates Jerusalem's skyline, stands over the great rock that formed the altar upon which Abraham offered Isaac.

Now, imagine how Abraham must have felt upon hearing this command from God. The account does not describe Abraham's feelings. It doesn't need to. We don't need Abraham's anguish spelled out to us in so many words. The voice of God was unmistakable. Abraham had heard the Lord's voice many times, and he knew it well.

Genesis tells us clearly that this command was a test. First, it was a test of whether or not Abraham was willing to obey the first commandment: "Love the LORD your God with all your heart and with all your soul and with all your strength" (Deuteronomy 6:5). God seeks only what He deserves—first place in every human heart.

Second, it was God's way to find out if Abraham's confidence for the future was in his son Isaac or in God. If Abraham placed his confidence in Isaac, he would hold his son back and say, "No, Lord! He's the son you promised to me. If I slay him, I'll have no future, no descendants! How can you ask such a thing?"

But if Abraham's confidence was in the Lord, he would say, "I don't understand why you want me to do this, but I trust you to keep your word, even if Isaac is slain."

## ABRAHAM'S GETHSEMANE

The passage does not say, but we can well imagine that Satan may have suggested a number of doubts to Abraham's heart: "Your God demands too much of you! This command makes no sense! No human being could ever do what He asks you to do! And what about your wife, Sarah? What will she say when you return from the mountain alone? How will you explain to her what you have done? How will you face her?"

Abraham must have agonized over his decision to obey the Lord. Should he obey and slaughter his son or hold on to his son at the cost of his relationship with God? It's impossible to imagine a more horrible dilemma.

Abraham's agony parallels the awful struggle of our Lord Jesus in the Garden of Gethsemane. There, the Lord faced a similar test—a test in which God the Father asked Him to do something utterly horrible and unthinkable: God asked the most innocent Man who ever lived to submit to a criminal's death—execution by slow torture on the cross. In the process, all of humanity's sin would be laid on Him—and He would experience total separation from the Father. How could God the Father ask such a thing of Him?

Perhaps you have faced a dilemma like Abraham's even if to a lesser degree. You may have faced a situation in which you said, "Is *this* what God wants me to go through? Is this truly His will? How can He ask me to do such a thing? This makes no sense. This is unfair. Why is this happening to me?"

Trials and obstacles in life are much easier to bear when we can understand the reason for them. But when we are forced to endure suffering and catastrophes that seem meaningless and illogical, life seems unfair. Indeed, God seems unfair. That is when our faith is really put to the test, just as Abraham's faith was tested.

Imagine the strain on Abraham's faith, his emotions, and his mind on the morning he arose to carry out the awful command of God. His heart was torn, yet he obeyed God. I'm profoundly impressed with the obedience of Abraham. How many times had he acted in a cowardly, foolish, or disobedient fashion? How many tests of faith had he already failed? Yet here, in the most extreme test of all, he passed. He obeyed. He committed himself to carrying out God's will, even though it made no sense to him.

Here we find the secret of the Christian life. The reality of our faith is not demonstrated by the fervor of our prayers, the emotionalism of our worship, or the intensity of our witness to others. There is only one way to truly authenticate our faith: obedience. When God gives us a command, do we carry it out? Do we obey Him even when His orders make no sense to us?

Abraham heard God's command, and he obeyed.

## THE CALVARY OF ABRAHAM'S FAITH

Now we come to faith's Calvary:

> He said to his servants, "Stay here with the donkey while I and the boy go over there. We will worship and then we will come back to you."
>
> Abraham took the wood for the burnt offering and placed it on his son Isaac, and he himself carried the fire and the knife. As the two of them went on together, Isaac spoke up and said to his father Abraham, "Father?"
>
> "Yes, my son?" Abraham replied.
>
> "The fire and wood are here," Isaac said, "but where is the lamb for the burnt offering?"
>
> Abraham answered, "God himself will provide the lamb for the burnt offering, my son." And the two of them went on together.
>
> When they reached the place God had told him about, Abraham built an altar there and arranged the wood on it. He bound his son Isaac and laid him on the altar, on top of the wood. Then he reached out his hand and took the knife to slay his son. But the angel of the Lord called out to him from heaven, "Abraham! Abraham!"
>
> "Here I am," he replied.
>
> "Do not lay a hand on the boy," he said. "Do not do anything to him. Now I know that you fear God, because you have not withheld from me your son, your only son."
>
> Abraham looked up and there in a thicket he saw a ram caught by its horns. He went over and took the ram and sacrificed it as a burnt offering instead of his son. So Abraham called that place The Lord Will Provide. And to this day it is said, "On the mountain of the Lord it will be provided." (Genesis 22:5–14)

Again the Scriptures are silent regarding Abraham's emotions, but the narrative makes it clear that his heart was breaking. He avoided telling Isaac the fearful truth until the last possible moment. We can imagine the tears in Abraham's eyes and the trembling in his voice when Isaac asked, "Where is the lamb?"

What a profound question! Where is the lamb? The answer remained hidden from human eyes until two thousand years later, when John the Baptist, standing beside the Jordan River, pointed to Jesus of Nazareth and said, "Look, the Lamb of God, who takes away the sin of the world!" (John 1:29).

How do we explain what Abraham did next? Where did he find the emotional and physical strength to bind his son and place him on the rock? The answer is found in verse 5: "He said to his servants, 'Stay here with the donkey while I and the boy go over there. We will worship and then we will come back to you.' "

I don't believe Abraham was trying to deceive his servants. He was a friend of God. He knew the merciful, loving heart of his Lord. He didn't understand how it was possible, but somehow he knew that both he and Isaac would return from the mountain. I think that Abraham had an inkling, if not a certainty, about the resurrection. He believed in the power of God to raise the dead back to life again. In Abraham's day and in our own, faith in the resurrection gives us the peace to follow God's commands.

## ABRAHAM'S RESURRECTION HOPE

When I imagine Abraham's struggle over his decision to obey God, I think he must have racked his brain for a way to make sense of God's command. His thought processes might have gone something like this: "God has given me His promise. Experience has shown me He always delivers on His promises. He told me that, through Isaac, I would become a great nation and all the nations of the earth would be blessed. Isaac can't fulfill that promise if he is dead. Now God asks me to sacrifice Isaac. There is only one explanation: God intends to raise Isaac from the dead."

To arrive at such a conclusion would take incredible faith. Abraham had never heard of anyone dying and rising again. The resurrection of

Lazarus was still twenty centuries in Abraham's future. Yet Abraham had such a deep and abiding faith in the character of God that he could conceive of no other solution to the dilemma. The thought of God going back on His word and invalidating His promise never even occurred to Abraham. There had to be some other solution, and to Abraham, that solution could only be resurrection.

You don't have to take my word for it. The Spirit of God confirms that this was the logic Abraham followed as he prepared to offer up his son Isaac. In the New Testament book of Hebrews, we read, "Abraham reasoned that God could raise the dead, and figuratively speaking, he did receive Isaac back from death" (Hebrews 11:19). You see? Abraham reasoned his way to faith in the resurrection!

Where did Abraham derive the strength to lead his son up that mountain, bind him, and raise that knife? It came from Abraham's firm belief in the resurrection from the dead. Abraham risked everything on the character of God, and he found God to be the Lord of resurrection life. As Abraham was about to slay his son, an angel stayed his hand and pointed him to a ram whose horns were caught in a thicket.

In an unexpected way, God provided a sacrifice in Isaac's place. Abraham received back his son, who had been as good as dead. Because of the wonderful triumph Abraham experienced on Mount Moriah, he called that place "The Lord Will Provide."

Human disappointments are God's appointments. It is never too late for God. Even if Abraham had been called upon to carry the bloody business through to its end, Abraham believed that God would fulfill the promise He had made.

In response to Abraham's obedience, God reaffirms His promise:

> The angel of the LORD called to Abraham from heaven a second time and said, "I swear by myself, declares the LORD, that because you have done this and have not withheld your son, your only son, I will surely bless you and make your descendants as numerous as the stars in the sky and as the sand on the seashore. Your descendants will take possession of the

cities of their enemies, and through your offspring all nations on earth will be blessed, because you have obeyed me."

Then Abraham returned to his servants, and they set off together for Beersheba. And Abraham stayed in Beersheba. (Genesis 22:15–19)

Abraham offered his son back to God. In response, God told Abraham that the promise of fruitfulness would be fulfilled immediately. There would be no more delay. The rivers of living water would now begin to flow from him to bless all the nations of the earth. When Isaac returned from the dead in resurrection power, God said, in effect, "Now the fruitfulness of your life will be manifest." This is resurrection life.

God has given gifts to us all. But God's gifts are of no value until we are willing, if necessary, to let go of them so that God might reign in our lives without a rival. When we come to a place where we are willing to obey Him without question, when His will for our lives means more than anything, when we love Him with all our strength, then God will resurrect that gift within us. Through our yieldedness, He will make that gift a blessing to everyone it touches.

What is the gift God has given you? Is it a special talent or ability? Is it your wealth? Your career? Whatever gift God has given to you, give it back to God. Tell Him you are willing to lay that gift upon the altar, to slay it, to watch it die. Do that—and the God of resurrection will take that gift and return it to you and make it a blessing to everyone around you.

Our God is the God of resurrection. When it seems as if we are throwing away every chance of blessing, He transforms the act of sacrifice into resurrection power. He transforms death into life. When we dare to live as Abraham lived, risking everything on the God of resurrection, we discover the meaning of the words of the apostle Paul: "I want to know Christ and the power of his resurrection and the fellowship of sharing in his sufferings, becoming like him in his death, and so, somehow, to attain to the resurrection from the dead" (Philippians 3:10–11).

Three years before he was martyred in Ecuador for Christ, missionary Jim Elliot wrote in his journal: "He is no fool who gives what he cannot keep to gain what he cannot lose." When God asks you to face life's hardest trial and offer up what you cannot keep, what will your answer be?

# 17

# TILL DEATH DO US PART

*Genesis 23*

What a bitter day it is when a man buries his beloved wife! It's the sunset of all of life's hopes and dreams—and one of the lowest points ever reached by the human spirit.

As we come to Genesis 23, we stand beside Abraham as he weeps at the grave of Sarah. He is walking through the valley where death has cast its shadow. But as we continue through this chapter of Abraham's life, we will see a light that always shines even in the darkest shadows of his life.

The opening verses of Genesis 23 draw us into the shadowy valley of sorrow and loss where Abraham now lives: "Sarah lived to be a hundred and twenty-seven years old. She died at Kiriath Arba (that is, Hebron) in the land of Canaan, and Abraham went to mourn for Sarah and to weep over her" (Genesis 23:1–2).

Approximately seventeen years have passed since the end of Genesis 22. Though the Genesis account records the significant trials and triumphs of Abraham's life, it passes silently over the years of blessing and peace that Abraham enjoyed together with his wife.

Sarah was 127 years old when she died. Her son Isaac was thirty-seven. By this time, Abraham had moved his family back to Hebron from Beersheba. Once more, the friend of God was living by the great trees of Mamre, where he and Sarah had first lived when they came into the land of Canaan. There, Sarah died. As the name Mamre indicates, it was the place of fatness of soul and richness of fellowship with the Lord.

It was a good place to die.

## THE DEPTHS OF GRIEF

In accordance with the Middle Eastern custom of that time, the body of Sarah was placed in a tent by itself. Abraham went alone into the tent to weep and mourn over the body of his wife. Though Abraham had been through many sorrows and bitter disappointments in his life, this is the first time the Genesis account ever tells us that Abraham wept. This is significant, for it reveals the depth of love and grief he felt for Sarah.

The Scriptures do not tell us how long Abraham and Sarah were married. We do know they were joined as husband and wife in those early years when they lived in Abraham's father's house in Ur of the Chaldeans. We also know that it was the custom in the ancient Middle East for couples to marry in their teens. Abraham and Sarah probably celebrated their hundredth wedding anniversary some years before she died.

Imagine the depth of grief you would feel at the graveside of the one who had been your beloved spouse and companion for more than a century. Then picture Abraham as he bows and weeps over the body of Sarah. Imagine the multitude of memories that flooded his thoughts. No doubt, he recalled the images of Sarah as a beautiful young bride, a loving wife and homemaker, and finally, by the grace and power of God, a mother nursing her newborn son, Isaac.

Abraham and Sarah had seen triumphs and failures, joys and sorrows. They had endured many hardships along their sojourn together. Abraham especially remembered the bitter tears Sarah had cried, year after year, over her barren womb. Now she had gone to her eternal rest. The grand adventure that had taken them from Mesopotamia to Egypt to the promised land of Canaan had come to an end. Death had torn her from his arms, but death could never take her from his heart.

While Abraham was in the depths of his grief, it must have seemed to him that his own life was over as well. But God still had important work for him to do. Abraham's adventure of faith would go on.

## AN ALIEN AND A STRANGER

As we read this account, we gain new insight into the life of faith:

> Then Abraham rose from beside his dead wife and spoke to the Hittites. He said, "I am an alien and a stranger among you. Sell me some property for a burial site here so I can bury my dead."
> The Hittites replied to Abraham, "Sir, listen to us. You are a mighty prince among us. Bury your dead in the choicest of our tombs. None of us will refuse you his tomb for burying your dead." (Genesis 23:3–6)

Abraham had lived as a pilgrim in the land. He did not even own a burial plot in which to inter his wife's remains. So he rose up from beside his wife's body and went to the people who lived in that land, the Hittites. His words to them stand as a wonderful confession of faith: "I am an alien and a stranger among you."

This is a statement of a man who has obeyed God's calling to be a pilgrim and sojourner in the land of promise. He does not own property. He has not put down roots. He looks beyond all that earth has to offer, and out there in the mists of the future, he sees the city whose architect and builder is God.

Abraham has been grieving his loss in the valley of the shadow of death. Yet he somehow senses that there can be no shadow without light. Whenever shadows come into your life, it is a sign that somewhere a light is shining. Of course, if you and I turn our backs to that light, then the shadow we face is the shadow that we ourselves have cast. Many people live in constant shadow because they have made their own darkness. They have turned their backs to the light, and they live in the shadows cast by their own willfulness, bitterness, selfishness, pride, and sin.

God calls us to face the light, as Abraham did throughout his life.

When we, like Abraham, look to the light that streams from that eternal city whose architect and builder is God, then the only shadows we face will be passing and temporary shadows. We pass through the shadows when some momentary tragedy or trial obscures the light for a moment. These shadows may darken our lives for days or months or even years, but ultimately a light remains. The shadows pass.

That, after all, is what death truly is—a temporary obscuring of the light. But the person of faith looks beyond the shadow and sees the light still shining. By faith we can say to the people around us, "I am a stranger and a sojourner among you. I don't seek a permanent sense of satisfaction here on earth. My eyes are fixed on the light of the city to which God is calling me."

God has promised the entire land of Canaan to Abraham. But the death of his wife reminds him that it is not yet God's time for him to possess the land. Abraham's faith is not weakened by the loss of his wife. It is strengthened. He is reminded that he is a pilgrim and a stranger in the land of promise.

Many people, upon losing a loved one, seem to give up on life. Their hearts were closely bound to the one they have lost. That's understandable. But the loss of a loved one is not the end of life. It's not the end of the adventure God has planned for us. Like Abraham, we must lift our eyes beyond this present shadow to the light from the city beyond. Like Abraham, we must remind ourselves that this world was never intended to meet the deepest needs of our hearts. We are pilgrims. We are strangers passing through.

That is a confession of faith Abraham makes when he goes to the Hittites to purchase a plot of land in which to bury his beloved wife.

Dr. Donald Barnhouse told the story of a Christian young woman whose husband was killed in action during World War II. To save expenses during the war, she had been living with her parents. When the tragic telegram came, she read it through, then told her mother, "I'm going to my room. Please don't disturb me."

Her mother called the young woman's father at work and told him what had happened. He hurried home and immediately went to his daughter's room. He opened the door and saw her kneeling beside her bed. The telegram was spread open on the bed. He heard his daughter pray, "Oh, my Father, my heavenly Father . . ."

Without a word, the man softly closed the door, went back downstairs, and told his wife, "She's in better hands than mine."

That's the response of faith to the shadow of grief.

## A PRINCE AMONG THE PAGANS

Next, we see something of the independence of the man of faith:

> Then Abraham rose and bowed down before the people of the land, the Hittites. He said to them, "If you are willing to let me bury my dead, then listen to me and intercede with Ephron son of Zohar on my behalf so he will sell me the cave of Machpelah, which belongs to him and is at the end of his field. Ask him to sell it to me for the full price as a burial site among you."
>
> Ephron the Hittite was sitting among his people and he replied to Abraham in the hearing of all the Hittites who had come to the gate of his city. "No, my lord," he said. "Listen to me; I give you the field, and I give you the cave that is in it. I give it to you in the presence of my people. Bury your dead."
>
> Again Abraham bowed down before the people of the land and he said to Ephron in their hearing, "Listen to me, if you will. I will pay the price of the field. Accept it from me so I can bury my dead there."
>
> Ephron answered Abraham, "Listen to me, my lord; the land is worth four hundred shekels of silver, but what is that between me and you? Bury your dead."
>
> Abraham agreed to Ephron's terms and weighed out for him the price he had named in the hearing of the Hittites: four hundred shekels of silver, according to the weight current among the merchants.
>
> So Ephron's field in Machpelah near Mamre—both the

field and the cave in it, and all the trees within the borders of the field—was deeded to Abraham as his property in the presence of all the Hittites who had come to the gate of the city. Afterward Abraham buried his wife Sarah in the cave in the field of Machpelah near Mamre (which is at Hebron) in the land of Canaan. So the field and the cave in it were deeded to Abraham by the Hittites as a burial site. (Genesis 23:7–20)

Why does the account provide so much detail of the business transaction between Abraham and the Hittites? I believe that one reason is that this site, Ephron's field in Machpelah, has been historically authenticated. Many other traditional sites in Israel are a matter of speculation and doubt, but the cave of Machpelah, where Sarah and Abraham were both buried, has been verified. You can go to Israel and visit it today. An Islamic mosque has been erected above the cave, but historians do not doubt that this is the final resting place of Abraham and Sarah.

The Spirit of God, knowing that this site would be well preserved down through the ages, wanted us to have this specific and detailed account. In this way, the reality of these events would be firmly anchored in our minds.

The respectful haggling between Abraham and Ephron in this account is typical of the kind of bargaining that goes on to this day in the marketplaces of the Middle East. Abraham's pagan friends have a genuine feeling of respect and honor for this man of faith. "You are a mighty prince among us," the Hittites tell him. In this way, these pagans recognize that there is something different and special about Abraham. By honoring him in this way, they honor God, who has shaped Abraham's faith and character.

You may have had a similar experience in your Christian life. While it's true that being a Christian often makes us feel estranged from the world around us, there are also times when non-Christian people will recognize and admire what is different about us. Often, non-Christians will come to us and say, "I don't always agree with you, but there is much that I respect about you. I respect your integrity, your kindness, and the way you state your beliefs without being argumentative." The more we demonstrate genuine Christlikeness and Christian love, the more often we will hear such words.

The world wants to squeeze us into its mold, and the world hates us when we reject its pressure to conform. We must always stand firm for God's truth and resist the temptation to compromise our faith in order to gain the world's acceptance. If we stand firm with a Christlike and loving spirit, the time will come when we'll hear, "You are a prince among us. We honor and respect you because God lives in you."

Such respect is not given easily. It must be earned. Abraham spent decades among the pagan Hittites, demonstrating godly integrity and proving the reality of his walk with God. In the end, he won their trust and respect, and they treated him as a prince.

## NO MORE DEATH OR SORROW

The pagans offered Abraham a burial cave on a plot of ground free of charge. But Abraham would not consent to own one inch of real estate that he had not properly paid for. He courteously insisted that he would take nothing from the world. Whatever he had must come from God. So Abraham insisted on paying a fair market price for the cave in which to bury his beloved Sarah.

The New Testament book of Hebrews tells us that none of the men and women of faith in the Old Testament ever received the promise for which they waited. They spent their lives moving toward it, but the fulfillment of the promise always lay ahead of them, in the distant future. God calls us to maintain this same expectant attitude. Like the saints of the Old Testament, we are pilgrims and strangers passing through this land. The fulfillment of God's promise to us, the city of light that lies ahead of us, remains in our future as well.

If you are a student of history, you may be aware of the persecution of the Scottish Covenanters during the 1600s. The Covenanters were early Protestants, the forerunners of the Presbyterians, and they opposed the oppressive state church of England, Scotland, and Ireland. These Protestants were hounded and hunted throughout the lands and hills of Scotland. When captured, the Covenanters were imprisoned, hanged, drowned, or burned alive as martyrs for their faith.

Samuel Rutherford was one of those who stood firm for his faith against the wrath of King James VI of Scotland. Rutherford's letters preserve the thoughts and feelings of a man who was totally committed to Jesus Christ. As Rutherford lay dying in the prison at St. Andrews, Scotland, the king sent a messenger to summon him before the court to answer charges of high heresy. When the messenger delivered the summons to Rutherford, he replied, "Go tell your master I have a summons from a higher court. Ere this message reaches him, I'll be where few kings or great folk ever come."

Thus Rutherford rebuked a king of the earth who arrogantly thought he could summon a man of God, a man of faith. It is the response of a believer whose eyes are fixed on the city of God, not on the transitory shadows of this world.

Abraham was promised a land, a nation, a multitude of descendants. At the end of his life, he owned nothing but a burial cave. This does not mean the promise of God was invalid. Abraham died knowing that the promise was still to be fulfilled.

All we can ever own here on earth is what Abraham owned in the end: a burial ground in which our remains may rest until the resurrection. If all we have lived for is the acquisition of wealth and fame and earthly power, then we are doomed one day to lose everything. All the things this world has to offer will be stripped from us when we are lowered into the grave.

The book of Ecclesiastes tells us that we were created for everlasting life with him. The Lord God "has made everything beautiful in its time. He has also set eternity in the hearts of men; yet they cannot fathom what God has done from beginning to end" (Ecclesiastes 3:11). He did not create us to be trapped in this tiny span of space and time. We were never meant to be satisfied with a few short decades of life, followed by endless, silent eons of death. God put eternity in our hearts.

The great tragedy of the human race is that so many people settle for far less. They set their hearts on things that do not last and do not satisfy. As the apostle Paul wisely said, "Set your minds on things above, not on earthly things" (Colossians 3:2). When our minds are focused on the things that last, the things that matter for eternity, we have strength and peace, even in times of shadow and grief.

Even at times when our world is shaken, we have a foundation that cannot be shaken. Our faith rests upon the finished work of our Lord Jesus Christ. Our hearts have been captured by Him, and He will never let us go. Our eyes are fixed on the light that streams from the city beyond, and we press on toward that beautiful place where there is no more death, no more sorrow, and no more tears.

# 18
# HERE COMES THE BRIDE

*Genesis 24*

Daniel Webster was a nineteenth-century American attorney and states-man. While a young lawyer in Portsmouth, New Hampshire, he fell in love with a minister's daughter, Grace Fletcher. On one occasion during their courtship, he visited Grace at her parents' home and helped her by holding skeins of silk so that she could unknot the threads.

Finally, he said, "Grace, we have been engaged in untying knots. I would like to tie a knot with you that would last a lifetime." Then he reached into Grace's sewing basket and withdrew a length of ribbon. He began tying a knot in the ribbon; then he handed the ribbon to Grace. Without saying a word, she finished tying the knot that Webster had started. With that little ceremony, they became engaged.

Daniel Webster and Grace Fletcher were married in 1808. Their marriage did indeed last a lifetime, though, as it turned out, Grace's lifetime was cut short in 1828, after scarcely twenty years of marriage.

Webster survived his beloved wife by almost twenty-five years. After his death, his sons found a box marked "Precious Documents" among his personal papers. It contained the letters he had exchanged with Grace during their courtship—and the knotted ribbon, never untied.

The beauty of romance is timeless. In the previous chapter, we wit-nessed the conclusion of the romance between Abraham and Sarah. But here, in Genesis 24, we come to the beginning of a new romance—the story of Isaac and Rebekah. It's one of those tales we have known since childhood—truly one of the most beautiful stories in the Old Testament. It's a romance story rich in beautiful imagery and poetic grace. Yet it is also a story, like all the other incidences in Abraham's life, rich in meaning for our Christian lives.

## A PICTURE OF PENTECOST

We previously saw how the story of Abraham's willingness to offer Isaac as a sacrifice is a profound illustration of the Father's heart. In that story, we begin to understand what it meant for the Father to offer up His Son on the cross at Calvary. Through the anguish of Abraham, we can better understand the anguish of the Father.

Indeed, we have seen how each of the incidences in Abraham's life has become an illustration of some New Testament truth. With this precedent in mind, we approach the story of Rebekah and Isaac, not only seeing this story as the account of a lovely romance but also seeking the deeper truths God has embedded there. What New Testament truth does this Old Testament story illustrate for us? It is a picture of Pentecost, when God the Father sent the Holy Spirit to the church, as recorded in Acts 2.

At the beginning of Genesis 24, Abraham summons an unnamed servant and commissions him to go to a far country to obtain a bride for his son, Isaac. The servant is to select a young woman and invite her to come back to Abraham's house, where the son waits to claim his bride for himself. How do these events relate to the New Testament event known as Pentecost?

Let's look at the characters in the story and see what they symbolize. First, there is Abraham. He stands for God the Father. Abraham's son, Isaac, clearly stands for God's own Son, the Lord Jesus. And the servant? He symbolizes the Holy Spirit, whom God the Father, on the day of Pentecost, sent into the world. The mission of the Spirit: to call people to faith in the Lord, to win a bride for Christ. That has been the task of the Spirit for two thousand years. Meanwhile, the Son waits to receive His bride, the church.

The thrilling and joyful moment when the Son claims His bride is pictured for us in the book of Revelation:

> "Let us rejoice and be glad
>    and give him glory!
> For the wedding of the Lamb has come,
>    and his bride has made herself ready.
> Fine linen, bright and clean,
>    was given her to wear."
> (Fine linen stands for the righteous acts of the saints.)
> Then the angel said to me, "Write: 'Blessed are those who are invited to the wedding supper of the Lamb!' " And he added, "These are the true words of God." (Revelation 19:7–9)

When we study God's Word, we do not want to miss any morsel of truth that He has placed there for us to find. Read the Old Testament with this perspective, and you will find that the Spirit of God will open a floodgate of insight and wisdom for your life.

## THE COMMAND OF THE FATHER

I'm sure you can remember a time when you felt the calling of the Spirit of God. You remember, in effect, how God courted and called you both by revealing to you the Lord's attractiveness and appeal and by revealing to you your own utter need for Him. You were called to love someone you have never seen, and as the Spirit, the servant of the Father, called to you, your heart answered. You felt the urge to begin a journey to a new country, where you would at last meet the Son, who waited for you in His Father's house.

If you read this story carefully, you will see that the central character is not the bride, Rebekah. The passage does not record her thoughts and feelings in much detail. She plays a secondary role in this drama. The spotlight is on Abraham's servant. He is the central character because he represents the Holy Spirit.

God has given us, as Christians, the privilege and responsibility of serving as His instruments to call His bride out of the world and into a love relationship with the Son. In our own power, we can do nothing to achieve this mission. But God has given us His Spirit, and it is the Spirit who works through us to call the Lord's bride out of the world. In this way, we clearly see that this story is a beautiful picture of the process of evangelism, from the day of Pentecost right up to the present day.

Now let's look at the text of Genesis 24. We will see how the process of bringing others to Christ begins with the command of God the Father:

> Abraham was now old and well advanced in years, and the LORD had blessed him in every way. He said to the chief servant in his household, the one in charge of all that he had, "Put your hand under my thigh. I want you to swear by the LORD, the God of heaven and the God of earth, that you will not get a wife for my son from the daughters of the Canaanites, among whom I am living, but will go to my country and my own relatives and get a wife for my son Isaac."
>
> The servant asked him, "What if the woman is unwilling to come back with me to this land? Shall I then take your son back to the country you came from?"
>
> "Make sure that you do not take my son back there," Abraham said. "The LORD, the God of heaven, who brought me out of my father's household and my native land and who spoke to me and promised me on oath, saying, 'To your offspring I will give this land'—he will send his angel before you so that you can get a wife for my son from there. If the woman is unwilling to come back with you, then you will be released from this oath of mine. Only do not take my son back there." So the servant put his hand under the thigh of his master Abraham and swore an oath to him concerning this matter. (Genesis 24:1–9)

The initiative is Abraham's. He sends his servant to perform this task, and he binds the servant with an oath. The ritual act of placing the hand under the thigh was a Middle Eastern custom involving the belief that the loins are the source of life. For the servant, this act represented being bound in the very deepest part of his life. This was a solemn oath.

Applying these facets of the story to our lives, we see God the Father standing in the place of Abraham, asking every servant, including you and me, to give himself fully to this task. Notice that the servant is not named. I believe that this is so that you and I can place our own names here and see ourselves as the servant of the Father. God the Father has commissioned us to go out into the world in the power of the Spirit and bring back a bride for His Son.

## A STRANGE RESTRICTION

Notice the restriction Abraham places on the servant: "Make sure that you do not take my son back there." Because of this restriction, the servant must go into that far country and convince a prospective bride and her family to trust him, to allow him to take the young woman away to a distant land and marry her to someone they've never met. How will this young woman's family know the servant is telling the truth? It would be so much easier if the servant could take Isaac with him, and he could point to Isaac and say, "Here is the young man himself."

Abraham has placed a restriction on the servant that makes his task all the more difficult. This restriction is difficult to understand if we view this story as merely a narrative of ancient events. But once we view this story as an Old Testament picture of New Testament truth, this restriction makes perfect sense.

God the Father sends us, His servants, out into the world with instructions to tell people about a Son they cannot see. Moreover, He has given us the task of persuading men and women to commit their lives to this unseen Son. Clearly, it would be easier to persuade people if we could present the Son to them in the flesh. It would be easier to prove the claims of Christ if we could point to the wound in His side and the nail prints in His hands and feet.

But like Abraham's servant, we have been given a task with restrictions. From a natural perspective, this task seems impossible. But the

Lord has sent His own Spirit to be with us. In a way we can't fully understand, the Spirit of God makes Jesus Christ more real to the human heart than if He were standing among us in human flesh.

There is an imaginative and fictional account of the Lord's ascension into heaven. Upon his arrival, He was met by the angels. One of them said, "Lord, what is your plan for spreading the gospel throughout the world?"

The Lord said, "I've called twelve men to be my disciples, and I have taught them and lived with them for three years. They must carry on the work."

"But, Lord," the angel said, "what if they fail? What is your plan then?"

The Lord replied, "I have no other plan."

The point of this story is true, but it leaves out one important truth: The total responsibility for evangelizing the world does not rest on the shoulders of human beings. That responsibility belongs to the Holy Spirit. We are the tools in His hands. If we will obediently allow Him to use us as He pleases, the world will be reached. Like Abraham's servant, the Spirit will find the bride and bring her back to the Son.

This is the missing dimension of much of the evangelistic effort of our time. Christians hear the command of God to go into all the world and preach the gospel, but they try to obey that command as if it all depends on them. They neglect the crucial role of the Holy Spirit. As a result, many Christians have great zeal for the gospel but little knowledge in how to present it and little sensitivity to their hearers.

You are familiar with the image of the fever-eyed religious fanatic who buttonholes his victims, trying to intimidate them into receiving Christ. At the other extreme are those stammering, flustered Christians who know they should witness to others but have no idea how to go about it. These two opposing kinds of Christians have one thing in common: Both fail to rely on the power of the Holy Spirit. Both operate completely in the flesh, and that is why they fail.

The secret to effective witnessing and evangelism is the Holy Spirit. When we rely on Him to guide us, empower us, and speak through us, God can use us to reach the world for Him.

## STEP 1: EXPECTATION

This passage in Genesis gives us a five-step approach to sharing the gospel with the people around us. Let's look at each step in turn. The first step is expectation. This step is illustrated for us in the next few verses:

> Then the servant took ten of his master's camels and left, taking with him all kinds of good things from his master. He set out for Aram Naharaim and made his way to the town of Nahor. He had the camels kneel down near the well outside the town; it was toward evening, the time the women go out to draw water.
>
> Then he prayed, "O Lord, God of my master Abraham, give me success today, and show kindness to my master Abraham. See, I am standing beside this spring, and the daughters of the townspeople are coming out to draw water. May it be that when I say to a girl, 'Please let down your jar that I may have a drink,' and she says, 'Drink, and I'll water your camels too'—let her be the one you have chosen for your servant Isaac. By this I will know that you have shown kindness to my master." (Genesis 24:10–14)

Abraham's servant was a man of faith. He prayed, fully expecting God to work. He didn't go into that distant land and say, "It's all up to me. Somehow, I have to find this young lady, make sure she's the right one, and persuade her to come back with me and marry someone she's never met. How will I do that?" This servant knew he had an invisible partner. He expected God to prepare the way for him.

And so it is with you and me. God has commissioned us to take the gospel into the world, but He has not left us on our own. He goes before us, preparing the way. Evangelism is not a function of human persuasion but of a divine call. Converting others is God's work, not ours. Our job is to be available and obedient, and to look for indications that His Spirit is at work in the lives of those around us.

Remember the example of the servant: He began with prayer. His prayer revealed that he fully expected God to work. In his simple prayer, the servant asked God to make the way clear and to reveal to him the young lady God had chosen. I always try to remember this approach in my personal witnessing.

When I am on an airplane or sitting in a waiting room, I try to be alert to the people around me. I ask God to tell me if there is someone He wants me to talk to. Sometimes, I sense that God wants me to read or study. But often, my attention is drawn to one individual. I ask God to give me the words to say; then I say what comes to mind. More often than not, I discover that this is a person God has been preparing. This individual has been going through a time of struggle or questioning and is ripe to hear the good news of Jesus Christ.

In such situations, I never feel that the burden is on me. The Spirit alone does the work of evangelizing. I am simply an instrument in His hands.

## STEP 2: CONFIRMATION

This brings us to the second step, confirmation, which is illustrated in the actions of Abraham's servant. We see this step in the next few verses:

> Before he had finished praying, Rebekah came out with her jar on her shoulder. She was the daughter of Bethuel son of Milcah, who was the wife of Abraham's brother Nahor. The girl was very beautiful, a virgin; no man had ever lain with her. She went down to the spring, filled her jar and came up again.
>
> The servant hurried to meet her and said, "Please give me a little water from your jar."
>
> "Drink, my lord," she said, and quickly lowered the jar to her hands and gave him a drink.
>
> After she had given him a drink, she said, "I'll draw water for your camels too, until they have finished drinking." So she quickly emptied her jar into the trough, ran back to the well to draw more water, and drew enough for all his camels. Without saying a word, the man watched her closely to learn whether

or not the LORD had made his journey successful. (Genesis 24:15–21)

Now here is confirmation. It is immediate and explicit. The passage tells us, "Before he had finished praying, Rebekah came out with her jar on her shoulder." This servant's prayer was answered even before he had finished praying.

The passage adds, "Without saying a word, the man watched her closely." He gazed at her in silence. Perhaps he was amazed that the answer to his prayer had arrived so suddenly. Or he might have been astonished at this young lady's willingness to go out of her way to do a favor for a stranger and his livestock. I am told that a camel can drink twenty-one gallons of water at one sitting, and the text says that she repeatedly went to the well and brought water back to the trough, "enough for all his camels." Rebekah was willing to work very hard. No wonder he gazed at her in silence.

Of course, we're also told that the servant gazed at her to find out whether the Lord had made his journey successful or not. "Lord, is she the one?" the servant silently asked. There could be no question. She did everything he asked of the Lord as a sign.

I should add that I don't believe we should ask for particular signs from God in every case. Sometimes Christians will invent signs in their own minds as an excuse for not doing what they know they should do. They may pass up an opportunity to witness or serve some person in Christ's name, rationalizing, "Well, the Lord didn't give me a sign that I should do it." Usually, the only confirmation we need is some little, normal, commonsense indication that an individual is open to talking about the gospel.

I once waited in the airport at Honolulu for a plane to Tokyo. It was early in the morning, and the airport was nearly deserted. I bought a newspaper and read an account of a young Filipino eye doctor who had come to Honolulu for a medical conference. He was a gifted surgeon who had perfected an operation no one else had done, and he had been demonstrating it to a gathering of fellow surgeons. Eventually, I boarded my plane and sat down to await takeoff.

After I took my seat, another passenger sat down beside me, a Filipino man. We chatted, and I learned that he was a surgeon. "Oh?" I said. "What sort of surgery do you perform?"

"Eye surgery," he said.

The instant he said that, I knew he had to be the surgeon featured in the newspaper article. I asked him if he was that man, and he said yes, he was. So we talked, and the discussion came around to the Word of God. In the course of the flight, I gave him a New Testament.

I went on to Tokyo, then flew to Manila and looked him up. He told me he had been reading the New Testament every day and had given his heart to Jesus Christ.

The Lord gave me confirmation that I should speak to this man—not in the form of a miraculous sign but in a little commonplace coincidence. It was, I'm convinced, a coincidence arranged by God, as if He wanted me to know, "Here is a man whose heart I've been preparing, and here you are beside him."

The Lord can do wonderful things for us if we are alert to indications that His Spirit is already at work, bringing the circumstances and people together.

## STEP 3: PREPARATION

After confirmation comes the third step, which is preparation. The passage continues:

> When the camels had finished drinking, the man took out a gold nose ring weighing a beka and two gold bracelets weighing ten shekels. Then he asked, "Whose daughter are you? Please tell me, is there room in your father's house for us to spend the night?"
>
> She answered him, "I am the daughter of Bethuel, the son that Milcah bore to Nahor." And she added, "We have plenty of straw and fodder, as well as room for you to spend the night."
>
> Then the man bowed down and worshiped the LORD, saying, "Praise be to the LORD, the God of my master Abraham, who has not abandoned his kindness and faithfulness to my

master. As for me, the LORD has led me on the journey to the house of my master's relatives." (Genesis 24:22–27)

Abraham's servant had no doubt: The Lord had led him to the right young woman. But he approached her with care. He did not immediately start talking about Isaac and tell her that God had chosen her to marry a young man who lived in a distant land. That might have frightened her off! Instead, the servant wisely arranged to meet with the young lady's family, so that he could prepare her and her family to be receptive to the proposal he'd come to make. Moreover, he invested time in worship to the Lord, bathing the entire matter in prayer and thanksgiving.

The step of preparation is vitally important. Sometimes in our zeal and impatience, we jump into a situation with both feet. We frighten people and cause them to back away from us. Even though we have expected the Lord to work, and even though we sense God's confirmation, it's still important to make adequate preparation, especially when presenting the good news to other people.

Instead of sharing the gospel with your neighbor over the back fence in five minutes, consider inviting your neighbor over for dinner and an evening of conversation and relationship building. Show your neighbors that you truly care about them and want to get to know them. That is how you make preparation to share the good news.

## STEP 4: PRESENTATION

We see the next step, presentation, illustrated for us in the next section, as the servant now meets with the family of this young woman:

So he said, "I am Abraham's servant. The LORD has blessed my master abundantly, and he has become wealthy. He has given him sheep and cattle, silver and gold, menservants and maidservants, and camels and donkeys. My master's wife Sarah has borne him a son in her old age, and he has given him everything he owns. And my master made me swear an oath, and said, 'You must not get a wife for my son from the daughters of the Canaanites, in whose land I live, but go to my father's family and to my own clan, and get a wife for my son.'

"Then I asked my master, 'What if the woman will not come back with me?'

"He replied, 'The LORD, before whom I have walked, will send his angel with you and make your journey a success, so that you can get a wife for my son from my own clan and from my father's family. Then, when you go to my clan, you will be released from my oath even if they refuse to give her to you—you will be released from my oath.'

"When I came to the spring today, I said, 'O LORD, God of my master Abraham, if you will, please grant success to the journey on which I have come. See, I am standing beside this spring; if a maiden comes out to draw water and I say to her, "Please let me drink a little water from your jar," and if she says to me, "Drink, and I'll draw water for your camels too," let her be the one the LORD has chosen for my master's son.'

"Before I finished praying in my heart, Rebekah came out, with her jar on her shoulder. She went down to the spring and drew water, and I said to her, 'Please give me a drink.'

"She quickly lowered her jar from her shoulder and said, 'Drink, and I'll water your camels too.' So I drank, and she watered the camels also.

"I asked her, 'Whose daughter are you?'

"She said, 'The daughter of Bethuel son of Nahor, whom Milcah bore to him.'

"Then I put the ring in her nose and the bracelets on her arms, and I bowed down and worshiped the LORD. I praised the LORD, the God of my master Abraham, who had led me on the right road to get the granddaughter of my master's brother for his son. Now if you will show kindness and faithfulness to my master, tell me; and if not, tell me, so I may know which way to turn."

Laban and Bethuel answered, "This is from the LORD; we can say nothing to you one way or the other. Here is Rebekah;

take her and go, and let her become the wife of your master's son, as the LORD has directed."

When Abraham's servant heard what they said, he bowed down to the ground before the LORD. Then the servant brought out gold and silver jewelry and articles of clothing and gave them to Rebekah; he also gave costly gifts to her brother and to her mother. (Genesis 24:34–53)

Notice that the servant leaves nothing out. He is forthright and candid. He begins by describing Abraham's wealth, flocks, herds, silver, gold, servants, and livestock. Why are these details important? Because all of this constitutes the inheritance of the son, Isaac. Next, the servant recounts how God led him along the way. In other words, he gives his personal testimony. He ends by presenting to Rebekah the gifts Isaac had sent along—the merest sampling of the riches he was offering to her.

What is the significance of this story to our lives? The answer lies in the words and deeds of the servant. Notice that everything he says is focused on the attributes of his master, Abraham, and Abraham's son, Isaac. In the same way, when we witness to others, our focus should be on God the Father and on His Son, Jesus Christ.

Some Christians, in their witnessing, lose sight of what is truly important. They think, "This individual is a sinner! Look at all of these bad habits! I need to convince this person to change his life!" This approach to witnessing rarely moves anyone closer to Christ. In fact, it usually drives people away.

When we witness to non-Christians, it's not our job to change the way they live. It's not our job to convince people to stop drinking, smoking, or swearing. Our job is to tell people about Christ. Once people have made a decision for Christ, the Holy Spirit will convict them of sins and harmful habits.

## STEP 5: INVITATION

The fifth and final step is the actual invitation. Once again, Abraham's servant gives us insight into how God wishes us to invite non-Christians to commit their lives to the Lord:

Then he and the men who were with him ate and drank and spent the night there.

When they got up the next morning, he said, "Send me on my way to my master."

But her brother and her mother replied, "Let the girl remain with us ten days or so; then you may go."

But he said to them, "Do not detain me, now that the LORD has granted success to my journey. Send me on my way so I may go to my master."

Then they said, "Let's call the girl and ask her about it." So they called Rebekah and asked her, "Will you go with this man?"

"I will go," she said.

So they sent their sister Rebekah on her way, along with her nurse and Abraham's servant and his men. And they blessed Rebekah and said to her,

> "Our sister, may you increase
> to thousands upon thousands;
> may your offspring possess
> the gates of their enemies."

Then Rebekah and her maids got ready and mounted their camels and went back with the man. So the servant took Rebekah and left. (Genesis 24:54–61)

## HERE IS THE INVITATION

Both this young woman and her family had to be persuaded. Even after Rebekah's father, Bethuel, agreed to the marriage, her brother and mother hesitated. When they tried to delay Rebekah's departure, the servant gently but firmly rejected their appeal. The Lord had blessed the arrangement, he said, so there was no reason for delay.

This must have been a difficult decision for Rebekah. It's clear that she was the prized and protected jewel of the household. It was hard for her to accept the idea that she was now going to be whisked away from her home and taken to a far land to become the bride of an utter stranger. Yet there was something about the servant's forthright presentation of the offer that had won her heart. Rebekah was ready to go.

This story reveals a deep truth regarding the presentation of the good news of Jesus Christ. We need to always be aware that, when we invite people to accept Jesus as Lord and Savior, it's not an easy choice. We are asking individuals to make a revolutionary and life-changing commitment. We need to make sure they clearly understand what it means to be a Christian.

## LOVE AT FIRST SIGHT

The work of the Trinity is evident throughout this story. It begins with the command of the Father, proceeds with the work of the Spirit, and ends with the communion with the Son. This is a delightful scene where heart meets heart:

> Now Isaac had come from Beer Lahai Roi, for he was living in the Negev. He went out to the field one evening to meditate, and as he looked up, he saw camels approaching. Rebekah also looked up and saw Isaac. She got down from her camel and asked the servant, "Who is that man in the field coming to meet us?"
>
> "He is my master," the servant answered. So she took her veil and covered herself.
>
> Then the servant told Isaac all he had done. Isaac brought her into the tent of his mother Sarah, and he married Rebekah. So she became his wife, and he loved her; and Isaac was comforted after his mother's death. (Genesis 24:62–67)

Throughout this account, the central figure of the story has been the servant. In these final verses, his work is done. As the servant and Rebekah approach the field where Isaac has gone to meditate, Isaac and Rebekah see each other for the first time. She asks, "Who is that man in the field?" Her heart knows—but she wants to be sure.

The servant speaks his final line: "He is my master."

This is a profoundly significant statement. These are the very words that should culminate our presentation of the gospel: "Jesus is Lord. He is my master." That is the goal of evangelism. We seek to introduce others to the one who is our Master.

Up to that point, we share our personal testimony. We tell the story of what God has done in our lives. But a moment arrives when we must stop telling our story. We must point the listener to Jesus and say, "He is my master. Why don't you talk directly with Him? Tell Him what's on your heart."

What did Rebekah and Isaac talk about? Was Rebekah shy or bold? Was Isaac awkward or confident? We don't know. The passage does not tell us. She may have said, "My friends call me Becky." He might have answered, "You can call me Ike." All we know is that it was a tender and beautiful first meeting. It was love at first sight.

And what of the servant? He departs, leaving the young lovers to get acquainted. His heart is undoubtedly full of joy and praise to God. He has fulfilled his mission. He has returned with a bride for Isaac—a bride handpicked by God.

The joy this servant felt is much like the joy you and I feel when God uses us to share His good news with others. The prayer of his heart was like the praise and worship we offer to God when we have a hand in leading another soul to Christ. In the New Testament, John the Baptist described this inner tingle of joy and praise when he said: "The bride belongs to the bridegroom. The friend who attends the bridegroom waits and listens for him, and is full of joy when he hears the bridegroom's voice. That joy is mine, and it is now complete" (John 3:29–30).

There is no joy like that joy. There is no greater thrill than the excitement of being used by God to bring one more person into his kingdom. Jesus is our Master. We are His servants. And the story of Abraham, Isaac, Rebekah, and the faithful servant is our story as well.

# 19

# THE ABUNDANT ENTRANCE

*Genesis 25:1–8*

I have officiated at more funerals than I could possibly count. Every funeral is an occasion for sadness and mourning. But many a funeral I have conducted was also filled with great hope, fond memories, and even a note of joy, because it was a celebration of a life well-lived and triumphantly completed. For the believer, death is a transition, not a destination; it is a comma, not a period.

As we come to the final chapter in our journey alongside Abraham, we see that his funeral was such an occasion. Yes, there was sadness and mourning. But the death of Abraham was truly the completion of a triumphant life of faith. He set the pattern of faith for us all. No more fitting epitaph could be written them than the one written by the apostle James in his New Testament letter: "And the scripture was fulfilled that says, 'Abraham believed God, and it was credited to him as righteousness,' and he was called God's friend" (James 2:23).

In all of Scripture, no other human being is referred to as the friend of God. Abraham alone bears that title. There are few people in history more respected and renowned than Abraham. He is revered by the three great monotheistic religions, Christianity, Judaism, and Islam. Wherever his name is mentioned, he is regarded as a man of great integrity, honor, vision, and faithfulness to his God.

Yet, as we have walked alongside this man of faith through each episode of his life, we've seen that he was someone with whom you and I can easily identify. Abraham was no plaster saint. Though he was a great role model of faith and faithfulness, Abraham was flawed and human. He had his moments of moral weakness, lying, selfishness, self-deception, and failure of nerve. But God, in His grace, patiently restored and reinstated Abraham after each failure.

One of the great lessons of Abraham's life is that this same grace is available to you and me.

## THE FRUITFULNESS OF ABRAHAM'S LIFE

The rich and fruitful coda of Abraham's life is summarized for us in the opening verses of Genesis 25:

> Abraham took another wife, whose name was Keturah. She bore him Zimran, Jokshan, Medan, Midian, Ishbak and Shuah. Jokshan was the father of Sheba and Dedan; the descendants of Dedan were the Asshurites, the Letushites and the Leummites. The sons of Midian were Ephah, Epher, Hanoch, Abida and Eldaah. All these were descendants of Keturah. (Genesis 25:1–4)

At the beginning of Abraham's adventure of faith, when he was setting out from Ur of the Chaldeans, God promised him that he would become the father of many nations. We have already seen how this promise was fulfilled through Isaac and Ishmael. Now, Abraham's second wife, Keturah, bears six more sons, all of whom founded nations. God' promise was literally fulfilled, and through Abraham all the nations of the earth have been blessed and continue to be blessed.

The New Testament book of Hebrews tells us that by the time Isaac was born, Abraham was no longer able to father children. He was too old, at age one hundred, to be physically capable of impregnating his wife. From any medical and fertility standpoint, Abraham's body was "as good as dead." Yet, the writer to the Hebrews concludes, Abraham produced "descendants as numerous as the stars in the sky and as countless as the sand on the seashore" (Hebrews 11:11–12). So it was a miracle of sheer grace that Isaac was born.

How, then, was Abraham able to have more children by his second wife, Keturah? Evidently, when his youthful powers were restored to him so that he could become the father of Isaac, that same youthful fertility remained with him. As a result, six more boys were born to Abraham after Sarah's death. So Abraham had a total of eight sons— Ishmael, Isaac, and his six sons by Keturah. These eight sons speak of the fruitfulness of Abraham's life.

## THE SECRET TO A FRUITFUL CHRISTIAN LIFE

Throughout our journey with Abraham, we have seen how these Old Testament events take on a deeper significance when viewed through the lens of the New Testament. This principle holds true right to the end of Abraham's life. The eight children of Abraham are a beautiful picture of the fruitfulness of a life that is led by the Holy Spirit. Like Abraham, you and I can have many children in a spiritual sense.

The apostle Peter wrote about spiritual fruitfulness in his second letter:

> His divine power has given us everything we need for life and godliness through our knowledge of him who called us by his own glory and goodness. Through these he has given us his very great and precious promises, so that through them you may participate in the divine nature and escape the corruption in the world caused by evil desires.
>
> For this very reason, make every effort to add to your faith goodness; and to goodness, knowledge; and to knowledge, self-control; and to self-control, perseverance; and to perseverance, godliness; and to godliness, brotherly kindness; and to brotherly kindness, love. For if you possess these qualities in increasing measure, they will keep you from being ineffective and unproductive in your knowledge of our Lord Jesus Christ. (2 Peter 1:3–8)

Notice that Peter lists eight marks of the fruitful Christian life: faith, goodness, knowledge, self-control, perseverance, godliness, brotherly kindness, and love. I wonder if it is mere coincidence that these eight characteristics correspond to the number of Abraham's sons.

Peter begins with *faith*, a supreme ingredient of the spiritual life. Whatever his circumstances, Abraham had complete confidence in God. That is a realistic definition of faith: complete trust in God regardless of circumstances. By contrast, unbelief is trusting in circumstances regardless of God. Is your faith in God or in your circumstances?

You and I cannot truly be Christians if we do not believe God regardless of our circumstances. When our lives become turbulent and filled with obstacles, when all of the supporting pillars of our lives are shattered and we have nothing to cling to but the promises of God, what does faith really mean? It means that we believe God is telling us the truth about life, even when His promises seem remote and hard to believe in.

When Abraham and Sarah were far beyond childbearing years, God's promise of a son and of many descendants must have seemed like a bad joke. Despite a lapse of faith which resulted in the birth of Ishmael, Abraham renewed his faith in God and chose to believe that God was telling the truth about his life, regardless of his circumstances.

Next, Peter tells us to add *goodness* to our faith. This word *goodness* could also be rendered "virtue" or "moral character." Abraham was a man of virtue and character. He displayed the virtue of courage when he armed his servants and set out to rescue Lot from the clutches of the kings from the east. Elsewhere in the narrative of Abraham's life, we saw him demonstrate virtues of obedience, compassion, wisdom, justice, and more. Virtue is a key ingredient of a fruitful Christian life.

Peter goes on to tell us that we must also add *knowledge* to our lives. All knowledge is from God; ultimate knowledge lies not in any human textbook but in the revelation from God's Word. The apostle Paul tells us that knowledge of God makes our lives fruitful for Him: "And we pray this in order that you may live a life worthy of the Lord and may please him in every way: bearing fruit in every good work, growing in the knowledge of God" (Colossians 1:10).

Peter says that to knowledge we must add *self-control.* Abraham faced many obstacles and great opposition in his life, yet we never see him out of control. As Christians, we represent Christ. His name is stamped upon our lives. So everything we do reflects on Him. The character we show to the world must be a reflection of His character. When other people attack us, criticize us, or anger us, we must remember that we belong to God. He is the Lord of our lives, and we must place our emotions and our responses under His control. To be God-controlled is to be self-controlled. To be ruled by the impulses of the self is to be out of control.

Hudson Taylor, the pioneer missionary to China, once chartered a small boat to take him downriver to an appointment. As he stood on the wharf, waiting to board the boat, an expensively dressed Chinese official approached. The official had a couple of men with him. Ignoring Taylor, the official asked the driver, "Where are you going?"

The boat driver pointed to Hudson and said, "This foreigner has charted the boat. I am taking him downriver."

With a wave of disdain, the official said, "Leave him. I'm taking the boat."

Taylor later recalled feeling a surge of anger. He was so offended by the official's arrogance that he experienced an almost irresistible urge to shove the man into the river—but then he felt the restraint of the Holy Spirit.

Turning to the official, Taylor said, "I know you regard me as nothing but a white foreign devil, but I have chartered this boat and it is mine by right. The Jesus that is in me kept me from pushing you into the river just now. The Lord did not send me here to push people into the river but to win them for Christ. I need this boat, and I have already paid to use it, but I invite you to come with me as my guest—free of charge."

The official was stunned by this invitation and by Hudson Taylor's demonstration of Christian self-control. He accepted Taylor's offer, and the two men conversed about spiritual things all the way to their destination.

230 / FRIEND OF GOD

## THE EIGHTFOLD FRUITFUL LIFE

To self-control, says Peter, we are to add *perseverance*. Another word for perseverance is patience. Have you ever noticed that God cannot give us patience? He can only teach it. There is no use praying for patience. If you do, the Lord will send you tribulation, because "tribulation worketh patience" (Romans 5:3 KJV). So be careful what you pray for!

Consider for a moment the patience and perseverance of Abraham. He waited twenty-five years for a son. The promise had been given, but it was not fulfilled until a quarter of a century later. As we look at Abraham's life, we see how, again and again, the Spirit of God instructed this man in the way of patience.

Most of us are like the little girl who banged her cup on her highchair and demanded a glass of milk. Her mother sternly said, "You need patience, young lady!" The child replied, "I've got patience, but I don't have any milk!" We all need patience for those times when the thing we desire doesn't arrive on our timetable.

Next, Peter says that we must add *godliness* to our perseverance. What is godliness? It is an awareness of God's presence in our daily lives. Abraham was the friend of God because he was a godly man, a man who was continually aware of and sensitive to God's presence. He was the man with the tent and the altar. He built an altar and worshiped God wherever he went. Godliness is expressed in the apostle Paul's phrase, "whatever you do, do it all for the glory of God" (1 Corinthians 10:31b).

To godliness, Peter says, add *brotherly kindness*. This means that we are to share with one another through hospitality, words of encouragement, and acts of generosity. Such actions are practical demonstrations of the Spirit at work.

Finally, we are to add *love*. Authentic Christian love is the most unmistakable fruit of the Spirit. As Paul wrote in one of the most beautiful passages of Scripture:

> Love is patient, love is kind. It does not envy, it does not boast, it is not proud. It is not rude, it is not self-seeking, it is

not easily angered, it keeps no record of wrongs. Love does not delight in evil but rejoices with the truth. It always protects, always trusts, always hopes, always perseveres.

Love never fails. . . .

And now these three remain: faith, hope and love. But the greatest of these is love. (1 Corinthians 13:4–8a, 13)

This kind of selfless, righteous, forgiving, accepting love is the only love worthy of the name. It is the greatest of all the fruit of the Spirit. If your life is characterized by genuine Christlike love, you are well on your way to demonstrating all the fruit of the Spirit, because love is the foundation of all the other virtues of the Christian life.

This is the eightfold fruitful life, suggested by Abraham's eight sons. These eight beautiful virtues define what it means to walk in the Spirit.

## PRACTICAL FORESIGHT

Abraham has arrived at the entrance to the kingdom of the Father. Even now, as he stands at the doorstep of eternity, he takes time to ensure that he leaves no important practical details undone: "Abraham left everything he owned to Isaac. But while he was still living, he gave gifts to the sons of his concubines and sent them away from his son Isaac to the land of the east" (Genesis 25:5–6).

Abraham never forgot that Isaac was the son of promise and the divinely chosen heir. To protect the inheritance of God, Abraham wisely made provision for his other sons so that they would not destroy what God was doing in Isaac's life.

Throughout Scripture, Isaac is a symbol of Christ. We read that Abraham gave all that he had to Isaac, just as the Father gives all that He has to the Son. Abraham symbolically represents a life that is so Christ-centered it seeks to keep away anything that might harm the inheritance. He demonstrated practical foresight in dealing with the other sons.

The text tells us that Abraham sent the other sons away from his son Isaac and toward "the land of the east." Why is this detail significant? When Abraham first came into the land, he pitched his tent between Ai and Bethel, with Ai on the east and Bethel on the west. Ai means "ruin"; Bethel means "the house or place of God." Isaac was given the inheritance in the west, in the place of God, while the other sons were sent out to the east—that is, to the place of ruin. The place of ruin is a picture of the natural life, which is our inheritance from Adam.

In much the same way, the Bible urges us to show practical foresight in order to protect our spiritual inheritance. For example, Psalm 119:11 tells us that the best preventative against sin is to memorize and meditate on Scripture—to hide God's Word in our hearts. Paul, in Galatians 5:16–17, advises us to continually "live by the Spirit" in order to prevent falling prey to the "desires of the sinful nature." In 2 Timothy 2:16, he tells us to "avoid godless chatter" because it leads us into ungodliness. And Peter urges us to be "self-controlled and alert" because Satan, our enemy, "prowls around like a roaring lion looking for someone to devour" (1 Peter 5:8).

If we want to protect our inheritance and avoid falling into sin and destruction, we need to intentionally wall ourselves off from temptation. We have to place guardrails of Scripture around our minds. We must take care to walk only where the Spirit leads us. Seemingly minor sins like coarse jokes and idle talk can lead us deeper and deeper into ungodly attitudes and actions even before we know it. So, like Abraham, we must demonstrate practical foresight to guard our hearts and minds against temptation and sin.

When I was a young man in Montana, I heard of a cowboy who came into town every weekend. He'd tie up his horse in front of the saloon, go inside, and get drunk.

Then one day he gave his life to Christ in the little church at the end of the street. He became a godly man and stopped drinking. For some time after his conversion, however, he continued to tie up his horse at the hitching post in front of the saloon.

One day an older Christian took the cowboy aside. "Now, son," he said, "I know you never go to the saloon anymore. You're always at

Sunday meetings and prayer meetings, and the way you live your life is an example to everyone. But one thing bothers me: You still tie your horse up in front of the saloon. Keep that up, son, and one day you'll be tempted. So I have a suggestion: Change your hitching post."

Now, that's good advice for all true children of Abraham: Change your hitching post. Use a little practical foresight to guard yourself against temptation.

## GATHERED TO HIS PEOPLE

Abraham lived as full and rich a life as anyone could want. The next two verses tell us: "Altogether, Abraham lived a hundred and seventy-five years. Then Abraham breathed his last and died at a good old age, an old man and full of years; and he was gathered to his people" (Genesis 25:7–8).

If you and I had been with Abraham at the moments of decision in his life, we might have pitied him. When he left Ur, we might have said, "Abraham, you poor fool! Do you really intend to wander out there and live in a tent the rest of your life? You could have enjoyed the city of Ur and all of its advantages and blessings!" Yet Abraham chose wisely, and God blessed him.

When Abraham allowed Lot to choose the best of the land, we might have said, "Don't throw away your rights! You are the elder! You have the right to choose." But Abraham let Lot have first choice, and God blessed Abraham.

The king of Sodom offered the riches of the city to Abraham, but Abraham replied, "I won't take even one of your shoelaces. I don't want any of it." We might have said, "Abraham, you can carry principle too far! Why not accept the king's offer? You could make a hefty donation to the Lord's work and still have plenty left over to enjoy life!" But Abraham made the right choice, and God gave him a life of fullness and satisfaction.

Abraham lived 175 years. Every one of those years was packed brim-full of the joy of serving God. Abraham died an old man, full of days, rich in good memories, at peace with God. Abraham's life confirms these words of the Lord Jesus:

> "I tell you the truth," Jesus replied, "no one who has left home or brothers or sisters or mother or father or children or fields for me and the gospel will fail to receive a hundred times as much in this present age (homes, brothers, sisters, mothers, children and fields—and with them, persecutions) and in the age to come, eternal life." (Mark 10:29–30)

God promises us a full, satisfying life in the here and now—and even greater joy in the life to come.

Genesis 25:8 contains an interesting phrase: "and he was gathered to his people." Clearly, Abraham was not physically gathered to his people, because he was buried in Canaan, not in Ur, where his ancestors were buried. Nor does this mean that he was gathered into the same spiritual realm as his ancestors, for they were idolaters and Abraham died a godly man, a servant of the one true God. Abraham was not spiritually gathered to his ancestors.

What, then, does "gathered to his people" mean? It means that he was gathered into the company of all those before him who believed in God and followed Him. He was gathered in among all those righteous ones, from the time of Adam until his own time, who walked with God. Two such believers were Enoch and Noah—true men of faith and godliness. People such as these were Abraham's people.

We see this same idea expressed in the words of Jesus: "Here are my mother and my brothers! Whoever does God's will is my brother and sister and mother" (Mark 3:34b–35). The deepest, truest kinship we have with others is not genetic kinship but spiritual kinship. Blood may be thicker than water, but kinship in Christ runs deeper than blood.

Abraham was gathered to his people—his brothers and sisters in the Lord. What beautiful fellowship there will be on the day of resurrection when we are all gathered to our people! Sorrow and death will have no more hold over us—for even though Abraham's body was placed in the tomb, his life did not end.

In Jesus' day, He was opposed by a sect called the Sadducees. These people did not believe in the resurrection of the dead. They were constantly trying to trip Jesus up with difficult questions. After one such incident, Jesus said to the Sadducees, "Have you not read what God said to you, 'I am the God of Abraham, the God of Isaac, and the God of Jacob'? He is not the God of the dead but of the living" (Matthew 22:31b–32).

Notice carefully what Jesus said here: Abraham is alive. God is the Lord of the living, not the dead. On another occasion, Jesus said, "I say to you that many will come from the east and the west, and will take their places at the feast with Abraham, Isaac and Jacob in the kingdom of heaven" (Matthew 8:11). I already have a place reserved at that table. Do you?

Abraham's life provides us with pictures of our lives, both in the here and now and in the life to come. Abraham was not an extraordinary or saintly man. He was flawed and imperfect, just like you and me. But he believed that God's promises are true. He obeyed God even when obedience was hard and God's will seemed to make no sense. He trusted God's plan for his life.

The writer to the Hebrews, in that great "heroes of faith" chapter, said this about Abraham and other men and women of faith:

> All these people were still living by faith when they died. They did not receive the things promised; they only saw them and welcomed them from a distance. And they admitted that they were aliens and strangers on earth. People who say such things show that they are looking for a country of their own. If they had been thinking of the country they had left, they would have had opportunity to return. Instead, they were longing for a better country—a heavenly one. Therefore God is not ashamed to be called their God, for he has prepared a city for them. (Hebrews 11:13–16)

Abraham's life represents the life of every Christian. All who walk in faith with the Lord Jesus Christ are called to be His, to be possessed by Him, to live as pilgrims and strangers on earth. He is our pattern, our example of a life lived by faith and obedience to God. As we follow in the footsteps of Abraham, the friend of God, we will find the joy and abundance and fruitfulness we desire, both in this life and in the life to come.

# NOTE TO THE READER

The publisher invites you to share your response to the message of this book by writing Discovery House Publishers, P.O. Box 3566, Grand Rapids, MI 49501, U.S.A. For information about other Discovery House books, music, videos, or DVDs, contact us at the same address or call 1-800-653-8333. Find us on the Internet at http://www.dhp.org/ or send e-mail to books@dhp.org.